HAZLITT AND THE
SPIRIT OF THE AGE

ROY PARK

Hazlitt
and the
Spirit of the Age

ABSTRACTION AND
CRITICAL THEORY

CLARENDON PRESS · OXFORD

1971

Oxford University Press, Ely House, London W.1

GLASGOW   NEW YORK   TORONTO   MELBOURNE   WELLINGTON
CAPE TOWN   SALISBURY   IBADAN   NAIROBI   DAR ES SALAAM   LUSAKA   ADDIS ABABA
BOMBAY   CALCUTTA   MADRAS   KARACHI   LAHORE   DACCA
KUALA LUMPUR   SINGAPORE   HONG KONG   TOKYO

PRINTED IN GREAT BRITAIN
BY W & J MACKAY & CO LTD, CHATHAM

TO
JOHN BRYCE

My cloudy thoughts draw off, the storm of angry politics has blown over—Mr. Blackwood, I am yours —Mr. Croker, my service to you—Mr. T. Moore, I am alive and well—Really, it is wonderful how little the worse I am for fifteen years' wear and tear, how I come upon my legs again on the ground of truth and nature, and 'look abroad into universality', forgetting that there is any such person as myself in the world!

The Plain Speaker, xii. 123.

PREFACE

I AM greatly indebted to various scholars and friends who have helped me in the writing of this study. My especial thanks are to Dr. John Beer, Dr. Raymond Williams, Professor Robin Downie, and Dr. Stanley Jones, who read and criticized the work, in full or in part, at various stages. My greatest debt is to Dr. Ian Jack. Without his constant kindness, encouragement and faith it is questionable whether it would have been written at all. Dr. Douglas Duncan of McMaster University and his wife Janet came to my rescue in Canada and enabled the work to be completed in tolerable conditions. My wife's bibliographical services saved me many months of tedious research. I am indebted to the University of Glasgow for financial assistance in the earlier stages of my research and to Pembroke College and its Fellows for the Research Fellowship which enabled me to complete it. Mr. J. B. Bullen and Mr. E. R. Hallowell very kindly assisted in reading the proofs. For permission to use material that has already appeared in print, I am grateful to the editors of *PMLA*, *Journal of the History of Ideas*, *Journal of Aesthetics and Art Criticism*, and *British Journal of Aesthetics*.

Pembroke College,
Cambridge.

CONTENTS

ABBREVIATIONS

BNYPL	*Bulletin of the New York Public Library.*
EC	*Essays in Criticism.*
ELH	*English Literary History.*
JAAC	*Journal of Aesthetics and Art Criticism.*
JHI	*Journal of the History of Ideas.*
KSMB	*The Keats-Shelley Memorial Bulletin.*
MLN	*Modern Language Notes.*
MP	*Modern Philology.*
PBA	*Proceedings of the British Academy.*
PELL	*Papers on English Language and Literature.*
PMLA	*Publications of the Modern Language Association of America.*
PQ	*Philological Quarterly.*
RES	*Review of English Studies.*
SAQ	*South Atlantic Quarterly.*
SEL	*Studies in English Literature.*
SIR	*Studies in Romanticism.*
TLS	*Times Literary Supplement.*

INTRODUCTION

There is a manifest and recurrent tendency in the
history of culture to convert aesthetic into something
other than itself. Indeed, at various times aesthetic has
been reduced to sociology or psychology or morals or
metaphysics.

ISRAEL KNOX, *The Aesthetic Theories of Kant, Hegel and
Schopenhauer*

THE following chapters attempt to trace in William Hazlitt's
writings certain aspects of a particular problem, an understanding
of which is fundamental to an appreciation of the criticism and
poetry of the early nineteenth century: whether poetry is poetry,
or whether it is finally explicable only within the framework of a
more general metaphysic. The problem is an enduring and ubiqui-
tous one and is not peculiar to the nineteenth century. It is an issue
which has agitated poets, critics and philosophers alike for many
centuries. Nevertheless, there are certain features which are unique
in the nineteenth-century formulation of the problem. For the first
time the issue was crystallized and its various strands isolated in a
way which released forces still operative in contemporary discussions of the place of poetry (and all that it stands for) in modern
culture. The important role played by Hazlitt in this, although
hitherto largely unacknowledged, even by Arnold, with whom he
has perhaps the greatest affinity, is the subject of the chapters that
follow.

The philosophical climate prevailing in England at the turn of
the nineteenth century rendered inevitable the subversion of the
poetic. In the absence of a philosophy capable of challenging
effectively the dominant empirical philosophy, the task of protect-
ing the imaginative principle in poetry and in life from the
encroachment of inapplicable scientific criteria devolved directly
upon the poets and critics. The consequences for poetry and poetic
theory were unfortunate. The distinction which was drawn
between a mechanical philosophy and a dynamic philosophy in
the writings of Wordsworth, Coleridge, and Carlyle was inadequate for their purposes. They failed to perceive that the gravest

threat to the imaginative and dynamic was not science or a science-oriented philosophy but abstraction, of which the bias to mechanism was only one aspect. Abstraction, or the tendency to generality, does not characterize the scientific approach alone. It is also the chief characteristic of the various philosophical and theological solutions proposed by the poets and critics themselves. In abstraction, the scientific, philosophical, and religious solutions meet and are one. Poetry is inevitably subsumed under one or other of these more general metaphysics.

The aim of the present study is to indicate some of the principal ways in which Hazlitt vindicated the self-authenticating nature of the poetic principle against both a hostile empirical epistemology and what he conceived to be the misguided attempts of contemporary poets and critics to construct a non-scientific and extra-poetic alternative. He viewed the age in which he lived as one of abstraction. His conviction of the harm arising from the contemporary emphasis upon generality is the key to his entire critical outlook, theoretical as well as practical. To this conviction can be traced his dislike of systems, doctrines, theories, dogmas, parties and sects. The general role assigned to him in the following pages is similar in many respects to that occupied by Matthew Arnold later in the century. Hazlitt is unique in one respect, however. The theory of abstract ideas which is the principal theoretical justification for his criticism of all forms of abstraction is entirely original. Its implications, whether as a philosophical theory or as a psychology of artistic perception, are revolutionary, and it constitutes the most important single factor in an understanding of his literary criticism. It is essentially the theory of a painter trained originally as a philosopher, and emphasizes the important role played by painting and philosophy in the formation of the mature literary critic.

The opposition between poetry and science in the early nineteenth century is the most significant single characteristic of the period. Yet the opposition is not in itself peculiar to the period. This will be rather more obvious if, like Hazlitt, we view it as a tension between poetry and abstraction. A brief consideration of some other manifestations of this tension will reveal the perennial nature of the problem and its significance in relation to the cultural values of civilized society. It will also help to isolate the various strands in the opposition especially characteristic of the nineteenth-century form of the dispute. Finally, by establishing a basic terminology it will render more incisive the investigation into the nature of the triangular debate in the early nineteenth century itself.

The first classic example occurs in the *Republic* of Plato. On the basis of an assumed metaphysic of Ideal Forms which, in addition to being supported by the argument of the One and the Many, is also reinforced by arguments scientific and mathematical, Plato considers poetry as a copy at third remove from the divine original. Poetry is concerned with fact, with truth, with an 'is' of which it is an inferior copy. As an inferior copy, however, the uses to which art can be put in the happy society must be strictly controlled. By positing art not as copy but as imitation, Aristotle succeeded in dissociating poetry from fact, from what is the case, and hence from truth and falsity. A great deal of his success in establishing a case for poetry on the ground of probability stems from the care with which he chose to ignore the Platonic framework, since the danger of the category mistake which the latter involves is that while it provokes argument it does so in terms of the inapplicable criteria which it has itself established. Unlike Coleridge, Hazlitt was severely critical of Plato's view of art (v. 3; xii. 246). Its similarities with Bentham's view of poetry as misrepresentation, however divergent their philosophies, were obvious to him, and he referred at one point in a discussion of Bentham to his 'Platonic embraces' (xix. 205). They were also linked in another way: Hazlitt's sparing use of an imagery of mechanism was almost entirely confined to his criticism of Bentham and Plato.

The first instance in English literature of a similar tension occurs in Sir Philip Sidney's *Apologie for Poetrie*, and in relating Bentham to Sidney's Puritan opponents as well as to Plato (xii. 180, 248) Hazlitt reveals his awareness of the perennial nature of the problem, as well as its earlier manifestations. While Sidney utilizes the Aristotelian view of poetry in his preliminary definition, he is unable to free himself from the Platonic view of the relation of literature and life as one of instrumentality, and consequently engages directly with Plato on the latter's own premises. In so doing he places himself within the fallacy of the utility of poetry, with the result that his best defence, and that on which his whole case should have rested, remains buried in a series of charges and countercharges: 'Now, for the Poet, he nothing affirmes, and therefore neuer lyeth. For, as I take it, to lye is to affirme that to be true which is false. . . . But the Poet . . . neuer affirmeth.'[1]

It is upon the question of truth and falsity that one important aspect of the twentieth-century version of this dispute has centred. The end of the nineteenth century in England saw the predomin-ance of an idealist system of philosophy and aesthetics characterized to a very large extent by a host of doctrines unverified and un-verifiable. The emergence of a strong empirical reaction in the present century with the development of Logical Positivism was a natural outcome. By means of the Principle of Verification Logical Positivism attempted to bring the propositions of Idealism within the purview of observation and experiment. According to this principle no synthetic proposition, or proposition that is not just a matter of logic, is meaningful unless it can be verified or is at least capable of being verified. As a result, all propositions which are not concerned with matters of fact capable of proof or disproof are not statements at all, but are meaningless. As in the early nine-teenth century, this application of purely scientific criteria posed grave problems for poetry, morality, and religion. Like Plato and Bentham, Logical Positivism evaluated poetry on a factual rather than on an imaginative or poetic basis.

The great merit of modern empiricism lies in the positive asser-tions it makes concerning the scientific. If we see its development in the twentieth century within the context of its opposition to the philosophical theories of Bradley, Green, and Bosanquet, the de-mand which it makes for the verification of all propositions seems almost salutary. Unfortunately, in exacting this demand of some of the more bogus metaphysical views of the late nineteenth century, the empirical reaction threw out the genuine philosophical issues, as well as the inadequate solutions previously offered by the Idealists. Like its early nineteenth-century counterpart, modern empiricism failed to acknowledge the imaginative or spiritual plane outside the realm of science, fact, and experiment. Coleridge's characterization of empiricism applies with just as much force to Logical Positiv-ism: 'The leading differences between mechanic and vital philo-sophy may all be drawn from one point: namely, that the former demand[s] for every mode and act of existence real or possible visi-

---

[1] *Elizabethan Critical Essays*, ed. G. G. Smith (London, 1904), I. 184-5.

bility.'[2] By their contempt for what Hazlitt in a different context called the 'prurience of the optic nerve' (x. 202), the poets and critics of the nineteenth century affirmed their belief that human experience was not commensurate with experiment and observation.

The obvious solution to the dilemma posed by the empirical principle of verification is to deny with Sidney that poetry affirms, and in the present century this is the point which was taken up and elaborated by Wittgenstein. For Wittgenstein, poetry, morality, and religion operate on the level of being or existence as opposed to that of scientific fact. Hence they are 'existential'. They appertain to those areas of human experience not susceptible of scientific investigation, which the early nineteenth century had earlier characterized as 'imaginative', 'vital', and 'dynamic'. None is concerned with affirmation. They do not make statements, since statements are limited to facts, to the scientific, the verifiable. The Principle of Verification is therefore inoperative on the existential plane: 'The solution of the riddle of life in space and time lies *outside* space and time.'[3] Corresponding to his view that poetry does not make statements is his view that one cannot ask questions of it since 'statement' and 'question' are correlative: 'For an answer which cannot be expressed the question too cannot be expressed.'[4] The question 'what?' invites an answer in terms of verifiable facts. Thus the question 'what is poetry?' involves a category mistake. The existential falls outside the jurisdiction of interrogation for the reason that it does not affirm.

Yet in an age like the early nineteenth century dominated by an empirical philosophy, the urge to define the nature of poetry, to draw a distinct line between science and poetry was felt as irresistible. To approach the issue directly with an explicitly formulated question, as some of the Romantics did, implies that what is involved is an ignorance of facts, either psychological facts as in the case of the eighteenth-century associationists, or in terms of non-natural or supersensible facts. The sole virtue of the latter rests in its recognition of the existential nature of poetry.

The significance of Wittgenstein's middle position is that it

[2] *The Complete Works of Samuel Taylor Coleridge*, ed. W. G. T. Shedd (New York, 1853), I. 470. Cf. Hazlitt's view that 'these persons wish to get rid of occult causes, to refer every thing to distinct principles and a visible origin' (xvi. 186). See also xx. 375.

[3] L. Wittgenstein, *Tractatus Logico-Philosophicus* (London, 1922), p. 185.

[4] Ibid., p. 187.

enables us to perceive the historical relevance and permanent validity of the philosophical position adopted by Hazlitt in the early nineteenth century in his recognition of the authenticity of a situation in which no statement can be made and no question asked. This response I have termed 'experiential'. Wittgenstein expressed his experiential view in this way: 'We feel that even if *all possible* scientific questions be answered, the problems of life have still not been touched at all. Of course there is then no question left, and just this is the answer. The solution of the problem of life is seen in the vanishing of this problem. (Is not this the reason why men to whom after long doubting the sense of life becomes clear, could not then say wherein this sense consisted?)'[5] Art for Wittgenstein is a showing forth, a revelation of ontological reality, of the significance of human life. The sense of life becomes clear although we cannot *say* in what this sense consists. In the early nineteenth century the credit for the formulation of the philosophical basis of this approach to poetry as poetry and not as science, religion or anything else must go to Hazlitt.

In an attempt to do justice to the influence exercised by philosophy and painting on Hazlitt's critical writings, the present study is arranged in three parts. In the first part I have tried to delineate the epistemological and moral basis of his general philosophical position both in relation to his age and to the two principal figures representative of the contemporary extremes of empiricism and idealism—Bentham and Coleridge. Underlying the popular expression of the essays, reviews, and lectures is the questing, probing mind of one who never ceased to be, in the nineteenth-century sense of the word, a metaphysician. Still following the contours of his mind and the development of his thought, Part II traces his theory of abstraction to his lifelong interest in painting and examines the consequences for his literary criticism of this unique fusion of philosophy and painting. In these chapters the philosophical and historical emphasis of the first part shades into an aesthetic and historical one in which his criticism is seen as the culmination of a new critical tradition originating in the last decades of the previous century. Part III examines his criticism of English poetry, past and present, in the light of his distrust of abstraction and his demand for imaginative sincerity, a concept that in Hazlitt's writings fulfils a function somewhat similar to Keats's use of negative capability.

[5] Ibid., p. 187.

PART I

The Metaphysician

The empirical philosophers are like to pismires; they only lay up and use their store: the rationalists are like to spiders; they spin all out of their own bowels: but give me a philosopher, who, like the bee, hath a middle faculty, gathering from abroad, but digesting that which is gathered by his own virtue.

BACON

CHAPTER ONE

The Triangular Debate: Science, Poetry, and Religion

> And therefore it was most aptly said by one of Plato's
> school, 'That the sense of man carrieth a resemblance
> with the sun, which (as we see) openeth and revealeth
> all the terrestrial globe; but then again it obscureth
> and concealeth the stars and celestial globe: so doth
> the sense discover natural things, but it darkeneth and
> shutteth up divine.'   BACON

1. THE PHILOSOPHICAL VACUUM

ONE of the most striking features of the late eighteenth and early
nineteenth centuries is the almost total dearth of any philosophical
works of a high intellectual calibre. The philosophical activity of
the first half of the eighteenth century which we associate with
Locke, Berkeley, Shaftesbury, Hutcheson, Hume, Butler, and
Price gave way to an age so barren philosophically, 'a decrepit,
death-sick Era'[1] as Carlyle called it, that subsequent historians of
English philosophy have been able to dismiss it with little or no
discussion. The decline in the quality of philosophical thought was
matched by a corresponding decline in the popularity of philosophy
itself as a subject of serious intellectual interest. Francis Jeffrey, in
his review of Dugald Stewart's *Philosophical Essays* (1810), took up
the second of these points and commented:

The studies to which Mr Stewart has devoted himself, have lately
fallen out of favour with the English public; and the nation which once
placed the name of Locke immediately under those of Shakespeare and of
Newton, and has since repaid the metaphysical labours of Berkeley and
Hume with such just celebrity, seems now to be almost without zeal or
curiosity as to the progress of the Philosophy of Mind. . . . To us, the phenomenon . . . has always appeared to arise from the great multiplication

---

[1] *Critical and Miscellaneous Essays*, III. 74, in *The Works of Thomas Carlyle*, ed.
H. D. Traill (London, 1896–9).

of the branches of liberal study, and from the more extensive diffusion of knowledge among the body of the people.[2]

In this passage Jeffrey is principally concerned with the decline in the popularity of philosophy. Carlyle's main concern twenty years later, during which time the situation had further deteriorated, was for the very existence of philosophy: 'There is now no Philosophy visible in these Islands.'[3] His bleak view of the general position was one which was fully shared by Coleridge, Hazlitt, and De Quincey. Bulwer-Lytton in *England and the English*, a general survey of the period from 1800 to 1830, attempted to account in detail for the philosophical sterility felt to be so characteristic of the age. The terms of his analysis were similar to those of Jeffrey in 1810, but for Bulwer the greater diffusion of knowledge, the growth of a reading public, and the rise of the periodical press explained not only the decline in philosophy's popularity but its decline in quality as well.[4] The philosopher of the eighteenth century died that the periodical essayist of the nineteenth might flourish. Whatever the shortcomings of Bulwer's journalistic and often superficial account of the first thirty years of the nineteenth century, this view in particular is extraordinarily illuminative of the age and of its writers. His attempt to establish a causal connection between the disappearance of the eighteenth-century philosopher and the emergence of the nineteenth-century periodical essayist and critic is especially significant in relation to Hazlitt's development as a writer.

The eighteenth-century philosopher in Hazlitt did not easily acknowledge defeat. His first published work was a philosophical treatise the full title of which has a familiar eighteenth-century ring to it: *An Essay on the Principles of Human Action: Being an Argument in favour of the Natural Disinterestedness of the Human Mind. To which are added, Some Remarks on the Systems of Hartley and Helvetius.* Although it was not published until 1805, Hazlitt had worked on it intermittently since 1796, and it was not until 1812 that he finally abandoned a study which had been his chief preoccupation for almost twenty years. In 1809 he issued a *Prospectus of a History of English Philosophy*, and when his hopes in this direction failed to materialize, he consoled himself with the prospect of publishing a

2 *Edinburgh Review*, XVII (1810), 167–8.
3 Carlyle, *Essays*, II. 38.
4 E. L. Bulwer, *England and the English* (London, 1833), II. 51–3, 63–7.

volume of philosophical essays. The contents of both these projected works were finally delivered in a series of lectures in 1812. Like the *Essay*, the lectures were not successful and were published only after his death as part of *Literary Remains* in 1836. Hazlitt always entertained the highest regard for his first published work, even to the extent of summarizing it for the benefit of the editor of the *Quarterly Review* in *A Letter to William Gifford* in 1819. Its poor reception and his cultivation of a more popular style in his later work he attributed to the public neglect of philosophy. Yet even during the period of his greatest activity as a philosopher, he had already begun to show signs of that literary versatility which was such a marked characteristic of an age that had abandoned formal philosophizing and had embarked upon what Jeffrey termed 'Encyclopedical trifling'.[5] By 1812, Hazlitt as well as being a philosopher, was already an editor, historian, biographer, grammarian, and critic of social and political affairs.

In abandoning philosophy Hazlitt did not cease to philosophize. Almost all his important works are in a profound sense 'the thoughts of a metaphysician expressed by a painter' (xvii. 311). The philosophical ground of much of his later work was in general little appreciated during his own lifetime, but his subterfuge in tailoring his more mature philosophical speculations to the taste of his age and the conditions imposed by it was by no means peculiar to him. Literature had not merely replaced philosophy in the public esteem. It had also taken over its role. For Carlyle this movement away from philosophy to literature represented one of the most significant developments of the age: 'All Intellect has fused itself into Literature: Literature . . . is the molten sea and wonder-bearing chaos, into which mind after mind casts forth its opinion.'[6] Bulwer-Lytton's analysis went further. While prepared to grant that literature in the nineteenth century had engrossed all the intellectual effort which had previously helped to sustain philosophy in the eighteenth, he saw the consequences of the ascendancy established by literature as of even greater significance. Imaginative literature had not only 'arrogated the due place of the Philosophical'.[7] It had also assumed a new role. Pointing to the rise of a Utilitarian and materialist philosophy hostile to a full poetic awareness, he wrote: '[Wordsworth's] poetry has repaired to us the want

---

[5] *Edinburgh Review*, XVII (1810), 169. Cf. ibid., XIII (1809), 344.
[6] Carlyle, *Essays*, II. 370.   [7] Bulwer, *England and the English*, II. 104.

of an immaterial philosophy—it *is* philosophy, and it is of the immaterial school.'[8] The manner of his formulation is open to serious criticism, and its scope, limited as it is to the poetry of Wordsworth and Shelley, is altogether too restricted. Nevertheless, the basic idea is a fruitful one in relation to the literature of the early nineteenth century in general and is capable of further generalization: in the absence of a philosophy capable of combating the dominant empirical epistemology of the Utilitarians the responsibility for the defence of the 'existential', the 'imaginative', or the 'immaterial' passed to literature.

Hazlitt's practice both as a critic and as an essayist exemplifies this perfectly. There is, however, one important corollary. The philosophical element was seldom explicit, was often consciously minimized, and in some cases a quite deliberate attempt was made to disguise the ultimate import of a particular work. This emerges quite clearly in a letter written by Coleridge to Humphrey Davy in October 1800: 'I gird myself up to attack . . . the Essay on Poetry. . . . It's Title would be an Essay on the Elements of Poetry / it would in reality be a *disguised* System of Morals & Politics—'.[9] In another letter he defended a 'popular style' as one in which 'the Author has had his own eye fixed steadily on the *abstract*, yet permits his readers to see only the *Concrete*'.[10] These and similar observations by Hazlitt aptly characterize the subterranean methods adopted by literature at the turn of the new century in the fulfilment of its new role. Hazlitt's view of his work as 'the thoughts of a metaphysician expressed by a painter' has similar implications, and in the essay 'On Depth and Superficiality', he drew attention to 'the way in which I work out some of my conclusions underground, before throwing them up on the surface . . . tracing any number of particular effects to a general principle. . . . It is in fact resolving the concrete into the abstract' (xii. 347, 355). If we fail to perceive the general moral and spiritual preoccupations that are the source of his inspiration as an essayist, 'the moral fineness of the mind behind those noble essays of his last decade',[11] then we shall consider the essays as little more than impressionistic ragbags of the kind censured earlier by Dr. Johnson in the *Rambler*.

[8] Ibid., II. 101.
[9] *Collected Letters of Samuel Taylor Coleridge*, ed. E. L. Griggs (Oxford ,1956), I. 632.
[10] Ibid., III. 153.
[11] D. Grant, 'Wordsworth and Hazlitt', *TLS* (6 Sept. 1968), 1062.

As a critic and essayist Hazlitt occupied a key position in the new role assumed by literature, defending like Coleridge not just poetry narrowly construed, but the poetic, the existential, the quality of life and what makes that life worth living. Nowhere perhaps in all his work is there a passage comparable in explicitness to Coleridge's letter to Lord Liverpool:

I must have remain'd silent, my Lord, had not the history of all civilized nations in all ages supplied the decisive answer—if the recorded experience of Mankind had not attested the important fact—that the Taste and Character, the whole tone of Manners and Feeling, and above all the Religious (at least the Theological) and the Political tendencies of the public mind, have ever borne such a close correspondence, so distinct and evident an Analogy to the predominant system of speculative Philosophy . . . as must remain inexplicable.[12]

Or to the following passage in Carlyle:

We may trace this tendency in all the great manifestations of our time; in its intellectual aspect, the studies it most favours and its manner of conducting them; in its practical aspects, its politics, arts, religion, morals; in the whole sources, and throughout the whole currents, of its spiritual, no less than its material activity.[13]

Part of the reason for this lies in Hazlitt's view that science, mechanism or the contemporary emphasis on understanding and experience were not the only threats to the imaginative and spiritual life of man. Yet like Coleridge and Carlyle, and like Arnold later in the century, this sense of a threat to the quality of the whole of civilized living pervades his entire work. Chapter I attempts to isolate the unique nature of his philosophical position and its relation to the views of his contemporaries in terms of what is the most significant feature of the early nineteenth century: the tension which existed between the scientific and the existential.

2. POETRY VERSUS SCIENCE: BACON AND THE 'PHYSICAL ANALOGY'

In the absence of a non-empirical philosophy able to counter effectively the threat to the existential posed by the growing dominance of empirical epistemology, literature took upon itself the task of drawing and maintaining a strict division between

---

[12] Coleridge, *Letters*, IV. 759.
[13] Carlyle, *Essays*, II. 63.

poetry and science. It accomplished this in a variety of ways. The philosophical manner in which the division was enforced is, however, of primary importance.

There were at least two possible ways in which the Romantic poets and critics could enforce this distinction. They could draw attention to the defective epistemology on which the empirical case rested. Alternatively, they could emphasize the inadequacies of the moral theory which that epistemology entailed. In a number of cases they chose to do both. Few were prepared to speculate at any length in epistemological terms on a theory of the creative nature of the human mind. Assuming such a theory, however, the writers of the late eighteenth and early nineteenth centuries were able to direct a telling series of criticisms against what they regarded as the basic category mistake of the modern philosophy—the 'physical analogy' (xx. 15).

In view of the philosophical sterility of the period the concern expressed at the implications of empirical philosophy may appear exaggerated. The explanation of this fear is to be found not in the work of any single philosopher but in the deep-rooted nature of the physical analogy itself. By the beginning of the nineteenth century empiricism rested upon a tradition of almost two hundred years. By 1750 the task of tracing out its speculative implications was over, and with the formation of a new industrial society and its concomitant evils the second half of the century was ripe for the practical application of the dominant speculative philosophy to various aspects of the social system. The fear of the early nineteenth century was that if the basic view of man taken by Bentham, Condorcet, Owen, Godwin, and others was fundamentally wrong as a result of a gross epistemological error, then the benefits procured, although in some respects welcome, would be directed at the material man, at man as a physical rather than as a spiritual being. The work of Bentham, Paley, Priestley, Malthus, and Horne Tooke represented for the Romantics the empirical misrepresentation of human nature in a variety of spheres: in penal legislation, political and moral theory, theology, political economy and the nature of language itself. Of the critics of the physical analogy only Jeffrey failed to appreciate its remoter implications. For Jeffrey its significance did not extend beyond philosophy.

Jeffrey's failure in this respect stemmed from his denial of any connection between empirical epistemology and empirical moral theory.[14] In doing so he ran counter to the anti-empirical tradition of the late eighteenth and early nineteenth centuries. As early as 1757 Richard Price had insisted upon the basic epistemological error as the source of all the others, and in making the same point almost thirty years later Thomas Reid singled out Price's subtle analysis for special praise: '[Price] saw the consequences which these opinions draw after them, and has traced them to their source, to wit, the account given by Mr LOCKE, and adopted by the generality of modern Philosophers, of the origin of all our ideas, which account he shows to be very defective.'[15] By concentrating upon the primacy of the epistemological error the writers of the early nineteenth century were following a pattern of defence already well-established. There is, however, one important difference. Whereas the eighteenth-century criticism of empirical epistemology emphasized the significant role played by Locke's account of the origin of our ideas, the nineteenth-century criticism of the physical analogy concentrated principally upon Bacon and to a lesser extent Hobbes as the sources of the empirical fallacy. For Hazlitt, Hobbes rather than Locke was the founder of modern empiricism, and Locke's alleged plagiarisms from Hobbes is one of his favourite themes. Coleridge, although by no means so favourably disposed to Hobbes as Hazlitt and Mackintosh were, considered that Locke's stature as a philosopher required reappraisal: 'I suspect, that we should give the name of Newton a more worthy associate — & instead of Locke & Newton, we should say, BACON & NEWTON.'[16] Shelley held similar views.[17] Once the eighteenth century had grasped the implications of Hume's *Treatise*, Locke's decline was inevitable. The part played by Price and Reid in initiating this revaluation of English philosophical history was important, although it was James Beattie who popularized and simplified their view of Locke for the non-philosophical public. His distinction between the philosophy of Locke and the renown

[14] *Edinburgh Review*, X (1807), 197.

[15] T. Reid, *Essays on the Intellectual Powers of Man* (Edinburgh, 1785), pp. 726–7. See R. Price, *A Review of the Principal Questions in Morals* (1757), ed. D. D. Raphael (Oxford, 1948), pp. 17–40. Both Raphael (p. xii) and W. H. F. Barnes, 'Richard Price: a Neglected Eighteenth Century Moralist', *Philosophy*, XVII (1942), 159–73, stress the importance of the epistemological element in Price's criticism of empiricism.

[16] Coleridge, *Letters*, II. 686. See ibid., II. 676.

[17] *The Complete Works of Percy Bysshe Shelley*, ed. R. Ingpen and W. E. Peck (London, 1926–30), VII. 8.

and integrity of his personal and political character, which helped
to render the depreciation of Locke's status as a philosopher more
palatable, later became a commonplace.[18] Among the empiricists,
however, Locke's declining popularity did not go unnoticed, nor
was it meekly accepted.[19]

With the introduction of Bacon and the elimination of Locke
a new phase in the discussion of the empirical theory of knowledge
was initiated. The revival of interest in Bacon was a phenomenon
of the late eighteenth century. For James Beattie he was the 'great
reformer of philosophy'.[20] Nevertheless, his introduction into the
discussion and the shift of emphasis which this involved was
peculiar to the early nineteenth century. An understanding of his
role here is crucial to an appreciation of what was in effect a new
equation. Whereas Price and Reid had emphasized the shortcomings and implications of an empirical theory of knowledge,
the nineteenth century, by its emphasis on the physical analogy
and the significant role played by Bacon, wished to draw attention
to the source of the fallacy at the root of all empirical epistemology.

A laudatory reference to Bacon in Dugald Stewart's *Account of
the Life and Writings of Thomas Reid* (1803) occasioned what was
perhaps the first expression of the nineteenth-century view of the
matter. In his review of Stewart's book Jeffrey pointed out that
Bacon's sudden access of popularity since the time of Hume cut
across traditional philosophical allegiances. His stern general
warning became the dominant theme in the early nineteenth
century's epistemological attack on the modern philosophy:

Mr Stewart, however, follows up this observation with a warm
encomium on the inductive philosophy of Lord Bacon, and a copious
and eloquent exposition of the incalculable utility and advantage that
may be expected from applying to the science of mind those sound
rules of experimental philosophy that have undoubtedly guided us to all
the splendid improvements in modern physics. From the time indeed
that Mr Hume published his Treatise of human nature, down to the latest
speculations of Condorcet and Mr Stewart, we have observed this to be a
favourite topic with all metaphysical writers, and that those who have
differed in almost every thing else, have agreed in magnifying the

---

[18] J. Beattie, *An Essay on the Nature and Immutability of Truth* (Edinburgh, 1770),
pp. 8–9. Cf. Bulwer, *England and the English*, I. 374.
[19] W. Belsham, *Essays, Philosophical, Historical and Literary* (London, 1789–91),
I. 199.
[20] J. Beattie, *Elements of Moral Science* (Edinburgh, 1790–3), II. 575.

importance of such inquiries. . . . Now, in these speculations we cannot help suspecting that those philosophers have been misled . . . by a false analogy.[21]

For Jeffrey, the rules of scientific induction set out by Bacon do not apply to the analysis of the human mind; they do not apply to man as a spiritual being: 'We cannot decompose our perceptions in a crucible, nor divide our sensations with a prism. . . . The science of metaphysics, therefore, depends upon observation, and not upon experiment. . . . In this department the greater part of that code of laws which Bacon has provided for the regulation of experimental induction, is plainly without authority. In metaphysics, certainly knowledge is not power.'[22] In his *Philosophical Essays* (1810), Stewart replied by drawing attention to the same kind of warning against the misapplication of the scientific method in Bacon himself: 'When men of confined scientific pursuits afterwards betake themselves to philosophy, and to general contemplations, they are apt to wrest and corrupt them with their former conceits.'[23]

The quotation from Bacon in no way invalidated Jeffrey's original criticism of Stewart, for Jeffrey had carefully refrained from imputing the source of the 'false analogy' to Bacon himself. It merely reiterated more succinctly Jeffrey's main contention. In choosing to warn the Professor of Moral Philosophy of the grave dangers consequent upon the misapplication of empirical criteria Jeffrey risked being considered presumptuous. Yet in choosing Stewart as the target of his criticism he revealed considerable philosophical acumen, since in spite of an anti-empiricism which Carlyle considered a necessary preliminary to an understanding of Kant,[24] Stewart was capable of making damaging concessions to his opponents through his failure to grasp the full implications of the empirical position. On one occasion he drew a parallel between the improvements in the sciences and the arts in a way which ran counter to one of the central tenets of Romantic poetic theory. On another, he commended the 'late excellent Dr Paley' on the 'well-merited popularity' of his ethical teaching. Finally, he promulgated

---

[21] *Edinburgh Review*, III (1804), 273.
[22] Ibid., 275.
[23] D. Stewart, *Philosophical Essays* (Edinburgh, 1810), p. 142. See *Edinburgh Review*, XVII (1810), 190.
[24] Carlyle, *Essays*, I. 79 n.

a theory of imagination which drew down upon him the wrath of Ruskin, nurtured in the poetic faith of the early nineteenth century.[25] In citing Bacon in his defence, however, Stewart enabled Jeffrey, who also quoted the passage in his review, to disseminate to a far wider audience what was to become in effect the essence of the nineteenth-century case against the empirical theory of knowledge.

Jeffrey clearly perceived the tension between the scientific and the existential arising out of the empirical attempt to impose scientific criteria in areas of human experience outside the scope of their legitimate application. His discussion of the category mistake which this involved in relation to Bacon as the founder of experimental philosophy anticipated the more familiar accounts by Hazlitt and Coleridge.

Hazlitt began his *Lectures on English Philosophy*, delivered between January and April 1812, with a detailed account of the origin and growth of modern empirical philosophy. He concentrated from the outset on the analogy which he conceived to be its greatest weakness and its gravest threat to the existential. He traced the source of the modern empirical emphasis directly to Bacon, although he nowhere suggested in the lectures that Bacon himself was in any way responsible for its subsequent development as a philosophical theory. Modern empiricism, he says, arose 'at the suggestion of Lord Bacon, on the ruins of the school-philosophy' (ii. 124). His choice of words is deliberate and circumspect. Its growth and development he attributed to a too narrow interpretation of Bacon's emphasis upon experience in the natural sciences. Experience, for Hazlitt, signified more than physical experience:

Physical experience is indeed the foundation and the test of that part of philosophy which relates to physical objects. . . . But to say that physical experiment is either the test or source or guide of that other part of philosophy which relates to our internal perceptions, that we are to look to external nature for the form, the substance, the colour, the very life and being of whatever exists in our minds, or that we can only infer the laws which regulate the phenomena of the mind from those which regulate the phenomena of matter, is to confound two things entirely distinct. Our knowledge of mental phenomena from consciousness,

[25] Stewart, *Elements of the Philosophy of the Human Mind* (London, 1792–1827), I. 17, 475–9, II. 476; *Elements*, ed. G. N. Wright (London, 1843), p. 541.

reflection, or observation of their corresponding signs in others is the true basis of metaphysical inquiry, as the knowledge of *facts*, commonly so called, is the only solid basis of natural philosophy.

(ii. 124)

Hazlitt's analysis in 1812 is strikingly similar to Jeffrey's in 1803. There is in the tone of this passage, however, a much more passionate awareness of the full implications of the physical analogy. Jeffrey had already isolated the precise nature of the analogy. But he had also denied the existence of any connection between the empirical premiss and the Utilitarian moral theory, and by implication therefore the social and political theories dependent upon that moral theory. In the eyes of Hazlitt, Coleridge, Shelley, Schlegel, Carlyle, and many others such a concession was tantamount to a failure to perceive that the whole of French and Utilitarian moral theory, with its emphasis on man's selfishness, on pleasure and pain, and on consequences alone as the criterion of right action, was the direct result of its basic empirical epistemology. Schlegel summed up for the rest of the Romantics in this respect when he said that Bacon as the founder of modern experimental philosophy 'carried in his pocket all that merits the name of philosophy in the eighteenth century'.[26] Hazlitt set down as the greatest mark against the *Edinburgh Review* its failure to recognize and stigmatize the empirical ethic at the root of the social inferences drawn by Malthus from his principle of population growth. This, he emphasized, was a 'doctrinal' failure (xi. 129). Jeffrey was aware of the implications of the analogy within the sphere of formal philosophizing, and its influence on the work of Darwin, Hooke, Dr. Smith, and Horne Tooke. He remained unaware of its more remote and insidious influence upon what Coleridge termed 'the Taste and Character, the whole tone of Manners and Feeling, and above all the Religious ... and the Political tendencies of the public mind'.

Quite apart from the difference in tone, Hazlitt's analysis differs from Jeffrey's in other and no less important ways. In Hazlitt's account the growth of modern empiricism was viewed within a much wider context. It was not enough in his view merely to draw attention to the fallacious nature of the physical analogy. Some attempt had to be made to understand the enduring nature of the

---

[26] A. W. Schlegel, *A Course of Lectures on Dramatic Art and Literature* (London, 1815), II. 108. Cf. the views of Coleridge and Shelley, below, nn. 30, 32.

empirical tradition itself within its historical context, for in spite of its obvious defects it was still the dominant philosophy. In the late eighteenth century Reid, who had discussed the problem in terms of Locke's theory of ideas, explained it in this way: 'This proneness to resolve every thing into feelings and sensations, is an extreme into which we have been led by the desire of avoiding an opposite extreme, as common in the ancient philosophy . . . [with] mysterious notions of eternal and self-existent ideas, of *materia prima*, of substantial forms, and others of the like nature.'[27] Hazlitt likewise explained the growth and success of modern empiricism in terms of a reaction, but in Hazlitt's case it is a reaction conceived within a quite specific historical context:

> The schoolmen and their followers attended to nothing but essences and species, to laboured analyses and artificial deductions. They seem to have alike disregarded both kinds of experience. . . . [Bacon] did nothing but insist on the necessity of 'experience,' more particularly in natural science; and from the . . . prodigious success it has met with, this latter application of the word, in which it is tantamount to physical experiment, has so far engrossed the whole of our attention, that mind has for a good while past been in some danger of being overlaid by matter. We run from one error into another; and as we were wrong at first, so in altering our course, we have turned about to the opposite extreme. We despised 'experience' altogether before; now we would have nothing but 'experience,' and that of the grossest kind.
>
> (ii. 125)

In each of these passages the aim of the writer is clear. By viewing the history of philosophy in terms of reaction they wished primarily to dissociate themselves from either extreme and to declare their own neutrality. Both wished to facilitate in this way the acceptance of their own highly individual views as to what constituted a balanced philosophical viewpoint capable of harmonizing what Hazlitt as early as 1807 had termed the 'material' and the 'intellectual' (i. 127).

Hazlitt's own revolutionary solution was in terms of a theory of abstract ideas. By means of this theory he attempted in all his writings to counter not only the claims made on behalf of empiricism in philosophy, moral theory and aesthetics, but to prevent those who shared his anti-empirical outlook from adopting at the opposite extreme a retaliatory idealism. His criticism of the

[27] Reid, *Essays*, p. 727.

physical analogy in terms of an historical reaction is of the utmost significance for his criticism of Coleridge as well as of Bentham. The distinction that Coleridge and Carlyle attempted to establish between a philosophy that was mechanical and one that was dynamic was unacceptable to him: 'We run from one error into another; and as we were wrong at first, so in altering our course, we have turned about to the opposite extreme.' In all that he wrote Hazlitt strove to hold the balance. Coleridge once said that the real solution lay in a fusion of the philosophies of Bacon and Plato.[28] He himself never succeeded in establishing such a balance. His real allegiance, as J. H. Muirhead has pointed out, was to Plato's theory of ideas as constitutive,[29] and whatever benefit he might have derived from a closer adherence to the philosophy of Kant in the formulation of a philosophical viewpoint which did justice to the 'material' and the 'intellectual' was thereby lost. Hazlitt on the other hand, unfamiliar with the philosophy of Kant, found Bacon sufficient in himself and the solution which he attributed to Bacon was one which he himself attempted to establish and exemplify in every department of his critical and creative effort:

He was one of the most remarkable instances of those men, who, by the rare privilege of their nature, are at once poets and philosophers, and see equally in both worlds—the individual and sensible, and the abstracted and intelligible forms of things. . . . And thus, by incorporating the abstract with the concrete, and general reasoning with individual observation, to give to our conclusions that solidity and firmness which they must otherwise always want.

(xx. 13–14; see ii. 125)

Hazlitt's attitude to Bacon was not altogether free from ambiguity. The account given in the *Lectures* and repeated almost verbatim two years later in his review of Mme de Staël's *De L' Allemagne* contrasts sharply with the narrowly scientific interpretation of Bacon's work in the essay 'The Spirit of Philosophy'. This ambiguity is equally apparent in Coleridge who suggested that the responsibility for the elaboration of the scientific analogy rested with Bacon's followers rather than with Bacon himself: 'There are occasional expressions which seem to have misled many of his followers into a belief that he considered all Wisdom and all

---

[28] Coleridge, *Treatise on Method*, ed. A. D. Snyder (New Haven, 1934), p. 51.
[29] J. H. Muirhead, *Coleridge as Philosopher* (London, 1930), pp. 89–117.

Science both to begin and to end with the objects of the senses. In this gross error are laid the foundations of the modern French school.'[30] Elsewhere, however, he continued to question the real meaning of Bacon: 'He demands, indeed, experiment as the true groundwork of all real knowledge, but what does he mean by experiment?'[31] Shelley had no such reservations. Like the rest of the nineteenth century he saw the challenge of modern empiricism in terms of Bacon's philosophy rather than of Locke's theory of ideas, and like Schlegel attributed to Bacon the growth of eighteenth-century empiricism: 'Lord Bacon ... Hobbes. ... Then, with a less interval of time than of genius, followed [Locke] and the philosophers of his exact and intelligible but superficial school. Their illustrations of some of the minor consequences of the doctrines established by the sublime genius of their predecessors were correct, popular, simple and energetic.'[32] The guarded and restrained language of Hazlitt and Coleridge is altogether absent. Bacon and empiricism are directly equated. Leigh Hunt was in no doubt either on this point: 'It might have been better for Lord Bacon had his being all for experiment not tempted him to take leave of sentiment and imagination.'[33] The equation of Bacon and empiricism is unequivocal; the tone, unlike Shelley's, is less than reverential.

The preoccupation of the early nineteenth century with the fallacious nature of the physical analogy appears at first sight to have little relevance to the social, moral, political, economic and aesthetic problems of a new industrial age still engaged in the Napoleonic Wars and still trying to assimilate the lessons of the French Revolution. The irrelevance, however, is only apparent. The empirical challenge to the existential in the Romantic period was specifically a Utilitarian challenge. It was not overtly epistemological. The Utilitarian principle served to unify a series of social, moral, and political doctrines, but it did so only on the basis of an empirical premiss. To cast doubt on the principle of utility and the doctrines associated with it, it was first necessary to destroy the initial premiss. Far from being irrelevant the epistemological issue was fundamental to the Romantic criticism of Utilitarianism. The

[30] Coleridge, *Treatise on Method*, p. 51.
[31] Coleridge, *The Philosophical Lectures*, ed. K. Coburn (London, 1949), p. 331.
[32] Shelley, *Works*, VII. 8.
[33] *Leigh Hunt's Literary Criticism*, ed. L. H. and C. W. Houtchens (New York, 1956), p. 170.

sustained criticism of empirical epistemology at the beginning of the nineteenth century originated in the heightened awareness stimulated by the growing Utilitarian threat that there were certain things in life which did not belong to the world of fact and science, and that this world was not the sum of life. In isolating the factor responsible, the poets and critics of the early nineteenth century became aware that what had begun as a method designed to extricate philosophy from the terminological wrangles of the Middle Ages had developed into a doctrine which in the non-scientific field determined the conclusions of the philosophers who employed that method. The pejorative references to science and scientists that abound in this period are not aimed at science as such, but are designed to impress on us that the scientific interpretation of natural phenomena appeals to a limited faculty, that, as Arnold was to express it later, 'it is not Linnaeus or Cavendish or Cuvier who gives us the true sense of animals, or water, or plants, who seizes their secret for us, who makes us participate in their life; it is Shakspeare ... it is Wordsworth ... it is Keats'.[34]

The epistemological emphasis did not long survive. The spread of Utilitarianism in the 1820s demanded radical changes in the strategy of the anti-empiricists. The philosophical analysis of the false analogy was no longer sufficient. The Utilitarian doctrines were no longer the sole property of a select group of influential reformers. As a result of a realignment of allegiances within the press, greater publicity for these doctrines was assured. John Black began editing *The Morning Chronicle* in 1817. 1824 saw the establishment of *The Westminster Review*, and in the following year Henry Southern took over *The London Magazine* from John Taylor. In 1830 Albany Fonblanque became the proprietor of *The Examiner*. The need for a new strategy to meet this challenge was most clearly expressed in the early critical essays of Carlyle. Aware of the analogy, Carlyle was not concerned with the empirical theory of knowledge as such in relation to either Bacon or Locke. The tone too is different. Where Jeffrey's was judicial, Hazlitt's passionate, Carlyle's was desperate. Philosophical analysis was replaced by a despairing rhetoric which accurately reflected the increasing gravity of the situation. He exploited the tension between the scientific and the existential in a new way, but he did

---

[34] *The Complete Prose Works of Matthew Arnold*, ed. R. H. Super (Ann Arbor, 1960), III. 13.

so in a manner which could not obscure his debt to the previous generation of Romantic poets and critics:

> Men have lost their belief in the Invisible, and believe, and hope, and work only in the Visible.... Only the material, the immediately practical, not the divine and spiritual, is important to us. The infinite, absolute character of Virtue has passed into a finite, conditional one.... Our true Deity is Mechanism. It has subdued external Nature for us, and we think it will do all other things.[35]

The polarities which Carlyle exploits in this passage—the living and the dead, the creative and the mechanical, the visible and the invisible, the finite and the infinite—are all manifestations of the initial opposition between the scientific and existential. In explaining what he meant by the invisible, divine, spiritual, creative, infinite, Carlyle isolated the existential element in human nature, the defence of which creatively as well as critically was the self-appointed task of the Romantic poets and critics: 'There is a science of *Dynamics* ... as well as of *Mechanics*. There is a science which treats of, and practically addresses, the primary, unmodified forces and energies of man, the mysterious springs of Love, and Fear, and Wonder, of Enthusiasm, Poetry, Religion, all which have a truly vital and *infinite* character.'[36]

It would be difficult to overestimate the significance of the Romantic insistence on the need for a philosophy capable of harmonizing the material and the imaginative, the scientific and the spiritual, the individual and the universal. Literature in the early nineteenth century assumed a new role, but whether creatively in poetry or prose, or critically in essays, lectures and reviews, this insistence is the central demand. Once the distinction between the scientific and existential is grasped and the significance of the demand for their union adequately appreciated, the complexity of the literature and its variety of emphases, while not diminished, are rendered more meaningful and harmonious. The literature of the period at once becomes the expression of a response to life at its deepest level. Its character is determined by its attitude to life. Its critical demands do not exist in a vacuum but are related, however tenuously, to this basic desire for a philosophy which does justice to man as physical object and as existential being. On the theoretical plane this is evident in the importance attached by poets and critics

---

[35] Carlyle, *Essays*, II. 74.   [36] Ibid., II. 68.

alike to the distinctions between reason and understanding, imagination and fancy, reason and imagination, in the greater interest shown in philosophy and philosophers generally by the Romantics, and in the frequent recurrence of such aesthetic problems as art as imitation or copy, art as generalization, art as organic, the imitation of classical models, the psychology of artistic creation, the function of academies of art, whether the arts are progressive. It helps to explain a great many emphases especially characteristic of the age: the violence of its reaction to the tradition of the previous century, the revival of interest in Elizabethan and Jacobean literature, the interest aroused by the Pope–Bowles controversy, the significance attached by De Quincey to his distinction between a literature of knowledge and a literature of power, and in a number of cases the general reception accorded to the works of individual authors.

The pervasive nature of the empirical analogy defies eradication. In the present century Wittgenstein has combated the preoccupation with the method of science just as unsuccessfully as the literary critics of the nineteenth century. Marjorie Grene in a recent discussion of modern philosophical trends has suggested that it is because modern philosophy is still held captive by the alleged objectivism of science that it has been unable to develop an adequate theory of knowledge. She argues for knowing as a venture of living individuals endeavouring to make sense of their experience through the limited endowments of space and time, and concludes that philosophy in the tradition of Locke and Newton is incapable of interpreting living nature or knowledge as an activity of living beings. The terms which she employs in her analysis of the problem are by now very familiar: 'Seventeenth-century thinkers had to free themselves from the bonds of scholastic discipline, and we have had to free ourselves from the bonds of Newtonian abstraction, to dare . . . to *understand*.'[37] By emphasizing the importance of poetry and literary criticism and by referring also at a crucial stage of her argument to Coleridge's conception of imagination and fancy, she makes quite clear her own awareness of the nature of the early nineteenth-century attempt to interpret the existential as existential.

The immediate aim of the present study is to investigate some of the ways in which this central demand is exemplified in Hazlitt's

[37] M. Grene, *The Knower and the Known* (London, 1966), p. 13.

critical theory. To do so, however, without some prior general consideration of the factors which serve to differentiate the work of one writer from another would be to incur the charge that, while the distinction between poetry and science harmonizes a great many elements within the period, it does so at the risk of obscuring the unique nature of an individual writer's contribution to the controversy. While the poets and critics of the early nineteenth century were united in their opposition to empiricism and Utilitarianism, they were in no way similarly united in their views of what constituted the best means of defence. A philosophy capable of harmonizing the individual and the universal may be the central demand, but it is a demand susceptible of different formulations. There is, therefore, in addition to the primary tension between the scientific and the existential, a further secondary tension existing within the existential itself. Hazlitt's opposition to Bentham exemplifies the former; his opposition to the metaphysical abstraction of Coleridge is illustrative of the latter. Hazlitt perceived that the abstraction common to both extremes derived from the method of science. It is this perception which informed Arnold's distrust of metaphysics later in the century and led to his view of theology as the application of the scientific to the inexpressible.[38] As Wittgenstein has expressed it in the present century: 'Philosophers constantly see the method of science before their eyes, and are irresistibly tempted to ask and answer questions in the way science does. This tendency is the real source of metaphysics, and leads the philosopher into complete darkness.'[39] In the present context, the most significant of these questions for the nineteenth century was 'what is poetry?' and it is by considering the variety of responses to this most improper of improper questions that the forces operative behind the self-division of the Romantics can best be discriminated.

3. POETRY VERSUS POETRY: HAZLITT, KEATS, AND SHELLEY

In the course of his criticism of Sir Joshua Reynolds's theory of generality in the third volume of *Modern Painters*, Ruskin broached the question of the definition of poetry:

It seems to me, and may seem to the reader, strange that we should

---

[38] Arnold, *Prose Works*, VI. 171–2.
[39] Wittgenstein, *The Blue and Brown Books* (Oxford, 1958), p. 18.

need to ask the question, "What is poetry?" Here is a word we have been using all our lives, and, I suppose, with a very distinct idea attached to it; and when I am now called upon to give a definition of this idea, I find myself at a pause. What is more singular, I do not at present recollect hearing the question often asked, though surely it is a very natural one; and I never recollect hearing it answered. . . . In general, people shelter themselves under metaphors, and while we hear poetry described as an utterance of the soul, an effusion of Divinity, or voice of nature . . . we never attain anything like a definite explanation.[40]

Ruskin's intellectual bewilderment is the direct result of the impropriety of the question. The poetic response is an authentic one, but it is not one susceptible of direct interrogation. Moreover, his comments at the end of the passage are more than a little disingenuous. The question 'what is poetry?' figured prominently in the literary criticism of the early nineteenth century. The Romantic critics were agreed on one point: poetry was opposed to science and not to prose. They were not content, however, to have this important distinction rest upon an epistemological critique of the empirical theory of knowledge. It was not enough merely to criticize the invalid nature of empirical criteria in non-empirical spheres. A more positive defence of the existential was necessary. For the literary critic this entailed an investigation of the essence of poetry, of what poetry was. The poetic, being one aspect of the existential, a justification of the one was a justification of the other. To defend the poetic was to vindicate the imaginative and spiritual dimensions of man generally. Poetry as Hazlitt once remarked 'is not a branch of authorship: it is "the stuff of which our life is made" ' (v. 2). For Hazlitt, man was not a social or rational animal but a poetical one. Consequently the Romantic response to the question 'what is poetry?' was governed by their response to the much more general question of what it is to be a spiritual being. Critics, like poets 'receive their distinctive character, not from their subject, but from their application to that subject of the ideas . . . "On God, on Nature, and on human life", which they have acquired for themselves'.[41] Differences at the level of critical theory reflect differences at this more fundamental level. The unanimity evident in the Romantic criticism of the physical analogy was

---

[40] *The Works of John Ruskin*, ed. E. T. Cook and A. D. O. Wedderburn (London, 1902–12), V. 28.
[41] Arnold, *Prose Works*, I. 210.

notably absent in the variety of responses to the question 'what is poetry?' The evidence in support of this view cannot be confined to the poetic narrowly construed. It must have reference to the existential generally.

Hazlitt's response to the question was unequivocal. He rejected any attempt to define the poetic in terms of empirical fact. Poetry was not misrepresentation as Bentham maintained; nor was it explicable in terms of empirical psychology. His views in this respect were perfectly consonant with those of his Romantic contemporaries. Although consonant, however, they were not the same. Hazlitt's criticism of the empirical conversion of the poetic operated on a different plane. The premiss from which he conducted his argument differed radically from the premiss utilized by Coleridge and Carlyle. The correct response to the empirical challenge was not to advocate a definition in terms of non-natural or supersensible facts. To do so was merely to exchange one extreme of abstraction for another. Both were equally guilty of converting the poetic into something other than itself, and however divergent the solutions might appear, both shared a common basis in scientific abstraction. They assumed the validity of a question in a situation in which no question could be legitimately asked since no statement could be made. In Hazlitt's view, the correct response was to deny the validity of the question and to reject the view that poetry was in any sense definable.

This emerges clearly from Hazlitt's reply to the *Quarterly Review*'s criticism of the *Lectures on the English Poets* (1818).[42] The anonymous reviewer's principal objection to the first of the lectures, 'On Poetry in General', was that Hazlitt had attempted to define poetry on no less than three occasions, and that not only had he failed to do so, but that in each instance he had provided three conflicting definitions. Hazlitt replied in the following year in *A Letter to William Gifford*. In his reply he exercised admirable restraint. He resisted the temptation to add anything to his previous statement. He resolved the alleged contradictions by pointing out that his 'definition' had a different subject in every case—the poet, the poem and the subject matter of poetry. He denied that his discussion of these had been intended to elicit the specific nature of the poetic, and he went on to turn the general question of definition back upon his critic by impugning the basic assumption behind his

---

[42] [E. S. Barrett], *Quarterly Review*, xix (1818), 424–34.

demand for definition: 'Do you mean that the distinguishing between the compositions of poetry, the talent for poetry, or the
subject-matter of poetry would have told us what *poetry* is? This
is what you would say' (ix. 44). Hazlitt's point is a valid one. Its
significance, however, extends far beyond its limited function
within this local dispute with an anonymous reviewer. It is an
equally effective counter to Coleridge's claim in the *Biographia*,
published only a few months before Hazlitt's first lecture, that the
question 'what is poetry? is so nearly the same question with,
what is a poet? that the answer to the one is involved in the solution
of the other'.[43] To juxtapose the two quotations in this way, one
from Hazlitt and the other from Coleridge, is to crystallize in as
concrete a form as possible the rift among the poets and critics of
the early nineteenth century. Although united in their opposition
to the dominant empirical philosophy, they lived in an age where
as a result of that dominance the urge to define the nature of the
poetic, to draw as distinct a line as possible between science and
poetry, was felt as irresistible. Hazlitt resisted the temptation;
Coleridge did not. He approached the problem with an explicitly
formulated question which implied that what was involved was an
ignorance of facts, albeit in Coleridge's case non-natural, non-
empirical facts. The precise nature of the solution proposed by
Coleridge is considered in detail in Chapter III.

Hazlitt's response to the more general existential issue was
equally unequivocal. It was not the task of the philosopher any
more than of the poet or critic to explain or define those areas of
human experience insusceptible of scientific investigation. In the
essay 'The Spirit of Philosophy', published posthumously in 1836,
Hazlitt made this point explicitly: 'Instead of taking for his motto,
"I will lead you into all knowledge", he should be contented to
say, "I will show you a mystery". The more we are convinced of
the value of the prize, the less we shall be tempted to lay rash and
violent hands on it' (xx. 371). Any attempt to render the poetic or
existential meaningful within a more general metaphysical or
theological framework elicited from Hazlitt an imagery designed
to emphasize the importunate, near-sacrilegious nature of the
attempt. His critical and philosophical position is thus strikingly
similar to that adopted later in the century by Matthew Arnold,
who in 1861 warned F. W. Newman that 'the critical perception of

[43] Coleridge, *Biographia Literaria*, ed. J. Shawcross (London, 1907), II. 12.

poetic truth,—is of all things the most volatile, elusive, and evanescent; by even pressing too impetuously after it, one runs the risk of losing it'.[44] This perception of the self-authenticating nature of poetry and of life is the principal source of the anti-scientific, anti-metaphysical bias evident in the contribution of both to the triangular debate in the nineteenth century. There is nothing in Hazlitt comparable to Arnold's general attack on metaphysics in *God and the Bible*,[45] but the cumulative effect of vocabulary, imagery, tone and use of quotation in his criticism of writers whom he considered guilty of the metaphysical conversion, for example, Reynolds, Schlegel, Coleridge, and Shelley, is perhaps an even more telling testimony to his almost obsessive preoccupation with this particular form of abstraction.

The specific nature of the vocabulary which he employed for this purpose varied in accordance with his estimate of the crudity or subtlety of the particular attempt to 'constrain' or 'lay a trap for truth' (xx. 373). Where the abstraction took the form of a crude religiose orthodoxy as he considered to be the case with the later Wordsworth, he emphasized the 'dogmatic' element with its train of related terms: *inquisitorial, bigoted, narrow, catechising*. He rejected the 'bread-and-butter', the 'Sunday-school' philosophy of *The Excursion* (xix. 73; iv. 46 n) and in his review of the poem itself he made explicit a tenet central to an understanding of his critical theory and practice: 'A speculative bigot is a solecism in the intellectual world' (iv. 116). Where the abstraction was of a metaphysical cast the vocabulary differed, but the suggestion of simplification, distortion and violence was still present in such phrases as 'metaphysical crucible' (viii. 149), 'sublimed into a high spirit of metaphysical philosophy' (xvi. 265), 'pounded . . . in the same metaphysical mortar' (xviii. 55) and 'subjected the Muse to *transcendental* theories' (xi. 30). In his criticism of Coleridge, Schlegel, and German philosophy he stressed the 'abstruse' and 'mystical': terms which, while they served to register his own disagreement, indicated at the same time a certain measure of his appreciation of their subtlety and complexity of thought. His anonymous critic in the *Quarterly Review* did not, however, receive even this modicum of comfort. He had assumed the validity of the question but had not proposed any specific answer. In this instance,

[44] Arnold, *Prose Works*, I. 174.
[45] Ibid., VII. 173.

therefore, it is the tone of Hazlitt's reply that is significant. The dismissive note of the contemptuous and interrogatory 'Do you mean ... ?' was sufficient to indicate his sense of the critic's inherent unfitness to deal with the delicate issues involved.

Hazlitt attributed freedom from this kind of philosophical abstraction to two groups of people: women and painters. In the essay 'On the Ignorance of the Learned' he wrote of the former: '[They] are less implicated in theories; and judge of objects more from their immediate and involuntary impression on the mind, and, therefore, more truly and naturally' (viii. 77). It was to this freedom from abstraction that in the essay 'On Manner' he ascribed the soundness of feminine prose style: 'Women generally write a good style, because they express themselves according to the impression which things make upon them' (iv. 371–2). The relation between abstraction and painting is considered in Part II.

His greatest fear was that in the attempt to express the sense of his awareness of life he might slide over, or be interpreted as sliding over, into mysticism. Leigh Hunt perceived the fine balance which he succeeded in sustaining between the two extremes of abstraction: 'It is not extravagance; it is not mysticism, of which he is sometimes inclined to suspect himself: it is but the doing justice to that real and interior spirit of things, which modifies and enlivens the mystery of existence.'[46]

[46] Hunt, *Literary Criticism*, p. 250. E. W. Schneider, *The Aesthetics of William Hazlitt: a Study of the Philosophical Basis of his Criticism* (Philadelphia, 1933), p. 42, Hazlitt's most enlightened and sympathetic critic has given her support to the view that there is in his work a tendency towards pantheism, although in the main she is an advocate of a 'pluralist' reading very much in harmony with that being put forward. Her motives in adducing two passages (iv. 20, viii. 82–3) which appear to run counter to her general argument are admirable, but her excess of frankness is too damaging to Hazlitt to be allowed to pass without challenge. A footnote reference to the two passages without any attempt to discover whether they can be reconciled with his general viewpoint cannot be allowed to possess the same stringency as the vast quantity of evidence which can be cited in support of the 'experiential' or 'pluralist' point of view. The ease with which she accepts the two passages as evidence of pantheism almost suggests that, subtle and acute as her general analysis is, she was not at that time aware of the implications of Hazlitt's general viewpoint for his theory of poetry as symbol. The ease with which J.-C. Sallé, 'Hazlitt the Associationist', *RES* xv (1964), 38–51, has shown both passages to be reconcilable with the major emphases in Hazlitt's work and to stem from them is sufficient evidence to support this. Although his argument is in the main a psychological one based on Hazlitt's associationism, it is the psychological counterpart of the experiential view at present being urged on the ontological plane. The suspicion that Professor Schneider has failed to grasp the significance of symbol for Hazlitt is

Hazlitt's experiential response to both these issues of the poetic and the existential, with its emphasis on poetic intuitiveness, is clearly important in relation to the philosophical and aesthetic theories of Bentham and Coleridge. Its relevance to the other Romantic poets and critics is perhaps less obvious. Nevertheless, its significance within the wider context of Romantic poetic theory generally is just as great, for although it is a response which underlies the whole of his critical theory and practice, and although he was its original, most articulate and most consistent advocate in the early nineteenth century, he was not alone in his advocacy. In spite of Carlyle's specific rejection of Hazlitt's solution as a valid alternative to a purely empirical interpretation of poetry and life, it was one that was warmly espoused by Keats in his letters, and by Shelley in the *Defence of Poetry*.

To Hazlitt's ability to sustain a balance between the two extremes of abstraction throughout his literary criticism and his other writings, his refusal to show what Bacon had termed 'an impatience of doubt and haste to assertion without due and mature suspension of judgment', can be attributed the extraordinary influence which he exercised upon the mind and thought of Keats. Until this shared experiential response to these two fundamental issues is fully appreciated the most exhaustive listing of parallels and influences must remain of very limited value. Hazlitt initiated the response and developed it to its utmost in a variety of ways, but it is to Keats that we owe the classic formulation of the experiential standpoint in his characterization of negative capability as a condition in which 'man is capable of being in uncertainties, Mysteries, doubts, without any irritable reaching after fact and reason'.[47] This characterization of the true poetic response to the mystery of living is equally effective as a counter to the metaphysical as well as to the scientific 'solution', and is little more than a restatement, in heightened language, of Hazlitt's view that the motto of the philosopher and poet should be ' "I will show you a mystery" ', rather than ' "I will lead you into all knowledge" '. By his immediate reference to Coleridge to exemplify his meaning, Keats was obviously not referring to the empirical brand of factual

heightened by her view that for Hazlitt 'intrinsic value resides in the world primarily' (p. 43). See Chapter II, p. 65.

[47] *Letters of John Keats, 1814–1821*, ed. H. E. Rollins (Cambridge, Mass., 1958), I. 193.

explanation: 'Coleridge, for instance, would let go by a fine
isolated verisimilitude caught from the Penetralium of mystery,
from being incapable of remaining content with half knowledge.'[48]
The substance of Keats's criticism is obvious: the essence of poetry
and of life are lost in Coleridge's attempts to explain them. His
language too is significant: 'a fine isolated verisimilitude caught
from the Penetralium of mystery' is no mere poetic affectation, but
an essential part of the thought being expressed, formally reinforc-
ing the substance of the charge which he is bringing against
Coleridge. The language is suggestive of his awareness of the
subtlety and complexity of thought which Hazlitt so prosaically
distinguished as 'mystical', 'abstruse' or 'transcendental'. Yet Keats
does so while still locating the essential differences between the
poetic and philosophical viewpoints.

The language of Keats's formulation is of interest from another
point of view. For the concept itself he was indebted to Hazlitt.
In its expression he may very well have been influenced by Bacon.
According to P. G. Gates, it is reasonable to assume that Bacon was
a frequent topic of discussion in Hazlitt's conversations with
Keats.[49] Such a view, although conjectural, is not without justification. Their shared experiential response to literature and life
would have made Bacon a natural subject of conversation, since
Bacon, in Hazlitt's view of him, was the most influential advocate
of that response in the whole of English literature. He was both
poet and philosopher, one who saw 'equally in both worlds—the
individual and sensible, and the abstracted and intelligible forms of
things' and one who 'by incorporating the abstract with the concrete, and general reasoning with individual observation [gave] to
our conclusions that solidity and firmness which they must otherwise always want'. He saw in Bacon a philosopher and writer who
rejected both the empirical and metaphysical extremes, who while
reacting against the metaphysical ingenuities of the mediaeval
schoolmen was just as critical of the empirical attempt to subject
all of human experience to the scientific model. One of Hazlitt's

---

[48] Ibid., I. 193–4.

[49] P. G. Gates, 'Bacon, Keats and Hazlitt', *SAQ* XLVI (1947), 239–51. The copy of
the 1629 edition of *The Advancement of Learning* now in the Keats Library in Hamp-
stead was shown by Gates to have belonged to Hazlitt and to contain his marginalia.
E. W. Schneider, *Aesthetics*, p. 42, n. 88, was the first to suggest that Hazlitt's general
attitude found much that was kindred in Bacon.

favourite passages in Bacon occurs in Book One of *The Advancement of Learning*: 'Another [error] is an impatience of doubt and haste to assertion without due and mature suspension of judgment. . . . If a man will begin with certainties, he shall end in doubts; but if he will be content to begin with doubts, he shall end in certainties.' This passage was quoted at length in the *Lectures on the Dramatic Literature of the Age of Elizabeth* (1820) (vi. 331–2), and in Hazlitt's own copy of the 1629 edition this paragraph was singled out by a line drawn in the margin and the comment that it was 'all good'. The language and import of the passage are clearly relevant to Keats's concept of negative capability. It recalls his remark that 'the only means of strengthening one's intellect is to make up ones mind about nothing',[50] and can be interpreted as a criticism of those who, like Coleridge, required specific answers to their questions and were 'incapable of remaining content with half knowledge'. The language of Bacon is also important. It is in the language with its reference to 'doubts' and to 'certainties' that we may find the source of Keats's formulation of negative capability. Hazlitt may also have influenced the manner of its expression. In his essay 'The Spirit of Philosophy' he had expressed the same idea in terms of a philosophy of 'knowledge' and a philosophy of 'mystery', and he did so within the context of a discussion of Bacon's role as a philosopher.

In all this there is much that must remain purely conjectural. We know for certain that Keats admired Hazlitt perhaps more than any other contemporary.[51] He referred to him frequently in his letters and quoted from him extensively. He possessed one of the few copies of Hazlitt's *Essay on the Principles of Human Action*, and in April 1818 he decided to 'prepare myself to ask Hazlitt in about

[50] Keats, *Letters*, II. 213.

[51] The full extent of Keats's critical debt to Hazlitt has only become apparent within the last thirty years. See K. Muir, 'Keats and Hazlitt', in *John Keats: a Reassessment*, ed. K. Muir (Liverpool, 1958), pp. 139–58; R. T. Davies, 'Keats and Hazlitt', *KSMB* VIII (1957), 1–8; R. Müller, 'Some Problems concerning Keats and Hazlitt', *KSMB* VIII (1957), 33–7. An attempt has been made to trace Hazlitt's influence on Keats to a shared attitude to life by C. L. Finney, *The Evolution of Keats's Poetry* (Cambridge, Mass., 1936) and J. R. Caldwell, 'Beauty is Truth', *University of California Publications in English*, VIII (1940), 131–53. Although negative capability has been interpreted in purely psychological terms by W. J. Bate, *John Keats* (Cambridge, Mass., 1963), pp. 233–63, and H. M. Sikes, 'The Poetic Theory and Practice of Keats: the Record of a Debt to Hazlitt', *PQ* XXXVIII (1959), 401–12, the critical tradition since S. Colvin, *John Keats: his Life and Poetry* (London, 1917) and through the work of J. M. Murry, H. I'A. Fausset, C. D. Thorpe, and C. L.

a years time the best metaphysical road I can take'.[52] Like Hazlitt he admired Bacon, and his two references to him in the letters are complimentary. We know too that the copy of *The Advancement of Learning*, now in the Keats Library and for long thought to have belonged to Keats and to contain marginalia by him, in fact belonged to Hazlitt. In view of this, and in view also of the striking similarity of their response to literature and life, it is not improbable that Keats's characterization of negative capability owed much to unconscious echoes from his reading of Bacon and his conversations with Hazlitt.

Hazlitt's objection to abstraction can now be rendered more specific. It was specifically an objection to all closed systems of thought in which the whole of human experience was interpreted in the light of the system's initial premiss, empirical or metaphysical, with scant regard to the individuality, complexity and diversity of 'the truth of things'. It was a rejection of closed systems as such. The implications of this rejection for his work as a critic and essayist are far-reaching. Abstraction for Hazlitt constituted the gravest threat to the quality of man's response to life, and to the quality of civilized living generally. In an age so dependent on systems, theories, dogmas, creeds, doctrines, and party-phrases that he designated it an age of abstraction (xviii. 305), it seemed to him that 'perhaps nine-tenths of the exertions of the human intellect have been directed . . . to prove the truth of doctrines' (xx. 372). His self-appointed task as philosopher, critic and essayist was to warn and to counter in every way possible the pernicious con-

---

Finney, has emphasized Keats's concern with reality. In the main the stress has been laid on a transcendental or mystical interpretation in which Keats's experiential view is seen as a belief in a 'vast invisible reality', C. D. Thorpe, *The Mind of John Keats* (New York, 1926), p.188. The validity of Caldwell's study of the beauty-truth equation depends upon his implicit recognition of an experiential response, the most explicit recognition of which is to be found in N. F. Ford's 'The Prefigurative Imagination of John Keats', *Stanford University Publications in Language and Literature*, IX (1951), 81–246, where the author argues that 'no colorless, incorporeal, Platonic heaven beckons to . . . Keats' (p.115). U. Amarasinghe's theory that Hazlitt's critical views were influenced by his personal association with Keats is original but unsupported by any evidence, *Dryden and Pope in the Early Nineteenth Century, 1800–30* (Cambridge, 1962), p.158. The personal relationship is stressed by C. D. Thorpe, 'Keats and Hazlitt: a Record of Personal Relationship and Critical Estimate', *PMLA* LXII (1947), 487–502. Irritated by this emphasis on Keats's 'debt' to Hazlitt, W. Garrett has replied with 'Hazlitt's Debt to C. W. Dilke', *KSMB* xv (1964), 37–42.

[52] Keats, *Letters*, I. 274.

sequences which he attributed to this perennial human tendency. He found an ally in Keats, but the contrast with Coleridge in this respect is striking. In a letter to Thomas Allsop in 1822 Coleridge confessed to being possessed of an 'intense craving after a resting-place for my Thoughts in some *principle* that was derived from experience, but of which all other knowledge should be but so many repetitions . . . as circles, squares, triangles, etc., etc., are but so many positions of space'.[53] Coleridge did not object to systems or abstraction, only to inadequate systems of abstraction. Yet the analogy which he employs in this letter is itself a clear indication of the circuitous and insidious manner in which science exacted its revenge. He wanted above all what Kant would have denied him: a science of metaphysics. Hazlitt's reply to this demand for one all-embracing truth is to be found once more in the little-known essay 'The Spirit of Philosophy':

> Another rule in philosophising is . . . to know where to stop. A man, by great labour and sagacity, finds out one truth; but from the importunate craving of the mind to know all, he would fain persuade himself that this one truth includes all others. Such has been the error of almost all systems and system-makers, who lose the advantage of the conquests they have achieved by pushing them too far, and aiming at universal empire.

(xx. 375)

The irresistible human urge to ask existential questions and to provide answers which by definition are factual, whether scientific or transcendent, was just as much appreciated by Hazlitt and Keats as it was by Arnold later in the century. Systems and theories represented the antithesis of the essential openness of the experiential or poetic response. This is the point of Keats's criticism of Coleridge, while it is Hazlitt's praise of the greatest artists that they are 'open to all impressions alike' (xvii. 148). His admiration for Montaigne, for example, stemmed from the view that he 'wrote not to make converts of others to established creeds and prejudices, but to satisfy his own mind of the truth of things' (vi. 93). The demand for an imaginative or poetic openness is the central characteristic of the experiential response, whether it appears as a demand for negative capability as in Keats, imaginative sincerity as in Hazlitt,

---

[53] *Letters, Conversations and Recollections of S. T. Coleridge*, ed. T. Allsop (London, 1836), II. 136.

or a 'dialectical open-endedness' as in the case of Arnold.[54] In the light of this demand Hazlitt's general and critical terminology acquires a new significance. His use of certain terms has never been adequately appreciated before owing to the failure to see them in relation to the ontological aspect of his critical theory, to the question of the essence of poetry, rather than the question of the means whereby that essence is embodied in concrete forms. It is a demand, moreover, that was made explicit, although within a limited context, as early as 1812 in the *Lectures on English Philosophy*: 'They [system-makers] have in fact always a purpose . . . [which] takes away that tremulous sensibility to every slight and wandering impression which is necessary to complete the fine balance of the mind, and enable us to follow all the infinite fluctuations of thought through their nicest distinctions' (ii. 261). This ability he attributed in 1819 in 'The Indian Jugglers' to the poet, and by implication to the poet in all of us. The poetic response alone possessed the 'trembling sensibility which is awake to every change and every modification of its ever-varying impressions' (viii. 83).

Keats's use of negative capability in his analysis of the character of Charles Wentworth Dilke and of the poetry of Wordsworth helps to clarify this point, and enables us to appreciate that Hazlitt's emphasis on imaginative open-endedness is no mere personal idiosyncrasy possessing little or no general critical relevance. Keats's objection in both these instances is to dogma and system. 'Dilke', he wrote, 'was a Man who cannot feel he has a personal identity unless he has made up his Mind about every thing. The only means of strengthening one's intellect is to make up ones mind about nothing—to let the mind be a thoroughfare for all thoughts. Not a select party. . . . They never begin upon a subject they have not preresolved on. They want to hammer their nail into you and if you turn the point, still they think you wrong. Dilke

---

[54] W. A. Madden, *Matthew Arnold: a Study of the Aesthetic Temperament in Victorian England* (Bloomington, Ind., 1967), p. 145. Madden argues that Arnold's principal allegiance is to the Romantics who believed that 'the aesthetic consciousness was capable of organizing and transfiguring the whole of human experience' (p. v). The priority which Arnold confers upon the aesthetic consciousness above all other forms of consciousness he holds to be the key to Arnold's work as a poet and critic. The role which Madden assigns to Arnold in this excellent study is similar in some respects to that envisaged by the present author for Hazlitt. Neither doubted for a moment the self-authenticating nature of poetry and they sought in all their writings to prevent its subversion by science, philosophy, and religion.

will never come at a truth as long as he lives; because he is always trying at it.'[55] For Hazlitt, the artist must be 'awake', 'alive', or 'open to all impressions alike'. For Keats, the mind must be 'a thoroughfare for all thoughts'. The demand is the same in both cases. As the implications of negative capability became clearer, Keats's view of Wordsworth altered dramatically. In January 1818 *The Excursion* was one of 'three things to rejoice at in this Age'.[56] By February of the same year he was unyielding in his opposition to what he conceived to be Wordsworth's subversion of the poetic:

> But for the sake of a few fine imaginative or domestic passages, are we to be bullied into a certain Philosophy engendered in the whims of an Egotist—Every man has his speculations, but every man does not brood and peacock over them till he makes a false coinage and deceives himself —Many a man can travel to the very bourne of Heaven, and yet want confidence to put down his halfseeing. . . . We hate poetry that has a palpable design upon us—and if we do not agree, seems to put its hand in its breeches pocket.[57]

'We hate poetry that has a palpable design upon us'—'They have in fact always a purpose'. The emphasis in both Keats and Hazlitt is the same. Their objection is not just an objection to poetry as didactic, but a total opposition to the philosophical viewpoint in any form. Keats's hostility is again formally reinforced by the language he uses to express the substance of his criticism. If we compare his criticism of Coleridge with his criticism of Dilke and Wordsworth, it is evident that his language alone would serve to discriminate the metaphysical on the one hand and the dogmatic on the other, between the subtle, sophisticated, and complex thought of Coleridge as opposed to the crude, literal orthodoxy of the later Wordsworth.

Hazlitt was the most consistent and articulate advocate of the experiential response in the early nineteenth century. Keats gave it classic shape in the concept of negative capability. It was Shelley, however, with whose poetry, politics, and personality Hazlitt had such an imperfect sympathy, who provided the most sustained, impassioned and eloquent defence of the poetic in *A Defence of Poetry*. Whatever construction may be placed upon his poetry, 'no colorless, incorporeal, Platonic heaven beckons' to Shelley in the *Defence*.[58] The language and imagery seem to suggest at times

[55] Keats, *Letters*, II. 213.   [56] Ibid., I. 203.   [57] Ibid., I. 223–4.   [58] See n. 51.

a mystical or *quasi*-philosophical standpoint. The poet is said to participate 'in the eternal, the infinite, and the one', and poetry to lift 'the veil from the hidden beauty of the world'.[59] Such metaphorical language was common to many of the Romantic poets and critics and is to be found even in Hazlitt.[60] Shelley's refusal to impose an alien pattern on poetic experience cut him off decisively from the philosophical abstraction of Coleridge and Carlyle: 'Poetry is a sword of lightning, ever unsheathed, which consumes the scabbard that would contain it.'[61] This clear statement of his allegiance to the experiential at the level of critical theory enables us to interpret other less concrete statements in a more concrete manner. Thus, when he says that the poet's auditors are 'as men entranced by the melody of an unseen musician, who feel that they are moved and softened, yet know not whence or why', or speaks of the poet's 'unapprehended inspiration',[62] he was indicating the indefinable, mysterious nature of the poetic experience and rejecting any attempt to find for it a pattern or explanation.

There is, however, one important difference between the response of Hazlitt and Keats and the response of Shelley. The former were critical of all forms of abstraction—commonplace dogmatism, religious orthodoxy, and metaphysical system-building. In the *Defence* Shelley on the other hand chose to concentrate exclusively upon religious abstraction. Dante, Calderon, and Milton are criticized for their distortion of reality in the interests of religious dogma: 'The distorted notions of invisible things which Dante and his rival Milton have idealised, are merely the mask and the mantle in which these great poets walk through eternity enveloped and disguised.'[63] It is clear that for Shelley the religious framework did not 'explain' the mystery of man's existence but succeeded only in distorting the reality of felt human experience. His language and the imagery of appearance and reality point to the essential falsification consequent upon the imposition of this more palpable pattern in terms of non-natural facts. In his comparison of Shakespeare and Calderon the language once more enforces the substance of the criticism:

---

[59] Shelley, *Works*, VII. 112, 117.

[60] Cf. Hazlitt: 'Art may be said to draw aside the veil from nature' (iv. 74). Schneider's pantheistic interpretation of two passages in Hazlitt, see n. 46, is indicative of the dangers inherent in this kind of language.

[61] Shelley, *Works*, VII. 122.   [62] Ibid., VII. 116, 140.   [63] Ibid., VII. 129.

Calderon, in his religious Autos, has attempted to fulfil some of the high conditions of dramatic representation neglected by Shakspeare; such as the establishing a relation between the drama and religion, and the accommodating them to music and dancing; but he omits the observation of conditions still more important, and more is lost than gained by a substitution of the rigidly-defined and ever-repeated idealisms of a distorted superstition for the living impersonations of the truth of human passion.[64]

For Shelley, as for Hazlitt and Keats, the tendency of abstraction towards reification is unnecessary. The human soul is not an invention of religion whatever religion may have engrafted upon it: 'There is no occasion to resort to any mystical union . . . nor to plant the root of hope in the grave, nor to derive it from the skies. Its root is in the heart of man: it lifts its head above the stars' (iv. 250).[65] Thus Hazlitt criticized Wordsworth's *Immortality Ode*. In the *Defence* Shelley attempted to correct the violent empirical reaction of his earlier writings against the religious characterization of reality, substituting a solution which, while it still rejected an explanation in terms of the supersensible, recognized the authenticity of an existential situation in which no question could be asked, and no answer given: 'But whilst the sceptic destroys gross superstitions, let him spare to deface, as some of the French writers have defaced, the eternal truths charactered upon the imaginations of men.'[66]

To juxtapose Hazlitt and Shelley in this way may seem surprising. It appears to bear little relationship to any of the more conventional categories and classifications of literary history. To Carlyle, however, who was fully conscious of all the implications of the triangular debate in the early nineteenth century, their juxtaposition was perfectly natural. Unlike Coleridge with whom he shared certain basic assumptions, Carlyle openly acknowledged the two fold nature of the challenge to his position: a challenge that emanated not merely from empiricism but from poetry itself. When Carlyle said that the poet was the interpreter of the 'Divine

---

[64] Ibid., VII. 120.

[65] Hazlitt considered that 'the theological doctrines of *Original Sin*, of *Grace*, and *Election*, admit of a moral and natural solution' (ix. 220). Cf. Keats: 'For as one part of the human species must have their carved Jupiter; so another part must have the palpable and named Mediatior and saviour, their Christ their Oromanes and their Vishnu', *Letters*, II. 103.

[66] Shelley, *Works*, VII. 132.

Idea'[67] that pervaded the universe, he meant precisely that, and although it is not possible to generalize about his philosophical or religious position, there seems to be little doubt that his characterization of reality is ultimately theistic.[68] Consequently his criticism of Hazlitt and Shelley while recognizing the common existential bond was unsparing in the severity of its attack on what he conceived to be their reduction of the divine to the human. Hazlitt feared mysticism in himself and criticized it in others. Carlyle was prepared to accept the mysticism which he considered inseparable from the excellences of the transcendental philosophy.[69] It was the 'faithlessness' of the experiential response which he would not tolerate in spite of the 'nobility' of its professors:

[They] dared to say No, and cannot yet say Yea; but feel that in the No they dwell as in a Golgotha, where life enters not.... Hard, for most part, is the fate of such men; the harder the nobler they are. In dim forecastings, wrestles within them the 'Divine Idea of the World,' yet will nowhere visibly reveal itself. They have to realise a Worship for themselves, or live unworshipping. The Godlike has vanished from the world; and they, by the strong cry of their soul's agony, like true wonderworkers, must again evoke its presence.... Hear a Shelley filling the earth with inarticulate wail; like the infinite, inarticulate grief and weeping of forsaken infants.... How many a poor Hazlitt must wander on God's verdant earth, like the Unblest on burning deserts; passionately dig wells, and draw up only the dry quicksand ... and die and make no sign![70]

Carlyle's confidence in his own case stemmed to some extent from the fact that like Arnold he took a limited view of the creative achievement of the early nineteenth century in England. Confronted by the massive creative achievement of Goethe and Schiller, he was not quite so confident, and in places appeared almost to doubt his own theistic interpretation of poets as 'the

---

[67] Carlyle, *Essays*, I. 58.

[68] C. F. Harrold, 'The Mystical Element in Carlyle, 1827–34', *MP* XXIX (1932), 475, has summarized some of the earlier and divergent interpretations of Carlyle, concluding that his mysticism 'shines like a golden gleam through the darker texture of his Calvinism'. René Wellek, *A History of Modern Criticism, 1750–1950* (London, 1955), III. 102, has pointed out that Carlyle in spite of his theistic interpretation can hardly be called a Christian in any orthodox sense of the word. J. E. Baker's view of Carlyle as a 'pure humanist' is a minority one, 'Our New Hellenic Renaissance', in *The Reinterpretation of Victorian Literature*, ed. J. E. Baker (Princeton, 1950), p. 227.

[69] Carlyle, *Essays*, I. 72.

[70] Ibid., III. 31–2.

dispensers . . . of God's everlasting wisdom':[71] 'When Goethe and Schiller say or insinuate that art is higher than religion, do they mean perhaps this? That whereas religion represents . . . the good as *infinitely* . . . different from the evil, but sets them in a state of hostility . . . art likewise admits and inculcates this quite infinite difference, but *without* hostility, with peacefulness. . . . *Sehr einseitig*! Yet perhaps there is a glimpse of the truth here.'[72] These doubts excepted, Carlyle's ultimate position must be characterized as a pugnacious and assertive theistic idealism essentially at odds with the experiential approach to poetry and life to be found in the writings of Hazlitt, Keats, and Shelley.

[71] Ibid., I. 58.

[72] J. A. Froude, *Thomas Carlyle: a History of the First Forty Years of his Life, 1795–1835* (London, 1882), II. 93–4. A similar doubt occurs a little later, ibid., II. 98.

CHAPTER TWO

Morality and Science: Hazlitt and Bentham

He turns wooden utensils in a lathe for exercise, and
fancies he can turn men in the same manner.
The Spirit of the Age, xi. 16

1. HAZLITT'S EARLY PHILOSOPHICAL DEVELOPMENT

THE most significant feature of Romantic poetic theory is the
tension between the scientific and the existential. The distinction
was enforced by the Romantic critics in a variety of ways: philosophical, aesthetic, and religious. The epistemological criticism of
the physical analogy was one facet of their philosophical defence.
This, in turn, was supplemented in a number of instances by a
criticism of empirical moral theory which, like its epistemological
counterpart, served to reinforce the basic dichotomy. The transition
from the epistemological to the moral will appear less abrupt if we
bear in mind the Romantic insistence that the source of the Utilitarian ethic lay in the scientific bias of empirical epistemology.
'Moral Newtonianism' is how one modern writer has characterized
the Utilitarianism of the early nineteenth century.[1] Moreover,
since the moral, like the poetic, is one aspect of the existential, and
since the character of the critic, like that of the poet, is determined
by his response to life and its fundamental issues, an examination
of Hazlitt's moral beliefs and the ethical theory underlying them
will be of the utmost significance for the subsequent analysis of
the concepts and terminology of the critic.

The self-division apparent in Romantic epistemology and poetic
theory is also present in the Romantic defence of the existential
nature of man as a moral being. There is no need, however, to
dwell on the precise nature of these differences since they are the
consequence, in part at least, of the divergences already evident at
the epistemological and aesthetic levels and mirror these fairly
accurately. It is entirely characteristic of these differences that
Hazlitt's criticism of empirical moral theory should be directed

[1] E. Halévy, *The Growth of Philosophic Radicalism* (London, 1928, 1952), p. 6.

primarily against the Utilitarianism of Bentham, and the criticism of Coleridge against the theological utilitarianism of Paley. The ultimate tendency of Coleridge's moral theory, which closely resembles Hazlitt's in some respects, will emerge indirectly in the analysis of his poetic theory in Chapter III.

For Coleridge and Carlyle the relationship between empirical epistemology and empirical moral theory was more than merely general. The demand for 'visibility' in epistemology corresponded to the demand for utility in moral theory. The empirical emphasis on verification implied a specifically utilitarian rendering of the moral imperative. The question 'what is rightness?' like the question 'what is poetry?' implied an ignorance of facts, and neither Coleridge nor Carlyle was prepared to accept an answer in terms of empirical facts. Coleridge traced the origin of Utilitarianism to its source in the physical analogy and commented: 'Dazzled by the real or supposed discoveries which it had made, the more the understanding was enriched, the more did it become debased; till science itself put on a selfish and sensual character, and immediate utility . . . was imposed as the test of all intellectual powers and pursuits. . . . [Understanding] was tempted to throw off all show of reverence to the spiritual and even to the moral powers and impulses of the soul.'[2] In making a similar point Carlyle explicitly established a parallel between the moral and poetic as twin aspects of the existential: 'Should Understanding attempt to . . . speculate of Virtue, it ends in *Utility*, making Prudence and a sufficiently cunning love of Self the highest good. Consult Understanding about the Beauty of Poetry, and it asks, Where is this Beauty? or discovers it . . . in rhythms and fitnesses.'[3] Implicit in Carlyle's statement is an important but easily overlooked distinction. By differentiating between two empirical approaches to the question of the essence of the poetic he is indicating an inner tension within empiricism itself. Logically at least, if not historically, the tension which Carlyle isolated in the empirical approach to the poetic exists also in relation to the moral. Thus in equating the empirical demand for verification in the epistemological sphere with a utilitarian inter-pretation in the moral, Coleridge and Carlyle were guilty of a slight

---

[2] Coleridge, *Works*, I. 463–4. Cf. Carlyle's view that 'to inquire after its *utility*, would be like inquiring after the *utility* of a God, or, what to the Germans would sound stranger than it does to us, the *utility* of Virtue and Religion', *Essays*, I. 56.
[3] Carlyle, *Essays*, I. 82.

over-simplification. A utilitarian rendering of the moral imperative is not the only possible empirical answer. The distinction between an extreme empiricism and a more moderate empiricism is important in relation to Bentham, whose interpretation of morality and poetry exemplifies the practical feasibility of an allegiance to both. His factual rendering of the moral in terms of utility was balanced by his unequivocal rejection of the poetic as misrepresentation.[4] It is true that Bentham allowed a utilitarian escape clause for painting, sculpture and music,[5] but this concession does not materially alter his position in relation to poetic or artistic value. Hazlitt's moral theory found its most mature expression in his opposition to Bentham's Utilitarianism. It is first necessary, however, to consider the implications of his first philosophical work for the more mature ethical theory which emerges in his later writings.

Hazlitt's *Essay on the Principles of Human Action* was first published in 1805. It was neglected during his lifetime, and although a second edition was published in 1836, it has never been reprinted separately since. The reasons for its unpopularity are fairly obvious. Its intrinsic merits as a work of philosophy are slight. It is largely derivative, and although it reveals Hazlitt as an acute philosophical critic, it can hardly be said to represent an original and constructive contribution to philosophical thought. It is not to be valued highly, therefore, as a positive investigation of metaphysical truth.[6] Its 'dramatic' significance, however, cannot be exaggerated. Dramatically, it is invaluable, both as an exhibition of character, beliefs and attitudes, and as representative of a perennial posture of mind in the youthful idealist. Philosophical neglect is understandable. Its neglect by literary historians and critics stems from the widespread failure to appreciate the central importance of Hazlitt's critical effort in English literary criticism and its relation to his general experiential viewpoint.

The importance of the *Essay* in the context of Hazlitt's mature ethical theory lies in the three principles that emerge from his attempt to construct a logical and epistemological framework for

---

4 ' "All poetry is misrepresentation" ', *Mill on Bentham and Coleridge*, ed. F. R. Leavis (London, 1950), p. 95. See also J. S. Mill, *Autobiography*, ed. J. J. Coss (New York, 1924, 1960), p. 78.

5 *Mill on Bentham and Coleridge*, p. 95.

6 J. Noxon, 'Hazlitt as Moral Philosopher', *Ethics*, LXXIII (1963), 279–83, praises Hazlitt's handling of abstruse philosophical concepts.

Butler's classic refutation of psychological egoism.[7] These principles are: the active nature of the human mind and its faculties;[8] the inability of associationism to give an adequate account of conscience, virtue and the intellectual faculties; and thirdly, the natural disinterestedness of the human mind which he elaborates in terms of the self-transcending nature of the imagination. Even to list the principles is sufficient to illustrate the absurdity of Bulwer-Lytton's attempted classification of the *Essay* as materialist.[9] Collectively they represent a systematic rejection as early as 1805 of the three basic tenets of the modern philosophy: its empirical epistemology, its empirical psychology based on Hartley's 'renovation' of Locke,[10] and its empirical ethic as exemplified by the moral theory of Helvétius and, more remotely, of Hobbes.[11]

The main interest of the *Essay* lies in Hazlitt's rejection of the doctrine of psychological egoism. Almost all his criticisms of Utilitarian theory can be traced ultimately to his objection to this psychological theory of the nature of man which Bentham expressed in the following way: 'Taking the whole of life together, there exists not, nor ever can exist, that human being in whose instance any public interest he can have had, will not, in so far as depends upon himself, have been sacrificed to his own personal interest.'[12] A few pages later Bentham returned to the charge and reiterated it more succinctly: 'In every human breast ... self-regarding interest is predominant over social interest: each person's own individual interest, over the interests of all other persons taken

[7] L. M. Trawick, 'Sources of Hazlitt's "Metaphysical Discovery"', *PQ* XLII (1963), 277–82, has shown that the framework as well as the substance of his argument was derived from Butler.

[8] Not until 1807 did Hazlitt view the mind as creative when for the first time he referred to Kant's view that 'the mind alone is formative' (i. 130). His slight acquaintance with Kant's philosophy is discussed by R. Wellek, *Immanuel Kant in England, 1793–1838* (Princeton, 1931), pp. 164–71.

[9] Bulwer, *England and the English*, II. 161–2. Hazlitt is discussed in conjunction with Bentham, James Mill and Austin.

[10] *Mill on Bentham and Coleridge*, p. 115.

[11] The evidence for the influence exercised by these writers on Utilitarian thought is to be found in Mill's various criticisms of Bentham. The influence of Hartley and Helvétius in particular is discussed fully by Halévy, *The Growth of Philosophic Radicalism*, pp. 5–34. The influence of Hobbes on the French philosophers so admired by the Utilitarians is considered by V. W. Topazio, *D'Holbach's Moral Philosophy* (Geneva, 1956).

[12] *The Complete Works of Jeremy Bentham*, ed. J. Bowring (Edinburgh, 1838–43), II. 475.

together.'[13] John Stuart Mill dissociated himself from the doctrine.[14] It is questionable, however, whether he ever really escaped from the egoistic psychology of Bentham and his father. In the *Essay* itself there is no mention either of Bentham or Paley.[15] Instead, Hobbes, Rochefoucauld, and Mandeville, the figures traditionally associated with the doctrine in the eighteenth century, together with Helvétius, provide the focal point of Hazlitt's criticism.[16] The main value of the *Essay* for the modern reader does not lie in its analysis of identity which in Hazlitt's view constituted its chief claim to originality, but in its expression of a view that was to become a lifelong conviction: that man is capable of the greatest self-sacrifice which cannot ultimately be reduced to self-interest.

In his criticism of psychological egoism Hazlitt developed a theory of imagination as the faculty of self-transcendence. Egoism was not only a libel on human nature. It excluded the possibility of moral action altogether by excluding the possibility of impartiality. By creating the possibility of impartial action, imagination ensured the morality of individual actions. The *Essay*, therefore, established the imagination as the moral faculty, and its central importance in this respect never altered in any of his subsequent ethical writings. He opposed imagination to reason in a manner similar to the opposition between reason and understanding proposed by Kant and adopted by Coleridge and Carlyle. In Hazlitt's moral theory on the other hand reason and understanding were synonymous. In spite of this he remained truer to the spirit of Kant's distinction than either Coleridge or Carlyle.

The term 'imagination' invites a psychological interpretation and emphasis, a danger which Carlyle recognized and avoided.[17] Hazlitt's account of imagination as the moral faculty, however, has philosophical as well as psychological implications. It is not just a psychological theory within a philosophical context, to be valued only for the way in which it prefigures the later emphasis on the role of sympathetic imagination in his psychology of artistic

---

[13] Ibid., II. 482.

[14] Bulwer, *England and the English* (Appendix B), II. 336–40.

[15] One of Hazlitt's main objections to Malthus was the latter's allegiance to Paley's theological utilitarianism in which self-interest was always the motive to right action (i. 346 n). Mill was equally critical of this element in Paley's theory, *Mill on Bentham and Coleridge*, p. 139.

[16] Hazlitt invariably grouped these writers together in his criticism of this doctrine (i. 83; ii. 225–6; ix. 184; xx. 36–7).

[17] Carlyle, *Essays*, I. 51.

creation. Its main value lies in the implications it has for his general philosophical position and for his critical theory considered onto-logically. Its philosophical importance is twofold. It emphasized self-transcendence as a necessary prerequisite for the achievement of the openness characteristic of the experiential stance, moral as well as poetic.[18] In addition, it has obvious affinities with Kant's concept of the autonomously legislative will operative within an ideal kingdom of ends in which the moral agent is both subject and legislator, willing for himself yet bound by the moral imperative willed. The role of practical reason in Kant's ethical theory and the role of imagination in Hazlitt's are essentially experiential. They are not concerned with knowing moral freedom cognitively as an idea as in Coleridge, but are faculties which realize that freedom in the moral life. Their roles are not to furnish an object of intuition but a law. Nevertheless, Hazlitt differed from Kant in other no less fundamental respects, since like Coleridge he did not conceive of the moral faculty merely as a mode of volitional consciousness, whilst, as the faculty of the poetic, imagination in its experience of reality was not confined to moral action.

The significance of the *Essay* in relation to Hazlitt's mature ethical theory is fourfold. It established imagination as the moral faculty. By insisting upon a principle of impartiality in any account of the moral imperative it established morality on the existential plane. The *Essay* exhibited the incompatibility of this principle with the doctrine of psychological egoism and evinced throughout the highest estimation of the moral potentialities of human nature. His belief that 'there is something really great and excellent in the world' (i. 115) was the source of inspiration for the two little-known works published shortly after the *Essay*—*Free Thoughts on Public Affairs* (1806), and *A Reply to the Essay on Population* (1807). One of his principal objections to Malthus's theory of population growth was that by heeding its social inferences 'we suffer ourselves to be wheedled into a silly persuasion, that the worst thing that could happen for the human race would be their being able to realise not in words only, but in deed all the fine things, that have been said of them' (i. 207).[19] Man, he once wrote, 'cannot entirely

[18] J. Kinnaird, 'The Forgotten Self', *Partisan Review*, xxx (1963), 302–6, is one of the few critics who has appreciated the philosophical implications of Hazlitt's insistence on self-transcendence, and in consequence has written a book review more significant than most scholarly articles.

[19] K. Smith's *The Malthusian Controversy* (London, 1951) opens and closes with

efface the stamp of the Divinity on him' (ix. 220), and it was this faith which was to provide the basis of the positive moral vision inspiring the greatest of his essays. It also has an important bearing on his criticism of certain writers who, he conceived, emphasized the impotence at the expense of the power of man.[20] His preference for 'that which confers dignity on human nature to that which degrades it' (ix. 198) is a factor in his philosophical and literary criticism which cannot be ignored.

2. HAZLITT'S MORAL THEORY

(i) *The Moral Imperative*

Hazlitt's criticism of Bentham is to be found in four major essays: 'Jeremy Bentham' in *The Spirit of the Age* (xi. 5–16), 'On Reason and Imagination', 'The New School of Reform', and 'On People of Sense' in *The Plain Speaker* (xii. 44–53, 179–95, 246–51). All of these essays were written in the 1820s and are Hazlitt's response to the alarming growth of Utilitarianism during that period. The significance of his criticism of Utilitarianism in these essays has never been appreciated either at the level of general philosophical history or, more surprisingly, by his own critics. It has, for example, become a commonplace in histories of English philosophical thought to refer John Stuart Mill's deviations from Utilitarian orthodoxy to the influence of the Romantics, especially of Coleridge and Carlyle. Yet neither critic ever specifically criticized Bentham's Utilitarianism, whereas every point raised by Hazlitt in his criticism of Bentham is to be found in one or other of Mill's defences where they are acknowledged as valid, or rejected and the basic doctrine reinterpreted to meet the criticism. His criticism of Bentham is important for a number of reasons. It has intrinsic and historical value as the first philosophical analysis of the weaknesses of Utilitarianism. The common view that Sidgwick was the first to expose the fallacies of the doctrine is unfounded. Hazlitt's own moral theory finds its most mature expression in opposition to empirical moral theory. To appreciate fully his experiential attitude to literature it is important to see its basis in his experiential view of

---

two quotations from Hazlitt's *Reply* expressive of his positive valuation of human life. Cf: '*Que peu de chose est la vie humaine*—is an exclamation in the mouths of moralists and philosophers, to which I cannot agree' (viii. 27).

[20] See Chapter VII, 'The Power and the Impotence', pp. 185–91.

the moral life as this emerges from his lifelong antagonism to the Utilitarianism of Jeremy Bentham.

The *Essay* argued for the existence of a moral imperative that could not be reduced to self-interest, explained in terms of association, or interpreted as a feeling or as a moral sentiment (i. 80). It did so in a highly abstract manner in keeping with the philosophical tradition of the previous century. The contrast with his criticism of Bentham twenty years later is striking. Literature had taken over philosophy's role in the defence of the existential. Hazlitt's criticism gave concrete expression to his view of the substance of moral action both with regard to respect for law and respect for persons and the basis of both in the good will.[21] It did so, however, in the form of essays written for the popular press and designed to make an immediate impact on a non-philosophical public. Consequently it is all too easy to underestimate the extreme subtlety behind the popular expression of what are in effect the first major criticisms of dogmatic Utilitarianism.

Since Hazlitt's moral theory found its most mature expression in his opposition to Bentham's Utilitarianism it is important that the ambiguity of this term be appreciated from the outset. The main danger in the use of the term 'utilitarianism' arises out of the tension between the original meaning of the word and its historical meaning. In the first sense utilitarianism refers to that class of moral theories which postulates a connection between the rightness of an action and its end. Hitherto, however, the term has not been used in its original but in its historical sense given currency by John Stuart Mill to indicate the much more specific form of universalistic hedonistic utilitarianism. When Hazlitt's ethical theory is later characterized as a 'reasoned utilitarianism',[22] the term is being used in its generic and original sense to indicate any theory which

[21] In view of Hazlitt's ignorance of Kant's ethical theory, the 'Kantian' elements in his own theory must be attributed to the anti-empirical tradition of Butler, Price, Reid, and Stewart whose deontological emphases have frequently evoked comparison with Kant, C. D. Broad, *Five Types of Ethical Theory* (London, 1930), p. 53; Price, *Review*, pp. ix–x; Reid, *Works*, ed. W. Hamilton (Edinburgh, 1863), p. 592 n; Carlyle, *Essays*, 1. 79 n. Except in the case of Butler, however, Hazlitt made no explicit acknowledgment of any debt. For his acquaintance with the work of Price and Reid, see H. Baker, *William Hazlitt* (Cambridge, Mass., 1962), pp. 22 n, 215 n. Price was a friend of his father. Hazlitt thought of his own philosophy as one which approached nearer to the 'commonsense' of mankind (ii. 124).

[22] D. H. Monro, *Godwin's Moral Philosophy* (Oxford, 1953), p. 31, coined the phrase 'reasoned utilitarianism' to indicate a moral theory that recognized a principle of impartiality as well as one of utility.

postulates a connection, direct or indirect, between the action and the end. If the term is interpreted to mean that the end is directly regulative of our duties, as is the case with Coleridge's definition of eudaemonism,[23] then it is misleading in relation to Hazlitt. The difference between Hazlitt's utilitarianism and Bentham's is the difference between a moral theory which operates with a deontological as well as a teleological principle, and one in which only the teleological principle is directly regulative of rightness. Operating with one principle only, Bentham's theory established a direct connection between rightness and goodness. The right act is the act which promotes the good construed as happiness: 'By the principle of utility is meant that principle which approves or disapproves of every action whatsoever, according to the tendency which it appears to have to augment or diminish the happiness of the party whose interest is in question: or . . . to promote or to oppose that happiness.'[24] By refusing to relate rightness and goodness indirectly by means of obligation Bentham was being perfectly consistent with his own doctrine of psychological egoism. The conversion of the egoistic element into a universalistic one was to be achieved artificially by a variety of sanctions or pressures—physical, religious, moral, and political. The logical status of this universalistic interpretation is, therefore, one of prescription: it asserts how we ought to act, not how we do act. In this respect it differs both from Hume where the utilitarian principle was descriptive of how we do judge morally, and from Mill who vacillated between both positions. By interpreting the question 'what is rightness?' factually or scientifically, and by rejecting the rationalist explanation in terms of non-natural facts such as 'conformity', 'fitness', 'congruity', and 'agreement' with truth, the nature of things, the law of Nature, or the will of God, Bentham provided a solution paralleled by the modern positivist rejection of late nineteenth-century idealism.[25] In throwing out such inadequate solutions, however, Bentham was just as guilty as his twentieth-century counterparts of ignoring the genuine philosophical issues involved. Herein lies the justification of Mill's criticism of Bentham's inept handling of the problem.[26] Richard Price's approach

[23] Eudaemonism is the theory 'which places happiness as the true source and regulator of duties, as the object and the aim of man', Coleridge, *Philosophical Lectures*, p. 210.

[24] Bentham, *Works*, I. I.   [25] Ibid., I. 8–10 and note.

[26] Bulwer, *England and the English* (Appendix B), II. 321–4.

to the same question in the previous century was much more subtle. No one, not even Hume, was more critical of the abstract nature of such concepts as 'congruity', 'fitness', 'agreement', and 'conformity'. Yet his rejection, unlike Bentham's, was accompanied by a reinterpretation of the imperative in terms of obligation and conscientiousness that steered between the extremes of empiricism and rationalism and recognized the existential nature of the problem.[27] The question 'what is rightness?' like its aesthetic equivalent 'what is poetry?' involves a category mistake. The indefinable nature of the imperative was grasped by Coleridge when he wrote: 'A pure conscience [is] that inward something . . . which . . . no man can describe, because every man is bound to know.'[28]

Like the ethical theories of Price and Reid, Hazlitt's 'reasoned utilitarianism' emphasized the necessity of two principles. In the eighteenth century the most famous expression of this demand is to be found in Dr. Johnson: '[Morality] answers two most important purposes: these are, the conservation of our happiness, and the test of our obedience . . . . Morality obliges men to live honestly and soberly, because such behaviour is most conducive to public happiness.'[29] Price also acknowledged the teleological principle as 'the most general and leading consideration in all our enquiries concerning *right*' when he wrote: 'I deny not, but that one circumstance of great importance, upon which is grounded the fitness of countenancing virtue and discountenancing vice among reasonable beings, is, the manifest tendency of this to prevent misery, and to preserve order and happiness in the world. What I assert is, that it is not *all* that renders such a procedure right.'[30] Reid was equally insistent that 'the notion of duty cannot be resolved into that of interest, or . . . happiness', although he was prepared to admit that 'what is good for us upon the whole' is one of the two ends of human action, the other being obligation.[31] For Hazlitt the deontological and teleological principles isolated by these writers in the eighteenth century stemmed from the dual nature of man as

[27] Price, *Review*, pp. 124–30.
[28] Coleridge, *Works*, II. 140.
[29] *The Works of Samuel Johnson* (Oxford, 1825), VI. 69. Like Belsham, *Essays*, II. 251, Mill adduced this passage from Johnson's review of Soame Jenyns's *A Free Inquiry into the Nature and Origin of Evil* in support of the principle of utility, *Mill on Bentham and Coleridge*, p. 54.
[30] Price, *Review*, pp. 153, 81.
[31] Reid, *Essays on the Active Powers of Man* (Edinburgh, 1788), pp. 228–9, 208.

spiritual and imaginative being and as physical and desiring object: 'Man is an intellectual animal, and therefore an everlasting contradiction to himself. His senses centre in himself, his ideas reach to the ends of the universe; so that he is torn in pieces between the two, without a possibility of its ever being otherwise. A mere physical being, or a pure spirit, can alone be satisfied with itself' (ix. 192). A number of his favourite quotations make the same point.[32] From the conflict of these two aspects arises the peculiarly 'moral' nature of the imperative itself: 'All morality . . . is the incessant struggle and alternate triumph of the two principles, the *ideal* and the physical' (xvii. 350). Although the deontological nature of the imperative was primary for Hazlitt, and indeed its essence since 'real morality . . . implies right conduct and consistent principle' (xx. 120), like Price and Reid he saw the end of moral action as the happiness of mankind. Of the principle of utility he wrote: 'This principle could be new to no one. . . . All the rest of the world were agreed in it long ago' (xx. 259).[33] He insisted upon the connection between right action and the principle of utility. At the same time he made it quite clear that the morality of the imperative derived from the primary principle of rectitude which alone regulated our regard for the end: 'If the *Westminster* reviewers insist that a creature like man is to make the good of the whole not only the remote and ultimate, but the immediate rule of his conduct . . . they are more mad or stupid than we thought them' (xx. 259).[34] Thus, there is a connection between the rightness of an action and the end construed as happiness, but it is always indirect. It is always mediated or regulated by the concept of the moral imperative, by the primacy of the deontological principle: 'Morality regulates our

[32] For example, ' "The web of our life is of a mingled yarn" ' (iv. 158, 225; vi. 92; viii. 263; xi. 167; xx. 37, 43, 349); ' "Video meliora proboque" ' (ix. 190; xvii. 346; xx. 292).

[33] Cf. Coleridge's view: 'What can be the object of human virtue but the happiness of sentient, still more of moral, beings?' *Notes, Theological, Political, and Miscellaneous*, ed. D. Coleridge (London, 1853), p. 351. 'The happiness of mankind is the *end* of virtue', *Essays on his own Times*, ed. S. Coleridge (London, 1850), I. 24. See also *Works*, VI. 369–70; I. 141–2. Mill chose the last of these four passages to compliment Coleridge on his philosophical acumen in supporting the principle of utility, *Mill on Bentham and Coleridge*, p. 161.

[34] Cf. Coleridge's view: 'No man doubts every sentient being must seek for a pleasurable sensation and avoid a painful sensation, but what has this to do with morality? Morality is to be the regulator of this which is only the aggregate of the passions and senses. They are the very things the moral principle is to conduct and regulate', *Philosophical Lectures*, p. 213. See also *Works*, VI. 370; *Essays*, II. 654–5.

sentiments and conduct as they have a connection with ultimate and important consequences' (xii. 217).

Hazlitt's insistence on the necessity and primacy of a deontological principle emerges in two main ways corresponding to the first two formulations of the categorical imperative in Kant's *Groundwork of the Metaphysic of Morals*. These are respect for law and respect for persons. Behind his emphasis on these two facets of the imperative was his recognition that the moral judgement is passed on the character of the will towards the end willed.

Operating with one principle, Bentham postulated that the right act was the act which promoted the happiness of the party concerned. Operating with two principles, Hazlitt insisted that the right act was the act which conformed to a moral rule. Herein lay what Johnson termed 'the test of our obedience' which evinces our respect for law formulated by Kant in the following way: 'Act only on that maxim through which you can at the same time will that it should become a universal law.'[35] The fulcrum of moral action for Hazlitt was the moral rule. The moral rule alone made an action moral through the introduction of obligation: 'The moralist can no more do without the intermediate use of rules and principles . . . than the mechanist can discard the use of wheels and pulleys, and perform every thing by simple motion' (xi. 9).[36] These intermediate rules mediating between rightness and happiness were not conceived by Hazlitt as *a priori*. They were not intuited but were the product of our own experience of what is most conducive to the promotion of human happiness: 'We must improve our concrete experience of persons and things into the

[35] *The Moral Law, or Kant's Groundwork of the Metaphysic of Morals*, tr. H. J. Paton (London, 1948), p. 88. In Coleridge's writings this became: 'So act that thou mayest be able, without involving any contradiction, to will that the maxim of thy conduct should be the law of all intelligent beings—is the one universal and sufficient principle and guide of morality. And why? Because the object of morality is not the outward act, but the internal maxim of our actions', *Works*, II. 180. See also *Notes*, pp. 384–5, and *Anima Poetae*, ed. E. H. Coleridge (London, 1895), pp. 200–1.

[36] J. O. Urmson, 'The Interpretation of the Moral Philosophy of J. S. Mill', *Philosophical Quarterly*, III (1953), 33–9, argues that Mill's reinterpretation of Bentham is a tiered or reasoned Utilitarianism which recognizes the necessity of moral rules. Replying, J. D. Mabbott, 'Interpretations of Mill's "Utilitarianism" ', *Philosophical Quarterly*, VI (1956), 115–20, suggests that Mill's view is still the more orthodox Benthamite one. It seems likely that Mill's theory, here as elsewhere, is a confused amalgam resulting from his attempt to reinterpret Bentham in the light of the criticism of the Romantics.

contemplation of general rules and principles; but without being grounded in individual facts and feelings, we shall end as we began, in ignorance' (xii. 46).[37] The justification of the rule was teleological. The rule itself, however, was objective and binding upon all: 'The rule is absolute. . . . If such things are ever done in any circumstances with impunity . . . it shows that there is an utter deadness to every principle of justice' (xii. 48).[38]

Morality for Hazlitt, therefore, was derived from the nature of man. The imperative was to be interpreted neither scientifically in terms of consequences, nor in terms of objective qualities intuited as ideas, since both interpretations, natural and non-natural, succeeded in explaining moral consciousness only by reference to a framework outside felt human experience. Coleridge, likewise, insisted upon the necessity of the two principles in his analysis of the imperative. His criticism of the rationalistic element in Kant's moral thought steered between both extremes of rationalism and empiricism: 'I know that in order to the idea of virtue we must suppose the pure good will, or reverence for the law as excellent in itself; but this very excellence supposes consequences though not selfish ones. . . . For if the law be barren of all consequences, what is it but words?'[39] The constitutive basis of Coleridge's philosophy, of course, ultimately entailed a moral theory differing radically from Hazlitt's in its implications. In his criticism of Kant, however, he was, like Hazlitt, insisting that moral rules could not be deduced

[37] Cf. Reid: 'It is a question in morals that admits of reasoning, Whether, the law of nature, a man ought to have only one wife? We reason upon this question, by balancing the advantages and disadvantages to the family, and to society in general. . . . If it can be shewn that the advantages are greatly upon the side of monogamy, we think the point is determined. But, if a man does not perceive that he ought to regard the good of society, and the good of his wife and children, the reasoning can have no effect upon him', *Essays on the Active Powers*, p. 240. A modern version of this view is to be found in S. E. Toulmin, *An Examination of the Place of Reason in Ethics* (Cambridge, 1950), pp. 141–2.

[38] Cf. R. S. Downie, *Government Action and Morality* (London, 1964), pp. 29–30: 'Our interests are furthered by the existence of moral rules, but a rule by its very nature is something which binds on all, and in so far as it does so it may be called "objective".'

[39] Quoted by J. H. Muirhead, *Coleridge as Philosopher*, p. 154. Cf. Croce's view that 'the criticism of ethical utilitarianism cannot begin by denying this truth and seeking out absurd and non-existent examples of *useless* moral actions. It must admit the utilitarian side and explain it as the concrete form of morality, which consists in this, that it is *inside* this form. Utilitarians do not see this inside', *Aesthetic as Science of Expression and General Linguistic*, tr. D. Ainslie (London, 1909, 1922 [rev.]), pp. 59–60.

from the mere necessity of obedience. An adequate moral theory requires both principles. Bentham's Utilitarian emphasis upon consequences represented for Hazlitt what in another context he called 'a river without banks' (xx. 188), and the category mistake which this involved he isolated correctly when he attributed it to the failure to perceive that 'logical reason and practical truth are *disparates*' (xii. 46).

Respect for persons as the second facet of Kant's analysis of the imperative presents the greatest challenge to dogmatic Utilitarianism: 'Act in such a way that you always treat humanity . . . never simply as a means, but always at the same time as an end.'[40] Hazlitt's expression of its supreme importance for an understanding of the imperative was unequivocal: 'I would not wish a better or more philosophical standard of morality, than that we should think and feel towards others as we should, if it were our own case. If we look for a higher standard than this, we shall not find it' (xii. 47–8).[41] In a later essay, 'On the Conduct of Life: or Advice to a Schoolboy', he termed this principle the principle of equality. He reminded his son to whom the essay was addressed that 'true equality is the only true morality or true wisdom. Remember always that you are but one among others' (xvii. 87–8). The effectiveness of the principle as a dialectical weapon capable of exposing mercilessly the central weakness of Utilitarianism was as obvious to Hazlitt as it had been earlier to Price.[42] The dilemma it posed for Utilitarianism was simple. If the doctrine has only one effective principle which establishes a direct connection between rightness and goodness, if the right act is the act which promotes the greatest happiness of the greatest number, then the sacrifice of the individual or the minority can be justified in the interest of the greater good derived by society as a whole. Hazlitt exploited this principle of impartiality or humanity in his discussion of the Utilitarian ethic in relation to slavery (xi. 10; xii. 47–51). The option which he provided there was either blood or sugar, or, as in the case of the Burke and Hare murders, blood or the progress of

[40] Kant, *Groundwork*, p. 96. Cf. Coleridge's view: 'Hence the sacred principle . . . which is the ground-work of all law and justice, that a person can never become a thing, nor be treated as such without wrong', *Works*, II. 175. See also ibid., II. 46, 51. Cf. Reid, *Essays on the Active Powers*, p. 240.

[41] Cf: '[Christ] redeemed man from the worship of that idol, self, and instructed him by precept and example to love his neighbour as himself' (vi. 184).

[42] Price, *Review*, p. 160.

medical science. The issue in his eyes was whether man is a person or a thing: 'But to take away life in order to *sell* the dead body, to be hacked and hewed, and turned to use that way . . . is the highest aggravation of the cruelty and insult. . . . We may see by this example (in spite of what the *Utilitarians* tell us) how impossible it is to sanctify the means by the end. . . . The abstract utility does not purify these men's motives. . . . There is then something besides Utility' (xx. 192).

John Stuart Mill subsequently denied the validity of this kind of criticism. Mill held that Bentham's principle that 'everybody [was] to count for one, nobody for more than one' safeguarded the rights of the individual. This principle he regarded as an 'explanatory commentary' on the principle of utility and not, as Herbert Spencer suggested, an anterior principle underived from it.[43] Mill's dilemma is that if he reinterprets Bentham's very weak form of the principle of impartiality in such a way that it can be derived from utility and made to mean 'equal amounts of happiness are equally desirable' instead of 'everybody has an equal right to happiness', it ceases to be a principle of impartiality since such an interpretation does not involve respect for others. Mill attempted just such a reinterpretation and as a result Hazlitt's criticism remains valid. If he does not reinterpret Bentham's dictum and continues to employ it as implying such respect—as he does[44]— then the principle is anterior to that of utility and not derived from it. If D. H. Monro is correct in his account of the utilitarianism of Godwin, then the latter was among the first to recognize the incompatibility of such a principle and the doctrine of psychological egoism.[45]

The significance of the moral imperative for Hazlitt cannot be measured only in terms of the frequency with which he formulated or the manner in which he expressed one or other of its two aspects in response to the Utilitarian challenge. Behind his emphasis on the two facets of the imperative was the recognition, one which he shared with Godwin, Coleridge, Shelley, and Carlyle, that the moral judgement is passed on the character of the will towards the end willed. The motive of the agent was therefore all-important.

[43] Mill, *Utilitarianism, Liberty, Representative Government,* ed. A. D. Lindsay (London, 1910), p. 58 and note.

[44] Ibid., pp. 29, 52.

[45] Monro, *Godwin's Moral Philosophy,* p. 15.

Bentham's interest in motives on the other hand was entirely psychological. A study of men's motives was necessary for the construction of an artificial community of interests in order to determine the amount of punishment necessary to counteract behaviour of a socially pernicious nature.[46] Mill's view that 'the motive has nothing to do with the morality of the action'[47] is one which was held both by Bentham and by James Mill. Outside of Utilitarian thought, however, there was general agreement that the ground of the imperative lay in the character of the agent's will.[48] Hazlitt frequently expressed this principle as a statement. Immorality was said to consist in 'the bias of their wills, not the deficiency of their understandings' (xx. 292). Virtue on the other hand entailed 'the absence of any *indirect* or sinister bias' (xx. 340). These and similar statements are, however, inadequate to express fully Hazlitt's sense of the evil consequent upon this bias of the will in favour of the self. This sense is part of the texture of his being and its traces are to be found in almost everything he wrote. Price said of the principle of impartiality that it included 'the careful avoiding of all secret attempts to deceive ourselves, and to evade or disguise the truth in examining our own characters.'[49] In so doing he was to characterize perfectly the precise relationship between Hazlitt as philosopher and moralist, and Hazlitt as essayist and prose satirist.

As an essayist Hazlitt was not concerned so much with the imperative itself as with its basis in the will of man, with the 'tacit' or 'secret' springs of action which bias motive in favour of the self and vitiate the rightness of action. Even to list the titles of those essays which he designated 'prose satires' (ix. 13), essays such as 'On Egotism', 'The Main-Chance', 'On Cant and Hypocrisy', 'On Religious Hypocrisy', 'On Envy', 'On the Pleasure of Hating', 'On Living to one's-self', 'On the Knowledge of Character', and 'On the Conduct of Life' is to realize something of the depth and extent of his intense conviction on this point and his awareness of the gulf which separated ostensible from real motive, the professions from the actions of men. He once wrote that 'if their passions or interests could be implicated in the question, men would deny

[46] See especially Bentham, *Works*, II. 192–266.
[47] Mill, *Utilitarianism*, p. 17.
[48] Price, Reid, and Stewart all emphasized the connection between the motive of the agent and the rightness of the action.
[49] Price, *Review*, p. 155.

stoutly that the three angles of a right-angled triangle are equal to two right ones' (xvii. 309). The imagery, language, tone and the ever-recurring quotations of the mature essays derive their intensity from fierce detestation of the gulf between appearance and reality in the matter of human motivation. For Hazlitt, the presence of the self blurred the essential openness characteristic of his experiential or 'pluralist' viewpoint, and man's capacity for experiencing morally the reality or significance of human life was so much the more diminished. This 'misanthropic' or negative strain in his essays is important. Unfortunately, the Utilitarians in their criticism of Hazlitt failed to see its real significance. Leigh Hunt caught perfectly the temper of the man when he wrote of Hazlitt as that 'splenetic but kindly philosopher',[50] and replying to the Utilitarian criticism that Hazlitt was 'at feud with the world', he pointed to the two aspects of his work and temperament: 'Love, hate, business, pleasure, books or no books, laughter and tears—nothing was indifferent to him that affected mankind. . . . Mr. Hazlitt was "at feud with the world" out of his infinite sympathy with them. . . . His regard for human nature, and his power to love truth and loveliness in their humblest shapes, survived his subtlest detections of human pride and folly.'[51]

The most obvious deficiency in Bentham's hypothetical rendering of the moral imperative, and one which did not escape Hazlitt, lay in the omission of conscience from his enumeration of 'external' sanctions. His specifically moral sanction, resting as it does on public approval and disapproval, was just as external as the physical, political and religious sanctions cited as incentives to right action. In his reinterpretation of Utilitarianism Mill subsequently introduced conscience as an 'internal' sanction in an attempt to counter the kind of criticism levelled against Bentham by Hazlitt. His account was still, nonetheless, a hypothetical one.[52] It is a subjective account the significance of which lies in its affinities with the eighteenth-century empirical tradition of Shaftesbury, Hutcheson, and Hume. Hazlitt's allegiance on the other hand, here as elsewhere in his moral theory, was to the rival tradition of Butler, Price, and Reid. Conscience in Mill's view of it is a complex of feelings with which we act in accordance from fear of the remorse resulting

50 Hunt, *Essays: The Seer, Part I* (London, 1842), p. 36.
51 Hunt, *Literary Criticism*, pp. 275–7.
52 Mill, *Utilitarianism*, pp. 24–32.

from our failure to obey its promptings. Our motive is pleasure and the avoidance of pain. It is still open, therefore, to Coleridge's criticism that 'the very fact of acting with this motive properly and logically destroys all claim upon conscience to give you any pleasure at all'.[53]

According to Price the empirical school was distinguished by the subjective nature of its view of conscience: 'Our perception of *right*, or moral good . . . is that agreeable *emotion*, or feeling, which certain actions produce in us.'[54] His own view of conscience was that it was a fusion of the affective and the rational, the subjective and the objective, feeling and judgement. In contemplating the actions of moral agents 'we have both a *perception of the understanding*, and a *feeling of the heart*'.[55] This awareness of the dual nature of the moral faculty likewise informed Butler's account of conscience as a rational sentiment: '. . . whether called conscience, moral reason, moral sense, or divine reason; whether considered as a sentiment of the understanding, or as a perception of the heart; or, which seems the truth, as including both.'[56] In his account of the criterion of right action Price had emphasized that he was not excluding the principle of utility. It was not the only consideration however. Likewise, in his account of conscience the question was 'not whether we owe *much* to implanted senses and determinations; but whether we owe *all* to them'.[57]

Hazlitt's response to Price's question was unequivocal. We do not owe all to the feelings. Nevertheless, his criticism of Bentham reveals an emphasis on the subjective or affective element in conscience sufficiently strong to render 'reasoned utilitarianism' inadequate as a characterization of his full ethical theory. Reference to Kant's various formulations of the moral imperative breaks down at that point where Hazlitt, building on the anti-empirical tradition of his English predecessors, extended the nature of conscience beyond the volitional consciousness of Kant's practical reason to embrace the subjective and empirical element, the omission of which, in Coleridge's view, constituted its greatest weakness: 'These emotions, affections, attachments, and the like, are the prepared ladder by which the lower nature is taken up

---

[53] Coleridge, *Works*, VI. 370.   [54] Price, *Review*, p. 15.

[55] Ibid., p. 62. Price's editor points out that there is no suggestion that the affective element is not rational, ibid., p. xxvii.

[56] Butler, *Works*, ed. W. E. Gladstone (Oxford, 1896), I. 399.

[57] Price, *Review*, p. 62.

into, and made to partake of, the highest room. . . . It is one of Kant's greatest errors, that he speaks so slightingly of psychology, and the weakest parts of his system are attributable to his want of the habits and facts of Psychology.'[58] Hazlitt's criticism of the moral theories of Bentham and Godwin emphasized their refusal to take advantage of man's feelings and affections in the promotion of the greatest happiness and, as a result, their failure to recognize their ultimate importance in the conception of the *summum bonum* itself.[59] In Hazlitt's view conscience was a sentiment as well as a judgement. It involved not only a judgement that an action was right or wrong but an intense feeling that it was right or wrong. Hence moral action extended beyond what he called 'the naked strength of the will' (xi. 23), embracing the affective and the volitional. Herein lay the significance of the moral teachings of Christ: 'His religion was the religion of the heart. . . . He was the first true teacher of morality. . . . He taught the love of good for the sake of good, without regard to personal or sinister views, and made the affections of the heart the sole seat of morality, instead of the pride of the understanding or the sternness of the will' (vi. 184). Such a view of morality could only strengthen his opposition to a Utilitarianism that altogether neglected the importance of man's affective nature. Replying to the Utilitarian criticism of his own 'sentimentalities', he wrote: 'I place the heart in the centre of my moral system, and the senses and the understanding are its two extremities' (xii. 193).[60] The heart and its feelings, affections and passions are the basis of the imagination as the moral faculty, and only through its reliance on these can it achieve the self-transcendence necessary for the achievement of the moral imperative.

[58] Coleridge, *Notes*, pp. 392, 407. Cf: 'I reject Kant's *stoic* principle, as false, unnatural, and even immoral, where . . . he treats the affections as indifferent . . . in ethics, and would persuade us that a man who disliking, and without any feeling of Love for, Virtue yet *acted* virtuously, because and only because it was his *Duty*, is more worthy of our esteem, than the man whose *affections* were aidant to, and congruous with, his Conscience', Coleridge, *Letters*, IV. 791–2.

[59] See Hazlitt, *Works*, xi. 10–11, xii. 50–1, 188–9. Cf. Coleridge's similar criticism of Godwin, *Letters*, I. 199; *Essays*, I. 24–5, 135.

[60] Cf. Hazlitt's view that 'the heart is the most central of all things' (xii. 310), and that 'the boundary of our sympathy is a circle which enlarges itself according to its propulsion from the centre—the heart' (xii. 55). Hazlitt, like Price, nowhere suggests that the feelings and affections are not rational. He is stressing here the living feeling. See 'On Genius and Common Sense' (viii. 31–50). Cf. Coleridge: 'Is it not this—to know what is right in the abstract, by a living feeling, by an intuition of the uncorrupted Heart?' *Letters*, II. 1000.

Hazlitt's criticism of the factual or scientific nature of Bentham's account of the moral imperative was twofold. The first was a philosophical justification of the imperative and of the criterion of right action in terms of respect for law and for persons and their basis in the good will. The second relates to Bentham's failure to take into account the 'sentimental' aspect of moral judgement. Consequences are not the only criterion of rightness: 'A calculation of consequences is no more equivalent to a sentiment, than a *seriatim* enumeration of square yards or feet touches the fancy like the sight of the Alps' (xi. 9). In 'On Reason and Imagination' the same point is made in similar terms, the object once more being Bentham's account of the imperative: 'Millions of acres do not make a picture; nor the calculation of all the consequences in the world a sentiment' (xii. 50). Moral truth and logical reason or understanding are disparates since the former, dependent for its essence on the feelings of the heart, cannot be measured by the faculties prized by the Utilitarians for the role which they play in the calculation of consequences. Passion or feeling is necessary for the existence of moral truth: 'So with respect to moral truth . . . whether a thing is good or evil, depends on the quantity of passion, of feeling, of pleasure and pain connected with it, and with which we must be made acquainted in order to come to a sound conclusion' (xii. 46). It was this affective element that the hypothetical rendering of the moral imperative in terms of facts or consequences failed to recognize. By linking rightness directly to goodness in the form of a mathematical equation Bentham gave a factual answer to an improper question. Mill's subsequent renovation of Bentham's theory failed to meet this criticism. His account of conscience is purely subjective. By rendering it as a 'sanction', even an internal one, he still viewed it as hypothetical. By dissociating motive and the morality of the action he was unable to give the same kind of weight and emphasis to the affections so characteristic of the Romantics: 'The levers with which we must work out our regeneration are not the cobwebs of the brain, but the warm, palpitating fibres of the human heart' (xvi. 268).

(ii) *The* Summum Bonum: *Hazlitt's Theory of Sentiment*

Hazlitt's criticism of Utilitarianism operates on two levels. It was critical not only of their criterion of right action but of their conception of the good which that action was designed to promote.

His strictures on the former had two aspects. One was a philosophical justification of the imperative. The other emphasized the
source of the imperative in man's affective nature. It is the second
of these, the emphasis on man's affective nature, that unites his
censure of Bentham's theory both on the level of the imperative
itself and of the *summum bonum*. While agreeing that the end of
virtuous action was happiness, Hazlitt took exception to the
Utilitarian conception of happiness as an algebraic sum of pleasures
and pains quantifiably measurable in accordance with a seven-point
felicific calculus,[61] and he did so because it ignored the existential
or imaginative element in life and its basis in the affective nature of
man. Thus, when he argued that no calculation of consequences
could ever constitute a sentiment, his criticism was effective against
both the Utilitarian criterion of right action and their conception
of human happiness. His criticism of the Utilitarian theories of
right action and of the *summum bonum* was the same: they operate
with one principle only instead of two and do so as a consequence
of their scientific rendering of human nature. A brief consideration
of Hazlitt's theory of sentiment will exemplify and substantiate
this point.

The place occupied by sentiment in Hazlitt's conception of
human nature is susceptible of two very different though complementary interpretations. The first is a psychological interpretation
concerned with the various ways in which sentiment plays such an
important part in his conception of human life and happiness. The
second is ontological in its emphases and relates sentiment to the
stress laid by Hazlitt on the imaginative nature of man and its
basis in his affective capacities. The first emphasizes imagination,
sympathy, the role of association and his associationist vocabulary.
The second accentuates the elements associated and the subsequent
transmutation of object into symbol. Recent critical discussion has
centred almost exclusively upon the analysis of the associative
nature of the imagination, and in so far as this approach has corrected
the previous bias towards the analysis of the imagination as sympathetic and has rendered the psychological interpretation more
balanced and complete, this new emphasis is welcome.[62] Two

[61] Bentham, *Works*, I. 16.
[62] J.-C. Sallé, 'Hazlitt the Associationist', *RES* xv (1964), 38–51; J. D. O'Hara,
'Hazlitt and the Functions of the Imagination', *PMLA* LXXXI (1966), 552–62;
R. E. Laughlin, 'The Influence of Eighteenth-Century Associationism on the
Criticism of Hazlitt' (Tulane University Dissertation, 1966 [unpbd]).

important distinctions, however, require to be made. To call Hazlitt an associationist merely because he exploited the vocabulary of eighteenth-century associationist psychology more fully than any other of his contemporaries is misleading. His theory of sentiment is associative only in a weak, not in a doctrinal sense. Imagination is associative (xii. 51), but cannot be explained in terms of association. Secondly, the investigation of the associative aspect of his vocabulary is beneficial only in so far as the psychological framework thereby constructed is not regarded as autonomous but is seen to derive its importance from its ultimate ontological implications. The elements which are associated in life, as in art, are derived from nature, the world of external nature and the nature of man. For Hazlitt, it was the heart, not the imagination, associative or sympathetic, that was the fount of man's moral and spiritual being. It was man in his 'sentimental' or existential role who conferred importance upon the associative and sympathetic vocabulary: 'Association has been assumed as the leading principle in the operations of the human mind, and then made the only one, forgetting first that nature must be the foundation of every artificial principle' (i. 76).

A sentiment in Hazlitt's view of the matter was not just a feeling of the heart but an habitual feeling, a strong inveterate habitual affection, the strength of which stemmed from man's nature and could not be explained in terms of association: 'By sentiment we would here understand the habitual workings of some one powerful feeling, where the heart reposes almost entirely upon itself' (xvi. 48). When he accounted for the human sentiment for natural objects, the element of association was present and was important, but what he was also stressing was its basis in man's affective nature: 'It is because they have surrounded us in almost all situations, in joy and in sorrow, in pleasure and in pain; because they have been one chief source and nourishment of our feelings, and a part of our being, that we love them as we do ourselves' (iv. 18). He was emphasizing that sentiment was a condition in which 'the heart reposes almost entirely upon itself'. The establishment of this existential or 'sentimental' relationship to the world around us, to our 'circumambient universe', was what Hazlitt in his *Lectures on the English Poets* termed the 'poetry' of life, that which made life worth living. Man is a poetical animal because he possesses feeling: 'Fear is poetry, hope is poetry, love is poetry, hatred is poetry;

contempt, jealousy, remorse, admiration, wonder, pity, despair, or madness, are all poetry' (v. 2). Sentiment and passion, therefore, are the basis of existential truth, moral as well as poetic (xii. 55): 'The more ethereal, evanescent, more refined and sublime part of art is the seeing nature through the medium of sentiment and passion, as each object is a symbol of the affections and a link in the chain of our endless being' (viii. 82–3). His perception of the affective basis of the existential enabled him to say of the poetic and the existential generally that 'the spirit of poetry, and the spirit of humanity are the same' (xix. 76).

J.-C. Sallé's emendation of Schneider's pantheistic interpretation of this last passage is evidence of the important role which close attention to Hazlitt's associative vocabulary can play in limiting possible ontologial interpretations of his real meaning. In life and in art, man, through the creation of symbol consequent upon the interaction of his spiritual being and the external world, transcends the confines of space and time and comes into contact with his noumenal, 'endless', 'immortal' being. Symbol in art, morality and life generally, is the result of the interaction of man as spiritual or existential being and man as physical object, between the ideal and the physical. The solution which Hazlitt offers here, like the solution offered in his interpretation of the imperative, is not scientific or constitutive but experiential. Panthesim, however vague its expression might be, is always essentially constitutive. For Hazlitt the gulf between what Kant termed the phenomenal and the noumenal was bridged not merely through the exercise of the categorical imperative as it is in Kant himself through practical reason, but by imagination having its source in man's affective nature and extending beyond volitional consciousness in the moral realm to include art and life generally.

Herein lies the significance of the past in his essays and his constant autobiographical emphasis: 'The future is like a dead wall or a thick mist. . . . The past is alive and stirring with objects' (viii. 25). These 'objects' he proffers to us in his essays not as objects but retrospectively as symbols. Life seen in this way becomes a fable: 'The change, from the commencement to the close of life, appears like a fable, after it has taken place' (xvii. 194). The object itself may be, and often is, intrinsically unimportant. It is the value that even the most trivial objects can embody which he asks his reader to weigh against the Utilitarian conception of human happiness:

I met Dignum (the singer) in the street the other day: he was humming a tune; and his eye, though quenched, was smiling. I could scarcely forbear going up to speak to him. Why so? I had seen him in the year 1792 (the first time I ever was at a play), with Suett and Miss Romanzini and some others, in NO SONG NO SUPPER; and ever since, that bright vision of my childhood has played round my fancy with unabated, vivid delight. Yet the whole was fictitious. . . . I place the heart in the centre of my moral system. . . . You leave nothing but gross, material objects as the ends of pursuit. . . . Is a man a mere animal? . . . Am I only as a rational animal to hear the sound, to see the object with my bodily sense? . . . And is it not better that truth and nature should speak this imperfect but heartfelt language, than be entirely dumb? And should we not preserve and cherish this precious link that connects together the finer essence of our past and future being by some expressive symbol?

(xii. 193–4)

The importance of childhood for Hazlitt lay in its symbolic fecundity and its subsequent symbolic richness. While he cherished Wordsworth's poetry for its reliance upon 'expressive symbol' he rejected Wordsworth's own account of childhood in the *Immortality Ode*. The object or incident in the past becomes a symbol of man's spiritual aspirations, a token of his divinity not explicable in terms of a mythological or theistic framework (iv. 250). The emphasis falls in every instance upon symbol and being, object and sentiment: 'Natural objects . . . form an ideal class; their repeated impression on the mind, in so many different circumstances, grows up into a sentiment. The reason is, that we refer them generally and collectively to ourselves, as links and mementos of our various being' (xix. 78). Their significance did not lie in the nature of the object as Schneider suggests, but in their role as 'expressive symbols'. They were epiphanies, moments in which, as Hazlitt expresses it, man feels his 'glassy essence'.[63] The task of expressing this revelation of the significance of human life was the function of poetry and, indeed, of much of his own work as an essayist. Leigh Hunt's perception of the fine balance sustained by Hazlitt in the expression of his apprehension of the significance of life, its avoidance of the scientific, philosophical, and religious varieties of abstraction, is of the utmost importance in this respect: 'It is not extravagance; it is not mysticism . . . it is but the doing justice to that real and

---

[63] A favourite quotation of Hazlitt's and like a number of others frequently used in this context. Cf: ' "Il y a des impressions que ni le tems ni les circonstances peuvent effacer" ' (iv. 91; vi. 362; vii. 128; xvii. 108).

interior spirit of things, which modifies and enlivens the mystery of existence.'

Hazlitt's emphasis on the 'holiness of the Heart's affections' and his refusal to countenance an interpretation of them in other than experiential terms has the most important consequences for his work as a critic and essayist. What he admired most in the work of Rousseau and Wordsworth was the creation of such 'expressive' or existential symbols, their ability as he expressed it in relation to Rousseau 'to gather up the past moments of his being like drops of honey-dew to distil a precious liquor from them' (viii. 24).[64] What he most admired in this respect was what he executed best himself as an essayist. The satirical or 'negative' aspect of his essays found its perfect counterpart in a positive moral vision of life, central to an understanding of which was his view of sentiment and his theory of symbol. This positive moral vision was embodied in either of two ways. In some essays it was stated directly. We are told explicitly in 'On the Feeling of Immortality in Youth' that: 'Truth, friendship, love, books, are also proof against the canker of time; and while we live, but for them, we can never grow old. We take out a new lease of existence from the objects on which we set our affections, and become abstracted, impassive, immortal in them. We cannot conceive how certain sentiments should ever decay or grow cold. . . . We . . . flourish and survive in our affections' (xvii. 195). The objects of such sentiments embody his positive valuation of life. They are his 'standing resource, [his] true classics' (xvii. 320), the 'lustres' (xii. 127) by which he estimated life as 'a strange gift, and its privileges . . . most miraculous' (xvii. 191). There are other essays, however, and these the greatest, which avoiding statement, are triumphs of realization, embodying his vision dramatically and themselves expressive of nature seen through the medium of sentiment. Paraphrasing and amending an earlier attempt to characterize the essence of the Romantic vision, J. H. Muirhead wrote: 'The writer goes on to find the essence of romance in a certain kind of faith in man depending upon some sense of the inherent greatness of his soul—a hope perhaps that he is more than mortal. "If the bend of a sunlit road, a bar of music,

---

[64] For Hazlitt, Rousseau was 'the father of sentiment' (xvii. 133). His affinities with Rousseau are discussed by J. Voisine, 'Un Nouveau Jean-Jacques: William Hazlitt', in his *J.-J. Rousseau en Angleterre à l'Epoque Romantique* (Paris, 1956), pp. 345–424.

or the glimpse of a face suddenly thrills with romance, it is because these things have brought some unexpected revelation of the value of human life. . . ." I think that this is profoundly true, but it requires to be added that what to the romantic spirit is of chief value in human life is the sense of the Infinite which is implicit in it, and is the source of all man's deepest experiences.'[65] Generalizations about Romanticism are always dangerous. In relation to Hazlitt's greatest and most mature essays in *Table-Talk*, *The Plain Speaker*, *Literary Remains* and *Sketches and Essays*, however, Muirhead's summing-up is more fruitful, apposite, and precise than many of the more specific attempts that have been made to isolate and articulate the unique nature of his achievement as an essayist.

Hazlitt nowhere attempted to formulate a theory of the *summum bonum* in a set philosophical manner. Nevertheless, it is obvious that Bentham's felicific calculus, whereby one pleasure was to be preferred to another in terms of a quantitative principle, is incompatible with the implications of Hazlitt's theory of sentiment according to which one activity is to be preferred to another in terms of the value which it has for us as complex and imaginative human beings. In spite therefore of the apparent agreement between Hazlitt and the Utilitarians that the rightness of action had some relation to the good construed as happiness, the disagreement as to wherein happiness consisted was just as fundamental as in the matter of the moral imperative. The precise nature of the disagreement is crystallized in the often quoted opposition set up by Bentham between push-pin and poetry.[66] This enables us to see that the empirical conception of human happiness advocated by the Utilitarians, like their failure to account for the moral imperative, derived from the strength of the 'physical analogy', from their refusal to recognize man's dual nature as physical object and existential being, from their repeated attempts in a variety of spheres to reduce the existential to the factual and scientific. The basic category mistake of empirical philosophy isolated in Chapter I is the recurring feature of Utilitarian social, moral and poetic theory. Their telescoping of the two principles of human nature into one was captured perfectly by Hazlitt when he said: 'Besides my automatic existence, I have another, a sentimental one' (xii. 192). In his criticism of the Utilitarian conception of human

[65] Muirhead, *Coleridge as Philosopher*, p. 28.
[66] Bentham, *Works*, II. 253.

happiness his strategy was to play off one against the other, the sentimental against the automatic, the living against the mechanical, physical object against affective subject: '[Burke] saw in the construction of society other principles at work, and other capacities of fulfilling the desires, and perfecting the nature of man, besides those of securing the equal enjoyment of the means of animal life, and doing this at as little expense as possible. He thought that the wants and happiness of men were not to be provided for, as we provide for those of a herd of cattle, merely by attending to their physical necessities. He thought more nobly of his fellows. He knew that man had affections and passions and powers of imagination, as well as hunger and thirst and the sense of heat and cold . . . affected by certain things from habit, from imagination, and sentiment, as well as from reason' (vii. 306). In 'The New School of Reform' Burke's organic conception of society once again formed the pivot of his attack on the Utilitarian conception of social man: 'This is their *idea of a perfect commonwealth:* where each member performs his part in the machine, taking care of himself, and no more concerned about his neighbours, than the iron and wood-work, the pegs and nails in a spinning-jenny. Good screw! good wedge! good ten-penny nail! Are they really in earnest?' (xii. 182). In the same essay he enlarged upon his distinction between man's 'automatic' and his 'sentimental' existence. In doing so he clearly revealed his awareness of the Utilitarian attempt to fuse the two principles into one and the consequences which this involved for their conception of the happiness of the individual as well as of society in general:

Things of the greatest use in reality are not always of the greatest importance in an imaginary and romantic point of view. . . . There are two standards of value and modes of appreciation in human life, the one practical, the other ideal. . . . Why then force these two standards into one? Or make the Understanding judge of what belongs to the Fancy, any more than the Fancy judge of what belongs to the Understanding? Poetry would make bad mathematics, mathematics bad poetry: why jumble them together? . . . Why then grudge them the pleasure they give to the human mind . . .? Why must I come to your shop, though you expressly tell me you have not the article I want?   (xii. 191–2)

3. POETRY AND UTILITARIANISM
Utilitarian moral theory was the natural outcome of the empirical premiss of Utilitarian epistemology. Utilitarian poetic theory was

likewise dependent on the same premiss. The ontological and moral implications of empirical epistemology are present in both. In opposing the early Utilitarian disregard for poetry, therefore, Hazlitt was also being consistent. His opposition to Utilitarian poetic theory and the manner in which he enforced his criticism of it are the direct result of his opposition to Utilitarianism at the level of epistemological and moral theory. To clarify the issues involved, however, it is first necessary to distinguish two very different questions and to appreciate the Utilitarian attitude to these. The first is the question of poetic value: whether poetry can, in any sense, be said to express the poet's awareness of the value of life. The second concerns the question of the uses or effects of poetry. On both these questions Hazlitt and Bentham were in fundamental opposition, and in both Hazlitt once again enforced his criticism in terms of the distinction between the empirical and scientific on the one hand and the poetic and existential on the other.

Hazlitt viewed poetry as imitation—the imitation of nature through the medium of sentiment and passion—as a result of which the object was transmuted into a symbol expressive in some sense of the poet's apprehension of the significance or value of human life. His view was expressive of the necessity of the conjoint operation of the external world subject to the laws of cause and effect, and of man's existential being and its affective basis. This ontological problem, which is the problem of the essence of poetry, because it cannot be stated, cannot be interrogated directly. It can be expressed only through poetry, and its perception by the critic demands, as Arnold later pointed out, the greatest tact, subtlety, and flexibility.[67] Bentham's view of the poetic involved the same dual reference: man and nature:

> Between poetry and truth there is a natural opposition: false morals, fictitious nature. The poet always stands in need of something false. When he pretends to lay his foundations in truth, the ornaments of his superstructure are fictions; his business consists in stimulating our passions, and exciting our prejudices. Truth, exactitude of every kind, is

[67] Arnold thought that 'the critic of poetry should have the finest tact, the nicest moderation, the most free, flexible, and elastic spirit imaginable'. Like Hazlitt (vi. 92–3), he turned to Montaigne to exemplify his meaning: 'He should be indeed the "ondoyant et divers", the *undulating and diverse* being of Montaigne', *Prose Works*, I. 174.

fatal to poetry. The poet must see everything through coloured media, and strive to make everyone else to do the same.[68]

The elements of poetry, object and feeling, are the same. The empirical logic, the application of a single scientific criterion, entails a radically different conclusion. Like Plato, Bentham acknowledged the imaginative element, but he diminished its status by opposing it to scientific truth. Poetry is a copy of reality, not an imitation. It is ' "not a true thing" ' (xii. 381).[69] Moreover the inspiration behind the copy being imagination with its reliance on the passions and feelings of man, the copy is a bad one: 'All poetry is misrepresentation.' The similarities with Plato are striking and the logic, granted the initial premiss, equally inexorable. Bentham's response to the second question of the effects or uses of poetry was just as uncompromising: 'Prejudice apart, the game of push-pin is of equal value with the arts and sciences of music and poetry. If the game of push-pin furnish more pleasure, it is more valuable than either. Everybody can play push-pin: poetry and music are relished only by a few.'[70] Mill subsequently attempted to minimize the alleged hostility to poetry of the early Utilitarians. His argument in mitigation, however, must be viewed against the unequivocal nature of Bentham's rejection of poetry in terms of poetic value and of its utilitarian function. Bentham himself once confessed that he 'never read poetry with enjoyment',[71] and Mill's own account of his early upbringing and the literary taste of his father has done little to dispel the popular conception of Utilitarianism that Mill challenged.[72] His attempt in Chapter II of *Utilitarianism* to effect a reconciliation of dogmatic Utilitarianism and poetry, to resolve in theoretical terms his own dual allegiance to Bentham and to Romantic poetic theory, was equally unsuccessful. By pleading the merits of poetry in terms of the quality of its pleasures he introduced a qualitative principle at odds with the purely quantitative assessment of Bentham's own felicific calculus. His analysis breaks down at this point as a direct result of

[68] Bentham, *Works*, II. 253–4.
[69] Hazlitt was critical of Byron's attempt to elevate didactic poetry on account of its truth: 'Is Lear a lie?' (xix. 68). He objected just as strongly to the notion of poetry being made the vehicle of ethical truths as he did to poetry seen in terms of philosophical and religious truths.
[70] Bentham, *Works*, II. 253.
[71] Ibid., x. 583.
[72] Mill, *Autobiography*, pp. 11, 78–9.

the irreconcilable nature of the opposition between the scientific and the existential. His attempt to marry doctrinaire Utilitarianism with the insights of the early nineteenth-century poets and critics only ends in a confused and unhappy amalgam of both.[73]

As a consequence of their dependence on a common empirical premiss Bentham's accounts of morality and poetry are strikingly alike. The deficiencies of the one are the deficiencies of the other. The major weakness in both cases can be traced to the role which he assigned to imagination and his assessment of its affective basis. In the moral imperative he ignored the imaginative and existential and by linking rightness directly with goodness transformed the moral into the hypothetical or non-moral. Although in the case of poetry he acknowledged the role of feeling, he diminished its existential significance and likewise rendered the poetic as non-poetic. Imitation became copy. His seven-point felicific calculus was only capable of measuring the quantity of pleasure accruing to man as physical object. His minimal regard for the utilitarian function or presumed effects of 'literary insignificancies'[74] rested on the same foundation.

Hazlitt's strategy in combating the anti-poetic strain within the Utilitarian movement in the early nineteenth century was to maintain a strict division between the issue of poetic value and that of the utilitarian function of poetry. He refused to be caught up in what Croce later called the pendulum of art as hetaira and art as pedagogue.[75] He refused to smuggle the concept of instrumentality into the sphere of poetic value. Just as the moral imperative was justified in terms of obligation and not of consequences, so too poetic value was validated in terms of the re-creation of the artist's vision. His answer to Utilitarianism is comparable to his answer to the *Quarterly Review*'s challenge to him to define the nature of poetry. In both cases he impugned the assumption at the root of his adversary's position. Reviewing an art exhibition in the *Scotsman* in April 1822, he wrote:

---

[73] D. D. Raphael, 'Fallacies in and about Mill's *Utilitarianism*,' *Philosophy*, xxx (1955), pp. 344–57, has defended Mill on the grounds that his qualitative principle can be reduced to one of quantity. R. S. Downie, 'Self-Realization', *Cambridge Review* (8 Oct. 1965), 7–9, attempts to show that although the qualitative principle is incompatible with Bentham's position, it is consistent with a theory of self-realization implicit in much of Mill's work.

[74] Bentham, *Works*, x. 540.

[75] Croce, *Aesthetic*, p. 160.

Scotland is of all other countries in the world perhaps the one in which the question, 'what is the use of that?' is asked oftenest. But where this is the case, the Fine Arts cannot flourish, or attain their high and palmy state, or scarcely creep out of the ground to expose themselves to the 'eager and the nipping air' of this kind of rigid catechising scrutiny; for they are their own sole end and use, and in themselves 'sum all delight'. It may be said of the Fine Arts that 'they toil not, neither do they spin', but are like the lilies of the valley, lovely in themselves, graceful and beautiful, and precious in the sight of all but the blind. They do not furnish us with food or raiment, it is true; but they please the eye, they haunt the imagination, they solace the heart. If after that you ask the question, *Cui bono?* there is no answer to be returned.

(xviii. 167)

Within the sphere of poetic value poetry is self-authenticating. The issue of pleasure or use is secondary and extra-literary just as in morality. A teleological principle is operative in both. Poetry, by calling into play the whole of man's imaginative capacities, contributes to the enrichment of his nature as a complex human being. It is still, however, just an effect. It is non-poetic as the other is non-moral. Yet it is of the utmost consequence to us as human beings, and they can be termed non-moral or non-poetic only if the terms 'moral' and 'poetic' are construed in the narrowest possible senses.

In Hazlitt's view the cultural implications of poetry for the individual and for society were vast. The Utilitarian denigration of the arts was his clearest evidence for their general unfitness to execute their self-appointed task of social reform in a manner flexible and adequate enough to meet the complexities of human nature: 'They propose to erect a Chrestomathic school ... to introduce a rabble of children, who for the Greek and Latin languages, poetry, and history, that fine pabulum of useful enthusiasm, that breath of immortality infused into our youthful blood, that balm and cordial of our future years, are to be drugged with chemistry and apothecaries' receipts, are to be taught to do every thing, and to see and feel nothing;—that the grubbing up of elegant arts and polite literature may be followed by the systematic introduction of accomplished barbarism and mechanical quackery. ... Instead of being legislators for the world, and stewards to the intellectual inheritance of nations, [they] are hardly fit to be parish-beadles, or pettifogging attorneys to a litigated estate!' (xii. 249). As a revelation of reality, as an expression of the poet's awareness of the significance and value of human life, the work of art itself became the bearer of symbolic significance. It nourished the imagination of man, symbolized certain values which ran counter to the tradition of English Utilitarianism and English religious dissent.[76] Its existence was essential to the full development of man's spiritual and imaginative potentialities and was central to his happiness. The openness characteristic of poetic vision at its most comprehensive, its non-dogmatic, non-assertive nature enabled man to achieve the same openness. Self, bias, whim, and prejudice vanished in the individual's awareness of his inter-relatedness with the rest of humanity and nature. It was in this sense, in part at least, that Shakespeare was for Hazlitt a great moralist and that poetry was an 'instrument' of moral regeneration. His defence of Sir Walter Scott against the criticism of the *Westminster Review* was founded on his profound appreciation of the effects of poetry (xii. 180, 183; xx. 258). He constantly emphasized the need for the humanizing influence of a literary and classical education: 'The habitual study of poetry and works of imagination is one chief part of . . . education. . . . Science alone is hard and mechanical' (iv. 200). Through such an education 'we imbibe sentiment with knowledge' (iv. 5; xvii. 92). The Utilitarian neglect of the existential and its basis in man's affective nature prompted Hazlitt to question the right of the Philosophical Radicals to legislate for the future good of man when their conception of that good rested upon a false estimate of human nature. He feared, moreover, that the Utilitarian concern for human happiness was merely speculative,[77] a fear borne out by Mill's account of his father who 'thought human life a poor thing at best' and of his own adolescence: '[My zeal] had not its root in genuine benevolence, or sympathy with mankind.'[78]

---

[76] Hazlitt's criticism of the English tradition of religious dissent in 'On the Tendency of Sects' in *The Round Table* is similar in many respects to his criticism of Utilitarianism: 'Their faculties are imprisoned in a few favourite dogmas, and they cannot break through the trammels of a sect. Hence we may remark a hardness and setness in the ideas . . . an aversion to those finer and more delicate operations of the intellect, of taste and genius, which require greater flexibility and variety of thought, and do not afford the same opportunity for dogmatical assertion' (iv. 49). In *The Plain Speaker* in the essay 'On People of Sense', he likewise remarked on the Utilitarian insensibility to 'the finer essences of thought' (xii. 248). The unique combination of Utilitarianism and dissent that was to emerge in Arnold's writings as Victorian Philistinism was anticipated by Hazlitt. Cf. xx. 264–7.

[77] Hunt, *Literary Criticism*, p. 278.

[78] Mill, *Autobiography*, pp. 34, 77. See also ibid., pp. 97–8.

Hazlitt's criticism of Bentham and Utilitarianism is important for a number of reasons, not least of which is that it represents the first sustained critique of dogmatic Utilitarianism. In his various essays he raised a great many of the points that Mill attempted to re-interpret or counter in his own revision of Bentham's theory forty years later. At the same time there emerges from his criticism of Bentham an ethical theory belonging to his maturity, at once individual and essentially English, based on the anti-empirical tradition of eighteenth-century moral thought. J. H. Muirhead attributed Coleridge's failure to develop just such a theory to the compelling influence exercised upon him by the moral thought of Kant, his ignorance of the previous English tradition as exemplified in Butler, and his preoccupation with religion.[79] In Hazlitt's case none of these factors is operative, and a theory, albeit neglected, satisfying both these conditions is to be found in his criticism of Bentham. Important as these considerations are, his criticism of Utilitarianism functions at yet another, and for critics of Hazlitt a much higher level. His attack on Bentham is not an isolated phenomenon but is a powerful expression of his general philo-sophical position. It has implications beyond the immediate problem represented by Bentham's scientific account of rightness and goodness.

The writings of Coleridge and Carlyle have furnished literary historians and critics with many instances of the alleged revulsion felt by the Romantics for their own age as one of mechanism. There is in Hazlitt, however, no passage comparable to the great set denunciations of Coleridge and Carlyle. An appreciation of the reasons for this is of fundamental importance in discriminating the ultimate aims and philosophies of the writers concerned. The concept of the spirit of the age is employed by all three writers in at least two distinct ways: either as a tension between two polar opposites or as an imbalance of one of these two factors. Coleridge and Carlyle conceived of this tension as one between the spiritual, imaginative, and vital on the one hand and the material, mechanical, and inanimate on the other. As an imbalance, the age was an age of mechanism. This conception is the motivating force behind the imagery of mechanism so characteristic of their social, literary and

---

[79] Muirhead, *Coleridge as Philosopher*, pp. 107, 139, 160. In 'My First Acquaint-ance with Poets' Hazlitt confessed that he had never read Butler's *Sermons* until Coleridge introduced him to them (xvii. 113).

philosophical criticism. In Hazlitt's writings the imagery of mechanism is negligible and perfunctory in comparison. This divergence is the direct consequence of a radically different view of the factors comprising the spirit of the age. Because of the difference in their views of the factors that constitute the tension, it is impossible to view Hazlitt as parasitic upon the philosophical and critical thought of Coleridge. In Hazlitt's writings the danger to the imaginative or dynamic, as Coleridge and Carlyle termed it, was not merely conceived as a threat from science or a science-oriented philosophy. The gravest danger to the imaginative in art and life was abstraction of which the bias to mechanism was only one aspect. Abstraction or the tendency to the general did not alone characterize the scientific approach. It was the chief characteristic of the philosophical and religious viewpoints adopted by Coleridge and Carlyle. There was not just one enemy for Hazlitt, but two. The first, of which Bentham is an instance, stands outside the imaginative or existential; the second, Coleridge, within the imaginative itself. Unlike Bentham, Coleridge recognized the authenticity of the imaginative experience but sought to explain it in terms outside of felt human experience.

The obsessive quality of Hazlitt's reiterated emphasis on the dangers of abstraction derived from his sense that the poets and critics of the early nineteenth century were betraying their own cause in attempting to defend it. It was not enough to discriminate the scientific and poetic. The poetic must be characterized in terms which are self-authenticating. Poetry and philosophy in the nineteenth century recognized the dangers of empirical philosophy. The tragic irony in Hazlitt's view of the matter lay in the manner in which the poets and critics chose to establish the distinction between science and poetry in their own work. Like the philosophy of Coleridge, their poetry was too dependent upon the general, the abstract, the systematic, and the theoretical—and ultimately, therefore, upon the scientific itself. Although the philosophies of Bentham and Coleridge appeared to be in radical opposition to one another, they had for Hazlitt a shared basis in abstraction. His criticism of Bentham is one aspect of his criticism of abstraction. It is, however, a crucial one for an understanding of his philosophical and critical theory. Coleridge represented a much more dangerous tendency because more insidious and less widely recognized as a danger.

CHAPTER THREE

Religion and Poetry: Coleridge and Hazlitt

> We can no more take away the faculty of the imagination, than we can see all objects without light or shade. . . . Poetry is one part of the history of the human mind, though it is neither science nor philosophy.
>
> *Lectures on the English Poets*, v. 9

ONE of the most disturbing features of English literary history in the past has been its tendency to group and unify, thereby simplifying, blurring, and in some cases distorting the unique nature of a writer's poetic or critical achievement. In literary history too the urge to seek unity and harmony, to reduce the many to the one, has its basis in scientific abstraction. Ironically enough, Hazlitt, the most outspoken and consistent English critic of abstraction in the early nineteenth century, has proved especially vulnerable in this respect. The tendency to view Romantic poetic theory in Coleridgean terms, in particular to assimilate Hazlitt's theory and practice as a critic to those of Coleridge, is detrimental to a real appreciation of the significance and independent nature of his critical effort. Fancy and imagination, the psychology of artistic creation, the organic metaphor, symbol and the antithesis between mechanism and dynamism are not the sum of Romantic critical theory. They do not exhaust the complexity of the early nineteenth century's critical achievement. They are an integral part of that achievement but are not to be used as standards against which the critical preoccupations of the age are to be assessed. They are merely one critic's response to a complex series of inter-related problems, a response moreover conditioned by a highly personal and original reading of certain fundamental philosophical issues. Since Hazlitt's interpretation of these issues and his attitude to life generally differ from those of Coleridge, it would be strange if the theoretical basis of his practical criticism and the emphases and terminology of that criticism did not also differ. It would be equally strange if two of the principal protagonists of the anti-empirical cause in the early nineteenth century did not have much in common. Both recognized after all the authenticity of the imaginative experience. The task of the present chapter, however, is to discriminate within this area of agreement, to draw attention to those elements in Coleridge's philosophy and critical theory that serve to differentiate them from the philosophical and critical views attributed to Hazlitt in the two previous chapters.

Since Coleridge's theory of poetry will be considered principally in terms of his theory of imagination and its affinities with Kant's concept of practical reason, it is necessary for Hazlitt's experiential account of imagination to be restated briefly in such a way as to facilitate comparisons. In his ethical theory imagination fulfilled a role analogous to that performed by practical reason in Kant. Both were experiential accounts of the nature of moral freedom. Neither was concerned with the intuition of non-natural or supersensible ideas. Imagination for Hazlitt was the bridge between man as phenomenal and man as noumenal being, resolving the perpetual contradiction of the duality of man's nature through the involution of the individual in the universal. Hazlitt, however, wished to extend the experiential nature of the imaginative faculty to embrace a conception of moral consciousness that was more than merely volitional by the inclusion of feeling or emotion. Yet he did so without in any way wishing to posit imagination as a faculty for the intuition of the noumenal. He also differed from Kant in that imagination was invested with a far greater sphere of influence. It was not restricted as was practical reason to the realm of the moral. Imagination bridged the gap between the sensible or physical and the ideal in art as well as in morality, and it did so with the emphasis once more falling upon its basis in man's affective nature. Coleridge's deviations from Kant on the other hand were much more radical, ultimately misconceived, and potentially subversive of the autonomy of all art.

Coleridge's main interest in *The Critique of Pure Reason* centred upon the 'Transcendental Dialectic' in which Kant developed the view that for pure reason in its speculative capacity the ideas of God, freedom and immortality are regulative and not constitutive. For the theoretical purposes of speculative reason the supersensuous or noumenal world, to which these ideas belong, is transcendent and cannot be known. They are assumptions. We must act as if they were true. They are merely regulative. That they were insusceptible of scientific proof, Coleridge accepted. In his view they could not, 'like the truths of abstract science, be wholly independent of the will'.[1] Freedom, for example, was a transcendental predicate of phenomenal beings and not a psychological property requiring an analysis of motives or of the soul. That they could not be known at all—once Kant had set out the limitations of pure theoretical reason—Coleridge could not accept. The crucial distinction for Coleridge between Aristotle and Kant on the one hand and Plato and the Platonists on the other, arose out of their respective attitudes to the ideas of pure speculative reason: 'Whether ideas are regulative only, according to Aristotle and Kant; or likewise constitutive, and one with the power and life of nature, according to Plato and Plotinus . . . is the highest problem of philosophy.'[2] For Coleridge these ideas were constitutive rather than regulative of our experience—the ultimate realities and the highest form of knowledge: '[Plato] leads you to see, that propositions involving in themselves a contradiction in terms, are nevertheless true; and which, therefore, must belong to a higher logic—that of ideas.' And again: 'He taught the idea, namely the possibility . . . of striving to contemplate things not in the phenomenon . . . but in their essential powers . . . chiefly as they exist in the Supreme Mind.'[3] This view, as he confesses in an unpublished manuscript note, 'is at once the distinctive and constitutive basis of my philosophy'.[4]

The importance of Kant for Coleridge is that although he denied these ideas as subjects of cognitive knowledge, he went on to show in *The Critique of Practical Reason* that freedom—at least in the realm of pure reason in its practical role, as distinct from its speculative or theoretical one—could be known, and not merely problematically thought. In addition, the fact that a being belonging to the world of the senses also belongs to the supersensible order was positively known. The supersensible world was known, and not merely transcendent as for theoretical purposes. It was, for practical purposes, immanent or experiential. For Kant pure practical reason is not concerned with objects so as to know them cognitively, but with its own faculty for realizing them. As practical, the role of reason was not to furnish an intuition but a law.

[1] Coleridge, *Biographia*, I. 135.

[2] Coleridge, *Works*, I. 484.

[3] Ibid., VI. 302; *Philosophical Lectures*, p. 166; cf. *Coleridge on Logic and Learning*, ed. A. D. Snyder (New Haven, 1929), p. 126.

[4] Quoted by J. H. Muirhead, *Coleridge as Philosopher*, p. 105.

This immanential or experiential 'compromise' was not adequate in Coleridge's view. For Kant practical reason, in the exercise of the categorical imperative, alone enabled man to pass beyond the world of sense and gave him a knowledge, albeit only experiential, of a higher reality or supersensible order. The knowledge which Coleridge required was an intuitive knowledge, wherein the role of practical reason was to furnish an intuition rather than a law. Experiential knowledge was not enough. Nevertheless the experiential knowledge of freedom which practical reason confers in acts of conscience was to provide Coleridge with his escape clause from the dualistic impasse which confronted him in Kant's denial of the possibility of a science of metaphysics. The importance of practical reason for Coleridge extends far beyond the ethical.[5] It was to furnish the principal ingredient in his elaboration of a higher reason capable of intuiting ideas as real and not merely regulative,[6] and at the same time it furnished him with the vital clue to faith in the religious sphere.[7] Its main interest for us in the present context, however, lies in its relation to Coleridge's theory of imagination, which can be construed on the basis of an analogy with the concept of practical reason. If it can be so construed, then are the changes which Coleridge effected with regard to practical reason, in his development of a constitutive theory of a higher reason intuitive of ideas as real, to be found reflected in the development of his theory of the poetic imagination?

Only in the exercise of our moral duty was Kant prepared to allow a bridge between the phenomenal and the noumenal, and even this admission was qualified by his view of the role of practical reason as the realization of a law rather than an intuition. The importance of practical reason for Coleridge derives from this admission. It provides the fundamental basis of his own philosophical and theological conclusions, even although these are diametrically opposed to the conclusions of Kant. This is nowhere so obvious as in his theory of imagination. For Kant both reason

---

[5] Muirhead, who offers a Platonic reading of Coleridge's philosophy, admits the importance of Kant in this respect (ibid., p. 107).

[6] See J. D. Boulger, *Coleridge as Religious Thinker* (New Haven, 1961), pp. 65–93. The recent shift in emphasis from the distinction between reason and understanding as the central point in Coleridge's philosophy to that of practical reason, which Boulger effected so successfully in elucidating Coleridge's development as religious thinker, represents a major change of direction in Coleridgean studies.

[7] See Coleridge, *Philosophical Lectures*, p. 389.

in its theoretical role and imagination are purely intellectual faculties. Imagination is the intermediary between the forms of sensibility and the categories of understanding. Croce's characterization of it as 'the sensible and imaginative vesture of an intellectual concept'[8] sums up Coleridge's own view of its limitations, since for Coleridge art was not a copy of the phenomenal world but an imitation. Like moral action, art for Coleridge, as for Hazlitt, offers a handhold into the world of noumena, bridging the gap between the ideal and the real, between subject and object. The essence of both in Coleridge's view lies not in a thing in itself but in an act of will, either moral or imaginative. For Kant man's contact with the noumenal was restricted to the moral. Whilst Coleridge employs practical reason in his development of an intuitive higher reason, the fact that his theory of imagination can be construed on an analogy with the same concept is highly significant. In the one he must escape from the dualistic impasse consequent upon Kant's view of ideas as regulative, and in the other from Kant's view of art as possessing only subjective validity. The part which practical reason plays in the breakthrough to the noumenal in Kant's ethical theory is crucial to an understanding of Coleridge's philosophical and aesthetic theories.

In the case of Coleridge's higher reason the result was a constitutive theory. In the case of his theory of imagination the important question is whether Coleridge remained content with Kant's experiential compromise or whether his view of imagination likewise developed into a constitutive one, in which art was the expression of a reality which could be known intuitively. Two points must be taken into consideration here. The first is Kant's view that practical reason alone enables us to pass beyond the world of the senses and gives us an achieved awareness of reality. The second is his view that practical reason shows that a human being, belonging to the world of the senses, also belongs to the supersensible world. If we bear in mind these two views in conjunction with Coleridge's contention that art deals with the objects of the senses but does so in their role as symbols, we shall be better able to appreciate that even if the seminal idea of Kant is not directly appropriated by Coleridge in the development of his theories of imagination and of art as symbol, they can be construed on an analogy with it. This being the case, any alteration effected in his

---

[8] Croce, *Aesthetic*, p. 275.

direct use of practical reason is likely to affect his view of poetic imagination.

Like the exertion of the will in the exercise of our duty, the exertion of the imagination in the creation of symbols 'realizes' the contradiction of participation in the ideal and the real, the noumenal and phenomenal, or as it is expressed more frequently in the context of literature, the individual and the universal, the external and the internal. As J. D. Boulger has shown, practical reason in the moral sphere did mean more for Coleridge than an experiential awareness of moral freedom. Rendering it constitutively, Coleridge fosters upon Kant his own use of it as the basis of religion: 'Here, then, he disclosed what I may call the [p]roof of his Christianity, which rendered him truly deserving the name philosopher.'[9] Coleridge's intuition of the ideas of God and immortality is founded upon his experience of moral obligation: 'The one great and binding ground of the belief of God and a hereafter, is the law of conscience.'[10] Not 'I am', but 'I ought' becomes the basis of his philosophical and theological speculations. As a result literature, morality, and religion share a common essence:

> Religion . . . [is] the consideration of the particular and individual . . . but of the individual, as it exists and has its being in the universal . . . and is the echo of the *voice of the Lord God walking in the garden*. Hence in all the ages and countries of civilization religion has been the parent and fosterer of the fine arts, as of poetry, music, painting, and the like, the common essence of which consists in a similar union of the universal and the individual.[11]

Imagination therefore operates in the same manner and upon the same basis as Coleridge's constitutive rendering of practical reason. It is practical reason in our lives that incorporates or fuses man as phenomenal and noumenal, man not just as object, mechanical, finite, a creature of understanding and fancy, subject to the laws of cause and effect, but man as free agent, with unconditioned causality resting in his will, man as organic, infinite, divine, a creature of reason and imagination. Imagination through the creation of symbols resolves the same contradiction in the specific form of art. The breakdown of Coleridge's analysis of imagination

⁹ Coleridge, *Philosophical Lectures*, p. 389.
¹⁰ Coleridge, *Notes*, p. 367. See also ibid., pp. 380, 384–95; *Letters*, IV. 756; *Works*, II. 376.
¹¹ Coleridge, *Works*, I. 457.

in the *Biographia* is due directly to his failure to relate it explicitly to the 'I ought':

> For the distinguishing characteristic of that faculty, as from the first conceived by Coleridge, had been its power of interpreting the world of experience as a manifestation of a spiritual principle. And the possibility of such an insight was dependent upon a previous spiritual experience of which it was the symbol and guarantee.[12]

What Shawcross fails to point out in this passage are the implications of such a connection between imagination and a view of moral consciousness which is also interpreted as the guarantee of the existence of a Christian God.

This can be made clearer if we compare Coleridge's view of art as a means of transcending the world of sense with the use which he makes of practical reason in his concept of a higher reason. In the latter the notion of ideas as regulative was insufficient. By insisting on the priority of practical reason Coleridge substituted an act of will for the thing in itself to render ideas constitutive, annexing to Kant's view of freedom and conscience the intuition of God.[13] This act becomes the prime source of our intuition of the ideas of reality. We have no longer an experiential awareness of freedom as in Kant but a real intuitive knowledge, not just of freedom but of God, immortality and the self. In view of the parallel nature of the roles fulfilled by higher reason and poetic imagination, in life and art respectively, the question can now be raised to what extent Coleridge's dissatisfaction with Kant's view of practical reason in the moral sphere is to be found reflected in his theory of imagination. A strict application of that concept to the elucidation of the nature of art (an application which Kant would not have countenanced in any case) results in an experiential theory of the poetic imagination such as we find in Hazlitt. Moreover in Hazlitt the questions of morality and religion are quite separate issues and he is able, unlike Coleridge, to establish the connection between art and life quite explicitly. Since such a theory is inadequate for Coleridge in the realm of philosophy and

---

[12] Coleridge, *Biographia*, I. lxxxiv–lxxxv.

[13] The substitution of act for thing, the superiority of the moral to the intellectual, marks the fundamental basis of the new dynamic philosophy for Coleridge. He attributes this advance on Kant's position to Fichte. See Coleridge, *Letters*, IV. 792, and *Biographia*, I. 101. In *Letters, Conversations and Recollections*, II. 137, Coleridge also emphasizes the '*transcendency of the moral to the intellectual*'.

religion, the question now is whether it is equally inadequate in the sphere of critical theory. Since Coleridge made no detailed application of his mature post-1817 philosophical insights to his earlier aesthetic, any bias towards a constitutive rendering of the reality revealed by art will remain only a bias. We cannot expect it to be embodied with the same subtlety and complexity. Indeed, Coleridge's growing constitutivism is totally inimical to what Shawcross has termed his earlier 'imaginative interpretation of nature',[14] for the one is essentially religious, the other essentially poetic. In the context of the thesis which is being put forward Shawcross's reasons for Coleridge's failure are significant:

> He realized more and more the paramount importance of emphasizing and appealing to the purely spiritual consciousness as a common possession of all men. Thus imagination, as the faculty of mediate vision, is thrust into the background, while reason, the faculty of direct access to truth, claims a more exclusive attention.[15]

But while remaining the most perceptive of all Coleridge's critics, aware of the ultimate implications of Coleridge's later philosophy, Shawcross constantly refuses to acknowledge openly the grave consequences which his constitutive philosophy has for literature.

If it is true that Coleridge's theory of imagination performs a function in his aesthetic theory analogous to the concept of practical reason in Kant's ethical theory, and that Coleridge's development of the latter in his construction of a mature philosophical viewpoint lay in the direction of a constitutivism which must ultimately affect his view of the ontological status of the work of art itself, it still remains to be shown what theory of imagination is of particular relevance in this context. Coleridge has two theories of imagination, or at least there are two facets to his theory. The first refers to the ontological aspect; the second to the psychological component. Practical reason here has reference only to the ontological nature of the work of art, and not to the psychology of its creation. Yet it is the psychological component which has hitherto received the greater share of critical attention. The failure to perceive the significance of practical reason, and of Coleridge's own idiosyncratic use of it in relation to his theory of poetic imagination, is the consequence of this neglect.

[14] Coleridge, *Biographia*, I. lxxxi.
[15] Ibid., I. lxxxiii.

The reason for this is not far to seek. If we have regard only to the more formal statements of the theory of imagination in the *Biographia*, the chief difficulty which presents itself is that Coleridge's discussion centres upon artistic psychology—the production of the work of art—not on the essence of that work. The ontological status of the reality revealed is only to be inferred. Shawcross's reading is in the main an experiential or immanential one, i.e. in terms of an achieved awareness of the spiritual verities; I. A. Richards ignores it; F. R. Leavis views it as irrelevant to Coleridge's practice as a critic.[16] An important distinction requires to be made at this point. Only thus can we appreciate the crucial role which Coleridge's theory plays in his critical practice. We must distinguish between (*i*) a psychological analysis of the faculty by means of which we break through to reality, i.e. an analysis of its *mode* of operation, and (*ii*) a philosophical analysis of the *role* of imagination as the faculty of the supersensuous. The essence of poetry, its ontological status, is the concern of Coleridge's theory of imagination in the latter sense and not the former. More especially it is the concern of the theory of art which developed from this view of its role and which is correlative to it. This is the theory of art as symbol. Poetry as symbol, as realizing the finite/infinite contradiction in symbol, is the product of imagination. Coleridge's concern is twofold: he must examine the role or nature of the faculty and its mode of operation.

The role of imagination, as we have seen, is similar to the role of the moral will; the work of art to the moral action. Coleridge's theory of imagination in this sense and his theory of art as symbol are correlative. They lead into one another, but do not exclude an analysis of the mode of that faculty's operation in psychological terms. When it is said that his theory of imagination has little relevance to his practice, the first step must be to discover whether the reference is to its role or to its mode of operation. If it is to the latter, then the charge is probably true but irrelevant, since as a psychological analysis it can hardly come within the scope of the ontology of poetry which is the concern of literary criticism. But if the criticism is directed at Coleridge's conception of the role of imagination, then the charge may appear at first sight to be substantiated by Coleridge's slight and fragmentary analysis in the

[16] Ibid., 1. xi–lxxxix; I. A. Richards, *Coleridge on Imagination* (London, 1934); F. R. Leavis, 'Coleridge in Criticism', *Scrutiny*, IX (1940), 57–69.

Biographia. If we would understand the relation between imagination in this sense and Coleridge's criticism, we must look not to
this slight sketch of its role but to the correlative theory of poetry
as ideal. It is Coleridge's attitude to poetry as the product of
imagination in its role as intermediary between the phenomenal
and noumenal, as revealing reality, that governs his entire conception of literature in his practical criticism. It is his theory of art
as symbol which enables us to confute the suggestion that his
theory of imagination has little or no practical relevance, since as
a theory it is the consequence of the high estimation which he
confers upon the role of the imaginative faculty.[17]

This distinction having been drawn, the question of the constitutive bias in his theory of poetic imagination still remains to be
answered. In this connection a late definition of imagination is
especially relevant. This reveals his attempt to fuse or incorporate
his theories of symbol and of imagination within a single definition,
thereby bringing his earlier psychology of art and 'imaginative
interpretation of nature' more into line with his developing views
of the nature of the reality revealed by art. His earlier psychology
of the creation of the work of art in terms of a dominant passion or
feeling is much more congenial to a purely experiential view of the
ontological status of the work of art, i.e. in terms of an achieved
awareness rather than of ideas intuited as real. In this late definition,
however, the affective basis of imagination is slighted. Instead it is
defined as:

> ... that reconciling and mediatory power, which incorporating the
> reason in images of the sense, and organizing ... the flux of the senses by
> the permanence and self-circling energies of the reason, gives birth to a
> system of symbols, harmonious in themselves, and consubstantial with
> the truths of which they are the conductors.[18]

This neglect of feeling is characteristic of the constitutive theory of
art and is in marked contrast with the constant emphasis on this
element in the work of Hazlitt and Keats. Even if we make allow-
ance for the fact that the definition was written under the influence

[17] The distinction between the role of imagination and the mode of its operation
is of the greatest importance in considering the literary criticism of the Romantic
period.
[18] Coleridge, *Works*, I. 436. Boulger cites this neglect of feeling as the central
weakness of Coleridge's later poetry and of his later religious views (*Coleridge as
Religious Thinker*, p. 199).

of Schelling—an influence to be so short-lived—it must be pointed out that what Coleridge finally objected to in the definition itself was not the incipient constitutivism which it betrays, but the pantheistic implications of that particular form of constitutivism.[19] The analogy with practical reason upon which his theory of imagination has hitherto been construed now appears to be an analogy with his own development of that concept in his elaboration of a higher and intuitive reason designed to explain how a knowledge of ideas, or a science of metaphysics, is possible. The consequence is that art becomes an expression of the artist's own intuitive insight into ideas as real—a conclusion which is borne out by his later poetry.

It is not necessary to argue that Coleridge identifies reason and imagination in this definition, or that he comes close to it. It is rather an attempt to view them as correlative, and is just one more obvious manifestation of his lifelong attempt to fuse literature and philosophy. It marks a watershed in his treatment of imagination, since it is an attempt to confer upon poetry an importance and equal status that is fundamentally at odds with a full constitutive theory, the inherent tendency of which, the more completely constitutive it is, is to effect a fusion at the expense of the poetic—to subordinate literature to philosophy and ultimately to religion. His rapid abandonment of this particular formulation is indicative of a realization not of the impossibility of such a fusion, but that this fusion of imagination and reason, of the poetic and religious spheres of the spiritual or dynamic as equal partners, was incompatible with his own conception of a Christian God. That he finally abandoned the definition was the result of his recognition of the impossible nature of the attempt to reconcile imagination as immanent or experiential and imagination as constitutive through reason. Such a curious hybrid of an extreme immanential theory and an incipient constitutivism can be achieved only at the price of a pantheistic conception of reality at odds with what has been called Coleridge's 'need for a real and knowable God'.[20] Thereafter

---

[19] See Coleridge, *Philosophical Lectures*, pp. 390–1.

[20] G. McKenzie, *Organic Unity in Coleridge* (Berkeley, 1939), p. 13. Cf. *Biographia*, I. lxxxiii, lxxxv) for Shawcross's view that 'aesthetic experience is subordinated to the experience in which the intuitions of reason find their surest witness, the "testifying state" of conscience.... The imagination, as creative artistically, does but seek to give outward expression to the harmony of the personal and divine will, which conscience enjoins.'

his interest in the poetic imagination declined, and with it his interest in poetry generally. We have thus neither a full statement of his final position nor any sustained piece of literary criticism which might have reflected any serious, although undefined, alteration in his theoretical position.

This view of the inevitable tendency of Coleridge's theory of imagination and of poetry as symbol illustrates precisely the same shift from an experiential rendering of practical reason to the constitutive construction placed upon it by Coleridge in his development of a higher reason. It is a view which finds considerable support in many of Coleridge's general comments on the relation of art to philosophy and religion, as well as in the whole tenor of his religious and philosophical views towards unity and comprehensiveness, harmony and subordination. In this the supreme idea is that of a Christian God dominant over his entire ontology. This is the reality which it is the task of the philosopher to elucidate and the poet to express. Coleridge yearned for just such a harmony when he wrote:

> The astronomer places himself in the centre of the system and looks at all the planetary orbs as with the eye of the sun. Happy would it be for us if we could at all times imitate him in his perceptions—in the intellectual or the political world—I mean, to subordinate instead of exclude.[21]

But it was a harmony only to be bought at a price—a price which Keats, Shelley and Hazlitt were not prepared to pay. Coleridge characterized his constitutive viewpoint perfectly when he confessed in the letter to Allsop that he had an 'intense craving after a resting-place for my Thoughts in some *principle* ... of which all other knowledge should be but so many repetitions'.[22] It is precisely this attempt, stated explicitly in so many parts of his writings, that Hazlitt was to criticize so severely in his essay, 'The Spirit of Philosophy'. The motto of the philosopher, the poet, and the critic is not ' "I will lead you into all knowledge" ', but ' "I will show you a mystery" '.[23] 'Systems and system-makers'[24] represent the antithesis of the essential openness to all experience characteristic of the experiential or poetic viewpoint. It is this insistence on Hazlitt's part that makes him, rather than Coleridge, Keats's natural ally.

[21] Coleridge, *Philosophical Lectures*, pp. 312–13.
[22] Coleridge, *Letters, Conversations and Recollections*, II. 136.
[23] Hazlitt, *Works*, xx. 371.
[24] Ibid., xx. 375.

Coleridge's demand for unification and harmony entailed the conversion of the poetic into something other than the poetic, its subordination to philosophy and ultimately to religion. Coleridge came to see literature and art with the eye of God, for it is God who is the central vantage point in the harmony he sought. The distinction between the experiential and the constitutive is fundamental to an appreciation of the essential differences between the literary, moral, social, political and philosophical theories of Hazlitt, Keats, and Shelley on the one hand and Coleridge on the other, and was drawn most emphatically by R. J. White when he wrote:

> It is a false dichotomy which would divide his metaphysics from his poetry, or his politics from either. ... Nor will the candid reader attempt to separate the religion, the metaphysics, and the poetic imagery from the politics. ... To Coleridge, the political world hung by the interwoven threads of religion, metaphysics and poetry, from the little finger of God.[25]

Within the scope of the present chapter it is not possible to consider even briefly the various ways in which Coleridge's constitutive bias is manifested in his literary criticism. Yet because literary history has tended to assimilate the criticism of the period to the critical theory of Coleridge, it is important that some indication, however perfunctory, should be given of those areas in his theory and practice where discrimination of this element is not only possible but essential. One of the most obvious and significant instances is his constant attempt, in his lectures, correspondence, and the *Biographia*, to define the nature of poetry. In the *Biographia* the problem is crystallized in the form of the question: 'What is poetry?'[26] Having committed this category mistake, Coleridge redeems himself by refusing to answer the question. The obliqueness of the analysis which follows is a testimony of his basic experiential distrust of the very question.[27] Ultimately of course he

[25] R. J. White, *The Political Thought of Coleridge* (London, 1938), pp. 23–4. J. Kinnaird makes the excellent point that Hazlitt's real objections to Coleridge centre upon his idealistic embroidery of the basically experiential text of Kant ('The Forgotten Self', *Partisan Review*, xxx (1963), 302–6). Hence he finds Hazlitt's review of *The Statesman's Manual*, printed before the latter's publication, the perfect, formal equivalent of a real and substantial dislike of Coleridge's 'immaculate conceptions'.

[26] Coleridge, *Biographia*, II. 8–13.

[27] In his lectures Coleridge characterizes his attempt as one of description rather than of definition.

did demand a transcendent solution, no less transcendent because it was intuitive. But in this part of the *Biographia* the whole interest centres upon the tension between his constitutive urge to ask and answer the question and his experiential bent, which prompts him to evade the consequences of the question. Closely related to this is the issue of his theory of poetry as ideal, which it was suggested earlier is correlative to his theory of the role played by imagination in art. Imagination may fuse the phenomenal and noumenal in the work of art through symbol, but what is the precise relationship between the individual or phenomenal and the general or noumenal? If we wish to disprove Dr. Leavis's view that Coleridge's theory is irrelevant to his critical practice, it is this aspect which must be emphasized, for it is the key to the whole of his critical effort. The relationship between the theory and practice is so close at this ontological level that the ambiguities to be found in his theoretical discussion are mirrored perfectly in his treatment of individual poets. A good example of this is to be found in the development of his views on the long philosophical poem, the evolution of which is best traced in his correspondence.[28] Especially relevant in relation to his progress towards a theistic characterization of the universal are his criticisms of Lucretius, Dante, Spenser, The Bible, Herbert, Milton, Bunyan, Wordsworth, and his own early poetry.[29]

An examination of his development as a critic of Wordsworth indicates that his critical attitude altered radically as a result of his later development as a religious thinker. The experiential rendering of poetry as ideal which characterizes his public criticism of Wordsworth is replaced in his correspondence and conversation by a constitutive interpretation in which the universal is viewed theistically. Coleridge's private opinions indicate that what he objected to in the poetry of Wordsworth was not its embodiment of truths, but the quality and nature of the truths and the inappropriate means of expression employed. Even where Coleridge's criticism of Wordsworth's orthodoxy, egotism, matter-of-factness, and pantheism overlaps with similar criticisms made by Keats or

---

[28] Coleridge, *Letters*, I. 215, 278–9, 397; II. 666, 864, 1034; IV. 564, 570–6. This issue is examined in more detail in my article, 'Coleridge: Philosopher and Theologian as Literary Critic', *University of Toronto Quarterly*, XXXVIII (1968), 17–33.

[29] Coleridge, *Miscellaneous Criticism*, ed. T. M. Raysor (London, 1936), pp. 31–3, 145–50, 159–66, 244, 393; *Letters*, I. 205, 281; IV. 574, 893.

Jeffrey or Hazlitt, the basis from which he is criticizing and the terminology which he employs are often radically different.[30]

The fundamental tension between the experiential and constitutive to be found in Coleridge's theoretical discussions also informs his questioning of the merits and standing of such diverse figures as Plato, Socrates, Aristotle, Bacon, Kant, and Sir Joshua Reynolds.

R. J. White's view therefore does require some qualification. In the period of his greatest critical activity the bias towards a constitutive theory fortunately remains only a bias. Yet the appreciation of this bias, which is always apparent in his philosophy from the beginning, and its influence on his theory of imagination and of art as symbol, does enable us to attain some understanding of certain emphases and inconsistencies in his work as a literary critic. His greatness as a literary critic is founded on his early experiential approach to the poetic, in which poetry is seen as the expression of a reality in terms of an achieved awareness, or experience, rather than of intuited ideas. The inherent tendency towards a constitutivist viewpoint, however, manifest in so many ways in his criticism, renders that criticism startlingly different from the criticism of his Romantic contemporaries.

[30] Coleridge, *Miscellaneous Criticism*, pp. 386, 397; *Letters*, II. 1013; IV. 564, 573; *Works*, II. 467; *Philosophical Lectures*, p. 129; *Letters, Conversations and Recollections*, I. 105–7. Coleridge's private and public criticism of Wordsworth's poetry is considered in my article, 'Coleridge's Two Voices as a Critic of Wordsworth,' *ELH* XXXVI (1969), 361–81.

PART II

The Painter

The painter does not view things in clouds or 'mist, the common gloss of theologians', but applies the same standard of truth and disinterested spirit of inquiry, that influence his daily practice, to other subjects. He perceives form; he distinguishes character. He reads men and books with an intuitive glance. He is a critic as well as a connoisseur. The conclusions he draws are clear and convincing, because they are taken from actual experience. . . . The habit of seeing for himself also disposes him to judge for himself.

Table-Talk, viii. 10

CHAPTER FOUR

The Painter as Philosopher

> They are not, then, so properly the works of an author
> by profession, as the thoughts of a metaphysician
> expressed by a painter. They are subtle and difficult
> problems translated into hieroglyphics. I thought for
> several years on the hardest subjects, on Fate, Free
> Will, Foreknowledge absolute, without ever making
> use of words or images at all, and that has made them
> come in such throngs and confused heaps when I burst
> from that void of abstraction. . . . Till I began to
> paint . . . I could neither write nor speak.
>
> *Uncollected Essays*, xvii. 311–12

1. HAZLITT'S THEORY OF ABSTRACTION

THE scientist's reliance on abstraction in non-scientific spheres,
according to Bacon, is the result of his training as a scientist:
'When men of confined scientific pursuits afterwards betake themselves to philosophy, and to general contemplations, they are apt
to wrest and corrupt them with their former conceits.'[1] Hazlitt, on
the other hand, attributes the painter's freedom from abstraction in
matters unrelated to his art to his experience as a painter: 'The habit
of seeing for himself also disposes him to judge for himself.' In so
doing Hazlitt invests painting with an influence especially relevant
to his own theory and practice as a literary critic. His training as a
painter not only helps to explain the distrust of abstraction evident
in all his writings; it is also the source of the theory of abstract ideas
by means of which he provided a philosophical justification of that
distrust.

Hazlitt was almost forty when he published his first work of
literary criticism in 1817. The next few years saw the publication
in quick succession of three series of public lectures, and within the
space of four years, his survey of English literature from Chaucer

[1] See above, p. 17, n. 23.

to Wordsworth was substantially complete.[2] His theory of abstraction and its origins in painting play an important part in considering the belated nature of his sudden emergence as a critic, the comparative brevity of the period of his critical activity and the maturity of a critical position which exhibits singularly little development. His maturity as a critic is apparent from the outset.

Until 1814, however, Hazlitt considered himself primarily a painter and philosopher. Between 1805 and 1812 he developed a highly individual and revolutionary theory of abstraction which was to become the basis of his response both to life and to art. Its origin can be traced to painting, but its elaboration is the consequence of his training as a philosopher, and its application to literature in the period after 1814 is the result of his awareness of its general critical implications. Only by emphasizing the conjoint operation of philosophy and painting in the earlier part of his career—as studies preparatory to the criticism of literature—can his sudden emergence as a literary critic be satisfactorily explained. He exemplifies Wallace Stevens's claim that since poetry and painting are twin facets of a unified poetic experience, 'it would be possible to study poetry by studying painting'.[3] Consequently it is necessary to examine his early preoccupation with painting in order to appreciate fully the dominant themes in his later literary criticism and the manner of their expression. Of his contemporaries, it was, significantly, a painter who was the most acutely conscious of the potential of his early familiarity with painting. Commenting on his transition from painting to literary criticism, Benjamin Robert Haydon wrote in his diary for 1816: 'He practised Painting long enough to know it; and he carries into Literature a stock which no literary man ever did before.'[4]

Even if his view of abstraction and its intimate relation to painting were disregarded, the important role which modern philosophy and psychology have conferred upon analogy and transfer in the processes of human learning is in itself a sufficient justification for emphasizing Hazlitt's twenty-year preoccupation

---

[2] *Characters of Shakespear's Plays* was published in 1817 and was followed by *A View of the English Stage* (1818), *Lectures on the English Poets* (1818), *Lectures on the English Comic Writers* (1819), and *Lectures chiefly on the Dramatic Literature of the Age of Elizabeth* (1820).

[3] Wallace Stevens, 'The Relations between Poetry and Painting', *The Necessary Angel* (London, 1960), p. 160.

[4] *The Diary of B. R. Haydon*, ed. W. B. Pope (Cambridge, Mass., 1960-3), II. 65.

with painting and philosophical speculation. A modern psychologist has observed that 'the learning of complex, abstract, meaningful materials and the solution of problems by means of ideas . . . are to a great extent functions of transfer. . . . It is, likewise, a basic factor in originality, the original and creative person having, among other things, unusual sensitivity to the applicability of the already known to new problem situations.'[5] To the original and creative mind no experience is entirely useless. The quotations from Bacon and Hazlitt, Haydon, and Wallace Stevens implicitly acknowledge the important role played by transfer and analogy in the development of human understanding. But the best justification for stressing the importance of painting is to be found in Hazlitt's own characterization of his work as 'the thoughts of a metaphysician expressed by a painter', and in his observation that 'till I began to paint . . . I could neither write nor speak'. Since his theory of abstract ideas has been neglected and misunderstood by literary historians and has not achieved any general critical currency, a simple exposition of it must be the first objective.

Unlike his moral theory, Hazlitt's view of abstraction cannot adequately be appreciated within the framework of eighteenth-century philosophical thought. In Locke's conceptualism and in the nominalism of Hobbes, Berkeley, and Hume, abstraction is conceived as a process of generalization. In Hazlitt, on the other hand, abstraction is a process of individuation. According to Locke, the concept of triangularity is formed by the abstraction of those elements common to our ideas of individual triangles, and by their combination to form a compound idea corresponding to the general term. In his criticism of Locke, Hazlitt rejects the view that we can have any concept which thus corresponds to a general term.[6]

---

[5] J. A. McGeoch, *The Psychology of Human Learning* (New York, 1942), pp. 445–6. Cf. D. Pole's doubly apposite view that 'in turning from one region of thought to another we carry over a whole set of pictures, for pictures govern much of our thinking', *The Later Philosophy of Wittgenstein* (London, 1958), p. 7.

[6] In Coleridge, *Philosophical Lectures*, p. 414, Kathleen Coburn mistakenly assimilates Hazlitt's theory to the conceptualism of Locke. While it is true that there is agreement between Locke and Hazlitt as to the existence of abstract ideas, the difference between their views as to what constitutes the abstract rules out any meaningful agreement. Like Coleridge, Hazlitt maintained that a compound image was an absurdity. It was not 'possible ever to arrive at a demonstration of generals or abstractions by beginning in Mr. Locke's method with particular ones' (ii. 191). He denies the possibility of compounding abstract ideas from individual ideas. A curious anticipation of his denial of generalization as a sign of intellectual maturity

Likewise, he rejects Locke's view of abstraction as the highest achievement of the human intellect. On the contrary, he suggests that it is the consequence of the limitations of the human understanding. Thus, like the nominalists, he denies that we have abstract ideas corresponding to general terms. For Hobbes, Berkeley, and Hume, all ideas are particular; it is their signification alone which is general. Abstraction is an operation of language, not of the understanding. Triangularity is not an abstract idea, but a general name corresponding to a particular idea. There are no abstract ideas. Hazlitt is in complete agreement with Berkeley's nominalist criticism of Locke that we do not have abstract ideas corresponding to general terms. He does not, however, argue for this on the grounds that all our ideas are particular. He agrees with Locke that we do possess abstract ideas, but for Hazlitt *all* our ideas are abstract. This radical solution of the traditional problem of universals rules out any meaningful agreement with either of the opposing theories of the eighteenth century. Ideas are not generalized in Locke's sense. They are individual, but each individual idea is indeterminate —'an imperfect and general notion of an aggregate' (ii. 191)— capable of infinite sub-division. It is in this sense that he views all our ideas as abstract. Thus, he writes:

I conceive that all our notions from first to last, are strictly speaking, general and abstract, not absolute and particular; and that to have a perfectly distinct idea of any one individual thing . . . would imply an unlimited power of comprehension in the human mind, which is impossible. All particular things consist of, and lead to, an infinite number of other things. Abstraction is a consequence of the limitation of the comprehensive faculty, and mixes itself more or less with every act of the mind. . . .

(ii. 191)

Abstraction, accordingly, is a category of the human mind—a built-in principle of perceptual ordering. This view of the subject, Hazlitt immediately confesses, is not 'very obvious at first sight', and his confession is significant. From this passage, and from one occurring later in the lecture, where he admits his inability to combat the nominalist view, or to indicate in what way his own solution can be said to clarify the issue, it is obvious that Hazlitt

is to be found in Hugh Blair, *Lectures on Rhetoric and Belles Lettres* (Edinburgh, 1783), I. 141–2. Blair likewise emphasizes the importance of individuation.

himself is not clear about the relation between his own theory and the theories of the eighteenth century. The reason for this is obvious. Within the context of the eighteenth-century discussion of abstract ideas, his solution is not a theory of abstraction at all. To the classic question what it is man does when he refers individuals to a class, his answer appears irrelevant. What he is saying is that all human ideas are indeterminate and complex, a vague and indefinite aggregate of a myriad of impressions. Intellectual progress is not towards abstraction, as Locke and the eighteenth century believed, but away from it towards individuation. Abstraction is implicit in every perception. His theory cuts across the classic form of the debate by denying the premiss common to nominalism and conceptualism alike, namely that abstraction is a process of generalization. In so doing he anticipates the findings of modern philosophy and psychology by more than a century.[7] This then is one reason for the disparity between the eighteenth-century theories and the solution which Hazlitt is proposing. An even more important reason for this disparity is his preoccupation with the psychological component of the theory considered as a theory of perception.

To attempt to relate Hazlitt to the eighteenth-century tradition, as Professor Coburn does,[8] is a serious misconception of his position, since it is only as an anticipation of more modern theories that his solution of the problem can be adequately assessed. But as a psychology of artistic perception, his theory connects with the past and the future. Viewed from a psychological standpoint, it is not a philosophical theory but the expression of a painter's insight into his art. Stripped of its philosophical context in the *Lectures*, the relation between his view of abstraction and the art of painting becomes clear:

Objects of sense are not as it were simple and self-evident propositions, but admit of endless analysis and the most subtle investigation. We do not see nature with our eyes, but with our understandings and our hearts. To suppose that we see the whole of any object, merely by looking at it, is a vulgar error. . . . This circle of knowledge enlarges with further

[7] Hazlitt's view of abstraction as a process from generalization to individuation is the theory favoured by most modern philosophers and psychologists. See Wittgenstein, *The Blue and Brown Books*, pp. 17–19; G. Ryle, *The Concept of Mind* (London, 1949), pp. 307–8; H. H. Price, *Thinking and Experience* (London, 1953); D. O. Hebb, *The Organization of Behavior* (New York, 1949), pp. 104 ff; R. Arnheim, *Art and Visual Perception* (London, 1956), pp. 27–31.

[8] See above, p. 97, n. 6.

acquaintance and study, and we then perceive that what we perhaps barely distinguished in the gross, or regarded as a dull blank, is full of beauty, meaning, and curious details. . . . Expression is the key to the human countenance, and unfolds a thousand imperceptible distinctions.

(xx. 388)[9]

In Hazlitt's view, as indeed in the view of most painters, no two leaves, no two grains of sand are alike. Each is composed of an infinity of parts, differing from one another, and even considered in isolation the same object varies infinitely in accordance with the time of day, the seasons of the year, the condition of the spectator, the angle of vision, and so forth. It is the task of the artist, more specifically of the painter, to express this unique existence:

> We do not see nature merely from looking at it. . . . In fact we only see a very small part of nature, and make an imperfect abstraction of the infinite number of particulars. . . . A painter, for instance, who has been working on a face for several days, still finds out something new in it which he did not notice before. . . . As he proceeds, a new field opens to him; differences crowd upon differences. . . . The combined genius and powers of observation of all the great artists in the world would not be sufficient to convey the whole of what is contained in any one object in nature.

(ix. 218)

Numerous passages of a similar import occur elsewhere in his writings.[10] Consequently, it would seem plausible to infer that his view of abstraction originated in large measure in his own experience as a painter. The internal evidence in favour of this inference is strong. Almost all the passages exemplifying the theory are couched in terms peculiar to painting, or are specifically related to it. His solution to the problem of abstraction is the basis of his views on genius and originality, in the illustration of which he almost invariably draws his examples from the great painters, and the art of painting.[11] Finally, his self-confessed inability to relate his findings in any meaningful way to the traditional dispute suggests that their origins were other than philosophical.

---

[9] The affinity of Hazlitt's theory of perception with the modern sense-datum theory is highlighted by H. H. Price's remark that 'the world as a painter sees it . . . does have to be described in a terminology of visual sense-data or something like it', *Perception* (London, 1954), p. vii.

[10] *Works*, ii. 207; iv. 73; viii. 8–10, 131–2; xx. 296–7, 445.

[11] Ibid., viii. 43; xx. 296–302, 391.

The external evidence is even stronger. *An Essay on the Principles of Human Action* in 1805, which was the fruit of his earliest philosophical speculations prior to his training as a painter, refers to abstract ideas in conventional philosophical terms, and evinces no dissatisfaction with the eighteenth century's handling of the problem of universals.[12] The reasons are not difficult to find. Hazlitt's mature view of abstraction postulates the creative nature of the human mind. In the *Essay* he was content to view the mind as active. His first reference to Kant's view of the creativity of the mind in 1807[13] coincides with the first fleeting reference to his own distinctive solution of the problem of abstraction in the preface to *An Abridgment of the Light of Nature Pursued* (1807).[14] He dealt with it again two years later in the *Prospectus of a History of English Philosophy*.[15] The first full statement of his own revised position in the *Lectures* of 1812 was almost certainly developed some time between 1810 and 1811 during which period he finally abandoned painting as a career.

Moreover, an examination of the writings of contemporaries and near contemporaries reveals that, as a psychology of artistic perception, Hazlitt's view is not in any sense unique. What is unique is the philosophical status conferred upon it, and the manner in which it is exemplified in his criticism. Furthermore, the writers who lay the greatest stress upon the necessity of individuation are painters and critics of painting. Blake's marginalia on Reynolds's *Discourses* is an obvious example of the painter-like emphasis on the need for the individual, and for a view of art as the minute discrimination of character. A century earlier, Dubos had written in much the same terms as Hazlitt, and, like Hazlitt, he related his views to a theory of genius and originality as manifested in the art of the painter:

Un homme né avec du génie ... découvre une différence infinie entre des objets, qui aux autres hommes paroissent les mêmes..........
Le Peintre habile a le talent de discerner le naturel qui est toûjours varié. ... L'experience aide encore beaucoup à trouver la différence qui est réellment entre des objets qui au premier coup d'oeil, nous paroissent les mêmes.[16]

Two more significant instances of the same viewpoint occur in Ruskin's *Modern Painters*:

[12] Ibid., i. 6 n, 23.   [13] Ibid., i. 130.   [14] Ibid., i. 124.   [15] Ibid., ii. 117.
[16] J. B. Dubos, *Reflexions Critiques sur la Poësie et sur la Peinture* (Paris, 1719), I. 210, 222.

WE NEVER SEE ANYTHING CLEARLY. . . . We suppose we see the ground under our feet clearly . . . there is literally *no* point of clear sight. . . . What we call seeing a thing clearly, is only seeing enough of it to *make out what it is*.[17]

and Constable:

The world is wide; no two days are alike, nor even two hours; neither were there ever two leaves of a tree alike since the creation of the world; and the genuine productions of art, like those of nature, are all distinct from each other.[18]

Likewise in the twentieth century, the greatest support for Hazlitt's theory is to be found among art critics, art historians, and psychologists concerned with artistic form. E. H. Gombrich summed up the general view when he wrote: 'There is a fallacy in the idea that . . . we slowly learn to generalize and to form the abstract idea. . . . We have seen that both philosophy and psychology have revolted against this time-honoured view. Neither in thought nor in perception do we learn to generalize. We learn to particularize, to articulate, to make distinctions where before there was only an undifferentiated mass.'[19] Hazlitt's theory of abstraction which would appear to derive from his own perceptual experiences as a painter has been confirmed by the experimental control of similar experience in psychological laboratories. Arnheim's characterization of this view as 'new' and 'revolutionary' supports the claim advanced earlier that Hazlitt's proposed solution placed the traditional discussion of abstract ideas on an entirely new plane.[20]

[17] Ruskin, *Works*, VI. 75–6. Cf. Hazlitt's view that 'people in general see objects only to distinguish them in practice and by name—to know that a hat is black, that a chair is not a table' (xvii. 223).

[18] C. R. Leslie, *Memoirs of the Life of John Constable*, ed. J. Mayne (London, 1951), p. 273. Cf. Hazlitt: 'There is no object whatever, the most minute and simple, but is the object of thought or of the senses, as a leaf, a grain of sand, a pin's head, and so on, that does not necessarily and strictly consist of a number of parts' (xx. 443). A. C. Quatremère de Quincy made a similar point: 'There are not, for instance, two leaves entirely alike', *An Essay on the Nature, the End, and the Means of Imitation in the Fine Arts*, tr. J. Kent (London, 1837), p. 18.

[19] E. H. Gombrich, *Art and Illusion* (London, 1960), p. 86. See also his *Meditations on a Hobby Horse* (London, 1963), p. 2. Similar views are to be found in C. Bell, *Art* (London, 1914), p. 77, and R. Fry, *French, Flemish and British Art* (London, 1951), pp. 101–2.

[20] 'The experimental findings demanded a complete turnabout in the theory of perception. It seemed no longer possible to think of vision as proceeding from the particulars to the general. . . . It became evident that overall structural features are the primary data of perception, so that triangularity is not a late product of intellectual abstraction. . . . The young child sees "doggishness" before he is able to distinguish one dog from another', Arnheim, *Art and Visual Perception*, p. 30.

Finally, there is the evidence of Crabb Robinson, who, in reporting a conversation between Hazlitt and Coleridge in 1811, wrote in his diary: 'Hazlitt said that he had learnt from painting that it was difficult to form an idea of an individual object, that we had first only a *general idea*, that is, vague broken and imperfect recollection of the individual object. This, I had observed, was what the mob generally meant by a general idea, and Hazlitt said he had no other. Coleridge spoke of the impossibility of referring the individual to the class without having a previous notion of the class.'[21] Hazlitt's manifest inability to show in what sense his new theory could be said to clarify the traditional view of the problem of universals is matched by Coleridge's inability to comprehend the point he was here trying to make. The relevance of a new theory to a more traditional one is always more obvious if the new theory adheres to the framework already established. Where it denies the underlying assumptions of the previous discussion, the possibility of a meaningful dialogue is seriously diminished. In this respect, Hazlitt's view of abstraction is comparable with his view of the imaginative element in life and in art. The central problem in each is discussed outside the traditional Platonic framework. The pluralist or experiental solution, which he proposed in relation to the imaginative or poetic, parallels and is indeed derivative from the experiential solution offered to the problem of abstract ideas. The opposition between his view of the poetic as self-authenticating and the constitutive theory of Coleridge that subordinates literature to philosophy and religion is now seen as the consequence of the similar divergence of their views on the much more fundamental question of universals. In Coleridge's writings, the major influence is that of neo-Platonic philosophy; in Hazlitt's, it is his experience as a painter.

Hazlitt's discussion of abstraction is important in itself. It has, however, other more far-reaching implications. It is fundamental to any satisfactory explanation of the preoccupations and terminology of his criticism and of the maturity and consistency of his belated critical activity. Considered historically, it also provides a philosophical and psychological rationale for the new critical movement towards particularity in the late eighteenth and early nineteenth centuries. Only within the context of this movement

---

[21] *Henry Crabb Robinson on Books and their Writers*, ed. E. J. Morley (London, 1938), I. 28.

away from Reynolds's ideal theory of art can the real significance of Hazlitt's theory of abstract ideas be fully appreciated.

2. THE NEW MOVEMENT

By the time Uvedale Price published *An Essay on the Picturesque* (1794–8), advocating an objective theory based in the main upon Burke, and like Burke's theory of the sublime drawing heavily upon the epistemology of Locke, the age had progressed so far in general sophistication and subtlety that even in its own day the work was something of an anachronism. Even before its publication, Twining and Alison had shown fairly conclusively that the picturesque was not a quality inherent in an object, but was the consequence of the influence exerted by painting on the way in which the ordinary person looked at nature.[22] Hazlitt fully agreed with this view,[23] and in an essay on Crabbe where he criticized the poet's attempt to emulate the close imitative effect of the painter, he pointed out that the increasing popularity of painting in the late eighteenth century had influenced the way in which the age now looked at poetry as well as at nature:

> We cannot help thinking that a taste for that sort of poetry, which leans for support on the truth and fidelity of its imitations of nature, began to display itself much about that time, and, in a good measure, in consequence of the direction of the public taste to the subject of painting. Book-learning, the accumulation of wordy common-places, the gaudy pretensions of poetical fiction, had enfeebled and perverted our eye for nature. The study of the fine arts, which came into fashion about forty years ago . . . would tend imperceptibly to restore it. Painting is essentially an imitative art; it cannot subsist for a moment on empty generalities: the critic, therefore, who had been used to this sort of substantial entertainment, would be disposed to read poetry with the eye of a connoisseur . . . and would turn with double eagerness and relish to the force and precision of individual details, transferred, as it were, to the page from the canvas.

(xi. 165–6)

[22] A. Alison, *Essays on the Nature and Principles of Taste* (Edinburgh, 1790), p. 29 ff; T. Twining, 'On Poetry considered as an Imitative Art', in *Eighteenth-Century Critical Essays*, ed. S. Elledge (Ithaca, N.Y., 1961), II. 984–1004. Richard Payne Knight's reply to Price in *An Analytical Inquiry into the Principles of Taste* (1805) is based largely on Alison's associationist interpretation.

[23] *Works*, iv. 73. Cf. Coleridge's view that 'Painting & Engravings sends us back with new Eyes to Nature', *The Notebooks*, ed. K. Coburn (London, 1957), II. 1907. See also Leslie, *Memoirs of Constable*, pp. 179, 279.

Hazlitt's emphasis upon the concrete and particular is the consequence of his own experience of painting. In this passage, he is prepared to generalize further, and to argue that a whole new critical tradition in literature began to develop as a result of the greater familiarity with paintings and prints. It is true that overt reference to painting declined in the early nineteenth century. This is still consistent, however, with his view that painting influenced poetry by its emphasis on concrete and particular qualities as the essence of the poetic. The importance of painting did not cease with the decline of *ut pictura poesis*. By its emphasis on particularity painting helped literature to assume its new role in the new century. It taught that art was not something thought, something true or false, but something felt and seen. Once that lesson had been learned, overt reference declined.

The emergence of a new critical tradition in the last part of the eighteenth century, which stressed the individual, and which Hazlitt isolated and attributed to the influence of painting, is significant in that it is within this mode (however much he transformed it) that he himself worked. Although he specifically refers only to its emphasis on the individual, the new criticism was also characterized by its emphasis on literary pictorialism—an adjunct which, as his criticism of Crabbe reveals, Hazlitt was not prepared to accept.[24] There is however no necessary connection between the two. This new mode employs two critical vocabularies: the first is a vocabulary of overt reference to painting; the second, by stressing the individual, is one of implicit reference. This second vocabulary in Hazlitt's criticism derives from his theory of abstract ideas. Even in the eighteenth century the poet's ability to present the concrete and particular was explicitly related to painting by Richard Hurd: 'The shapes and appearances of things are apprehended, only in the gross, by dull minds. They think they *see*, but it is through a mist, where if they catch but a faint glimpse of the form before them, it is well. . . . Every object stands forth in bright sunshine to the view of the true poet. Every minute mark and lineament of the contemplated form leaves a corresponding trace on his fancy. . . . This is what we call *painting* in poetry.'[25] Although William Duff,

[24] *Works*, xi. 166.

[25] R. Hurd, Q. *Horatii Flacci, Ars Poetica* (London, 1749; 2 vols, 1753), II. 133–4. Cf. Blair, *Lectures*, II. 371: 'To a Writer of the inferior class, nature . . . appears exhausted. . . . He sees nothing new, or peculiar, in the object which he would

in making the same point, does not explicitly relate the emphasis on particularity to the influence of painting, his reliance on visual metaphor justifies such an inference.[26] As in the case of Hazlitt, the abstract is attacked as the vague and the indefinite. An outstanding example of this demand for the individual and concrete is to be found in Joseph Warton, who complained that he could perceive 'many symptoms, even among writers of eminence, of departing from these *true* and *lively*, and *minute*, representations of Nature, and of *dwelling in generalities*.'[27] His criticism of Shakespeare, Homer, and Virgil echoes many similar passages in Hazlitt. In his *Essay on the Writings and Genius of Pope*, Warton wrote: 'What distinguishes Homer and Shakespeare from all other poets, is, that they do not give their readers *general* ideas: every image is the particular and unalienable property of the person who uses it. . . . Even Virgil . . . is frequently general and indiscriminating, where Homer is minutely circumstantial.'[28] For Kames, Hurd, and Walter Whiter, the excellence of Shakespeare also lay in his freedom from abstraction,[29] and among the Scottish theorists of the late eighteenth century, this emphasis is most marked in the work of Hugh Blair, George Campbell, James Beattie, and Adam Smith.[30]

Hazlitt's view that eighteenth-century literary criticism changed

---

paint, his conceptions of it are loose and vague; and his expression . . . feeble and general.'

[26] [W. Duff], *An Essay on Original Genius* (London, 1767), pp. 158–9: 'A person who is destitute of Genius, discovers nothing new or discriminating in the objects which he surveys. He takes only a general and superficial view of them, and is incapable of discerning those minute properties, or of relishing those particular and distinguishing beauties.'

[27] J. Warton, *An Essay on the Writings and Genius of Pope* (London,1756–82), II. 230.

[28] Ibid., I. 321–2. Warton criticized Pope for describing 'rural beauty in general, and not the peculiar beauties of the forest of Windsor' (ibid., I. 20).

[29] H. Home, Lord Kames, *Elements of Criticism* (Edinburgh, 1785), II. 352; Hurd, *Ars Poetica* (London, 1776), I. 59; W. Whiter, *A Specimen of a Commentary on Shakespeare* (London, 1794) reprinted in part in *Eighteenth-Century Critical Essays*, ed. Elledge, II. 1065–1103. Thomas Warton attributed this quality in Chaucer to his familiarity with tapestries, *The History of English Poetry* (London, 1774–81), II. 215. Whiter extends this to cover the writers of the sixteenth century as well.

[30] H. Blair, *Lectures*, II. 371–2; G. Campbell, *The Philosophy of Rhetoric* (London, 1776), II. 166; J. Beattie, *Essays on Poetry and Music* (Edinburgh, 1776), p. 97; A. Smith, *Lectures on Rhetoric and Belles Lettres*, ed. J. M. Lothian (London, 1963), pp. 67–8.

direction around 1770 is borne out not only by the demands made by the critics but by the changing conceptions of criticism itself. The early attack by Thomas Warton on 'panegyrical comments', and by Hurd on 'vague and superficial' criticism, were consolidated by Joseph Warton in his view that 'general and unexemplified criticism is always useless and absurd', and by Morgann when he wrote: 'General criticism is as uninstructive as it is easy: *Shakespeare* deserves to be considered in detail.'[31] William Richardson, whose analyses of Shakespeare's characters even Stockdale criticized as being too minute,[32] followed Morgann in this, and anticipates Hazlitt's own justification of detail by relating it to feeling: 'When emotions, by being expressed, become excessive, the mind passes from general reflections to minute and particular circumstances: and imagination . . . renders these circumstances still more particular.'[33] Like Hazlitt, Richardson frequently renders his perception of particularity through his use of a vocabulary of painting which does not in the slightest way entail support for a doctrine of literary pictorialism: 'Every passion is compounded of inferior and subordinate feelings, essential to its existence, in their own nature nicely and minutely varied, but whose different shades and gradations are difficult to be discerned.'[34] This passage embodies in a very simplified, and indeed an almost naïve form, that fusion of a vocabulary of particularity and a vocabulary of painting—owing no allegiance to pictorialism—which, so inexpressibly richer in Hazlitt, is the prime characteristic of his critical terminology. The decline of literary pictorialism in the early nineteenth century did not diminish the relevance of the analogy with painting. By drawing attention to the limited nature of the parallel between the two arts, the anti-pictorialist tradition paved the way for the transformation of the analogy in the literary criticism of the early nineteenth century.

[31] T. Warton, *Observations on the Faery Queen* (London, 1754; 2 vols, 1762), II. 263; Hurd, *Ars Poetica*, 1753, II. v; J. Warton, *Essay on the Writings and Genius of Pope*, II. 75; M. Morgann, *An Essay on the Dramatic Character of Sir John Falstaff* (1777), reprinted in *Eighteenth Century Essays on Shakespeare*, ed. D. Nichol Smith (Oxford, 1963), p. 211.

[32] P. Stockdale, *Lectures on the Truly Eminent English Poets* (London, 1807), I. 107–8.

[33] W. Richardson, *Essays on Some of Shakespeare's Dramatic Characters* (London, 1797), p. 81.

[34] Ibid., p. 15. Cf. his appeal to 'observe . . . the fine lineaments and delicate shadings of this singular character' (ibid., p. 336).

At its simplest level, the influence of painting on Hazlitt's critical terminology is most clearly evinced by his adoption of the pre-existing vocabularies of explicit and implicit reference. His use of 'gusto' in his literary criticism is the most obvious example of the transference of terminology characterizing the first of these two vocabularies. But his explicit vocabulary has a significance transcending the ramifications even of this key concept. It embraces most of the terms of eighteenth-century art criticism: atmosphere, light and shade, relief, perspective, finish, contrast, blending, historical painting, picturesque, gradation, chiaroscuro, drapery, grouping, disposition, composition, expression, sentiment, gusto, still-life, canvas, studies, colours, lines, contours, tints, portraits, outlines, shades, pencil, keeping, plaster-casts, and lay-figures. His exploitation of the vocabulary of painting on such a scale almost justifies Quatremère de Quincy's jaundiced view that in contemporary poetry and criticism 'the vocabulary of the art of painting is drained to exhaustion'.[35] By comparison, the eighteenth-century use of the same vocabulary of explicit reference is relatively feeble and half-hearted. Yet Hazlitt's handling of such an explicit terminology always evinces a respect for the differences as well as for the similarities of the two arts. The terms derived from painting are not employed indiscriminately but are always controlled by his conception of kinds of gusto. Implicit in all his literary criticism are equivalences between kinds of painting and kinds of literature —a correlation which excludes pictorialism. He always demands the gusto appropriate to the branch of literature he is considering, and the language which he employs in criticizing, for example, a drama approximates the vocabulary employed in criticizing an historical painting. It illustrates Prince Hoare's view that 'Painting, like Literature, includes various divisions, some of which . . . bear a relation to poetry'.[36] This correlation of comparable genres in painting and poetry confers greater structural unity upon his vocabulary than is the case with his eighteenth-century pre-

---

[35] Quatremère de Quincy, *Essay*, pp. 99–100: 'The author no longer draws his inspiration directly from the objects even of physical nature, but from the imitations and imitative processes of the artist. . . . He affects to model forms, trace contours, draw outlines, project shadows, and group masses. . . . He will not forget the vapours of the aërial perspective in the distance, nor the prominent objects in the foreground . . . nor the play of light on its windows. . . . The vocabulary of the art of painting is drained to exhaustion.'

[36] P. Hoare, *The Artist*, No. XIV (1809), 289.

decessors, and it does so without detracting from his subtle and sensitive handling of particular terms. The structural unity is expressive of his view of the essential unity of the two arts, resting in the need of both—as poetic—for the particular. The vocabulary of painting is frequently subordinated to the vocabulary of particularity, and becomes the medium through which he expresses the need for detail.

The second influence of painting on Hazlitt's expression of his experiential position is indirect and relates to the vocabulary derived from his theory of abstraction, which it was suggested earlier is essentially the theory of a painter. This vocabulary comprises a vast network of synonymous and related terms bearing on his view that individuals, and not kinds, are the essence of art. Nouns like detail, trait, trace, gradation, tint, finish, particular, distinction, discrimination, individual, variety, and part, are balanced against such qualifying epithets as local, concrete, subtle, delicate, minute, refined, exact, curious, nice, definite, particular, endless, numberless, infinite, and varied. This emphasis on the individual, in turn, gives rise to a further complex of terms parallel to the first, and used in opposition to them. This set of synonyms refers to the general, which Hazlitt construes as the abstract, vague, oracular, universal, indefinite, didactic, commonplace, flimsy, vapid, rhetorical, declamatory, critical, preconceived, predetermined, and theoretical. Plays, poems, or novels possessing such characteristics of generality are not literature but rather theses, dissertations, sermons, homilies, abstracts, lectures, descriptions, declamations, precepts, commonplace books, paraphrases, commentaries, theories, discussions, statements, reflections, dogmas, and creeds. The artist, for Hazlitt, is characterized by an openness to the whole of experience in all its complexity and variety as a result of his greater sensitivity of feeling. The effect of generality, whether it be manifested in a creed or dogma, party or sect, a system or theory, is to narrow the range of the artist's impressions. Abstraction diminishes the poet's 'imaginative sincerity' (xii. 328). Poets, critics, and philosophers preoccupied with the general, the theoretical, and the dogmatic 'have in fact always a purpose . . . [which] takes away that tremulous sensibility to every slight and wandering impression which is necessary to complete the fine balance of the mind, and enable us to follow all the infinite fluctuations of thought through their nicest distinctions' (ii. 261). In all Hazlitt's writings, there is no better expression of his experiential view of art than this. It reveals his insistence upon openness, upon the infinite detail and complexity of experience, and upon the prerequisite sensitivity of the artist. His view of art is tied firmly to his view of abstraction as a process of individuation and thereby to his early training as a painter.

M. H. Abrams has suggested that Hazlitt's demand for detail as the essence of the poetic is unqualified. Hazlitt and Blake alone among the major critics exemplify the late eighteenth-century demand for unqualified particularity.[37] Thus he sets up a radical opposition between Hazlitt and Blake on the one hand, and Coleridge and Wordsworth on the other. The latter are alleged to emphasize the generality of art.

It is extremely doubtful, however, that the demand for particularity in the late eighteenth century was unqualified. In the case of Blake and Hazlitt, this view is plainly mistaken. Their emphasis on the concrete and particular is not unqualified. It is equally misleading to say that by the phrase 'poetry is essentially *ideal*', Coleridge is proclaiming his allegiance to the general as opposed to the individual. We must distinguish between 'ideal' as general and universal, which is an eighteenth-century usage, and 'ideal' as it occurs in the critical terminology of Coleridge. 'Ideal' is used by Coleridge in at least two senses: (*i*) as an adjective derived from 'idea', and used interchangeably with 'subjective' or 'noumenal', and (*ii*) to characterize the 'involution of the universal in the particular'. When Coleridge says that poetry is ideal, it is in this second sense that he is employing the term. It is not, as is implied by Abrams, synonymous with the universal or general. Moreover, to the passage which Abrams cites, Coleridge appended a note which has the effect of qualifying the term ideal in the manner suggested: 'Say not that I am recommending abstractions. . . . In Geometry it is the universal truth, which is uppermost in the consciousness; in poetry the individual form.'[38] It was suggested earlier that there is a tendency in Coleridge towards a specifically theistic characterization of the universal at the expense of the particular and of feeling. There is no question, however, of his explicit demand for the individual: 'Nothing *lives* or is *real*, but as definite and particular.'[39] However much he admired the

---

[37] M. H. Abrams, *The Mirror and the Lamp* (New York, 1953), p. 56.
[38] Coleridge, *Biographia*, II. 33 n.   [39] Ibid., II. 187.

'semi-Platonism' of Reynolds, and the beneficial influence which the latter exerted on the arts in the eighteenth century, he rejected Reynolds's theory of generality on the grounds that 'the *essence* must be mastered'.[40] If Hazlitt's demand for the individual is not unqualified, and Coleridge's insistence on the ideal is not a demand for the general, then the opposition which Abrams establishes between them falls to the ground. Likewise, the opposition between the critical movement away from the general to the particular in the late eighteenth century and the literary criticism of the early nineteenth fails to convince. They are united in their rejection of the ideal as generality. In this, the influence of painting cannot be impugned. Hazlitt's perception of the continuity between the literary criticism of the late eighteenth and early nineteenth centuries and its debt to a greater familiarity with painting still holds good.

It is a false distinction which would oppose Hazlitt to Coleridge on the grounds of their respective allegiance to the individual and the general. The criticism of both is a search for the ideal as a synthesis of both, and it is within this area of agreement that their respective differences must be discriminated.[41] When they accepted Schlegel's characterization of modern literature as 'picturesque', the term meant more than an emphasis on the detailed, the minute, and the circumstantial. It also entailed a harmony and a balance.[42] The detail for Hazlitt was always a characteristic or essential detail, which it could be only if it were related to the whole. The need for unity and wholeness was a factor which neither Blake nor Hazlitt, as painters, could possibly overlook. There is always a difference in Hazlitt between a detail which is 'subtle', and one which is merely 'minute'. Moreover, it is a difference which he invariably works out in terms of painting: 'The difference between minuteness and subtlety or refinement seems to be this—that the one relates to the parts, and the other to the whole. Thus, the accumulation of a

---

[40] Coleridge, *Letters*, IV. 759; *Miscellaneous Criticism*, p. 208. Cf. his criticism of Opie, Lebrun, and Cipriani, *Miscellaneous Criticism*, p. 208; *Biographia*, II. 187; *Notebooks*, II. 2828.

[41] This was the object of the closing pages of Chapter II and the whole of Chapter III.

[42] Schlegel's distinction between ancient and modern art as picturesque is paraphrased at length and with approval by Hazlitt (xvi. 63–4). He was also to use it for his own distinction between ancient and modern drama (vi. 347). Coleridge frequently refers to the distinction, but insists that the term 'picturesque' involved a 'balance, counteraction, inter-modifications, and final harmony of differents', *Miscellaneous Criticism*, p. 190.

number of distinct particulars in a work, as . . . in a portrait of
Denner's, is minute or high finishing: the giving the gradations of
tone in a sky of Claude's from azure to gold, where the distinction
at each step is imperceptible, but the whole effect is striking and
grand . . . is true refinement and delicacy' (ix. 214). It is true that
the poet must always be 'open' or 'alive' to the infinite particularity
and ever-changing complexity of reality, but it is out of that very
openness that the universal emerges: 'The phenomena are infinite,
obscure, and intricately inwoven together, so that it is only by
being always alive to their tacit and varying influence, that we can
hope to seize on the power that guides and binds them together'
(xx. 373). In Hazlitt's view, the general results from an 'aggregate
of well-founded particulars . . . [not] an abstract theory' (xii. 246).
Although the painter is concerned at one level with the surface
details, nevertheless, he is also 'identified with the permanent form
of things' (x. 7). Like Barry before him, and like Constable and
Ruskin after him, Hazlitt did not counter Reynolds's theory by
advocating the merely particular against the general.[43] Separately,
neither constituted the ideal in his eyes. The imitation of the one
or the other exclusively resulted only in mannerism.[44] What he
did insist upon was that Titian, whom Reynolds had praised for
his general effect, was also characterized by his great care for detail
and finish.[45] For Hazlitt, the individual and general were not in
opposition to one another. The opposition was between the individual and the abstract, where abstract was construed as the vague
and indefinite. It is only in this limited sense that one can say his
demand for particularity was unqualified. It does not exclude the
general, only the vague and indefinite. His criticism of many
Dutch painters for their inability to organize detail into a plastic

[43] Hazlitt quotes from Barry's criticism of Raphael to illustrate his own view
that characteristic traits do not detract from ideal nature. Both are essential (xviii.
79–80). For Barry's own rejection of Reynolds's theory of generality, see *An Inquiry
into the Real and Imaginary Obstructions to the Acquisition of the Arts in England* (London,
1775), pp. 134–5. Ruskin likewise insisted on the need for both 'law' and 'individuality', but emphasized the individual more because 'more difficult of attain-
ment', *Works*, xv. 116. For Ruskin's emphasis on the individual in his criticism of
Reynolds, see *Works*, v. 23–33. Fry adopted a similar position in relation to
Reynolds, *Discourses on Art*, ed. R. Fry (London, 1905), pp. xiii–xviii.

[44] *Works*, xii. 297.

[45] Ibid., viii. 136. Hazlitt is supported by Constable in this, Leslie, *Memoirs of
Constable*, pp. 305–6. Reynolds's criticism occurs in *Discourses on Art*, ed. R. R.
Wark (San Marino, Calif., 1959), p. 195.

whole is incompatible with the view that he emphasizes the individual to the exclusion of everything else.

In literary criticism, his position is the same. It is only out of the artist's openness to nature in all her variety and detail that the 'fine balance' is to be achieved. The passage which follows is given at some length because it exemplifies so many of the points which have been made in the previous discussion:

> The genius of Shakespear was as much shewn in the subtlety and nice discrimination, as in the force and variety of his characters. The distinction is not preserved more completely in those which are the most opposite, than in those in which their general features . . . most nearly resemble each other. . . . His mind . . . was exquisitely alive to the slightest impulses and most evanescent shades of character and feeling. The broad distinctions and governing principles of human nature are presented not in the abstract, but in their immediate and endless application to different persons and things. The local details, the particular accidents have the fidelity of history, without losing any thing of their general effect.
>
> It is the business of poetry, and indeed of all works of imagination, to exhibit the species through the individual. Otherwise, there can be no opportunity for the exercise of the imagination, without which the descriptions of the painter or the poet are lifeless, unsubstantial, and vapid. If some modern critics are right, with their sweeping generalities and vague abstractions, Shakespear was quite wrong. In the French dramatists, only the class is represented, never the individual . . . they are nothing but the mouth-pieces of certain rhetorical common-place sentiments on the favourite topics of morality and the passions. . . . [In Shakespeare] those that are the most alike, are distinguished by positive differences, which accompany and modify the leading principle of the character through its most obscure ramifications.
>
> (v. 204–5)

With no apparent image derived from painting, it is obvious that it is a painter who is writing. Detail is subtle if it is the result of feeling or emotion, since it is passion which renders the detail, be it a word, an act, or even a gesture, significant, characteristic, and integral. It is, as Hagstrum has pointed out, a dramatic conception of particularity.[46] More specifically, however, it is a painter's conception. Particularity which does not satisfy his stringent conditions is unhesitatingly rejected.[47] This conception, originating in his

[46] J. H. Hagstrum, *The Sister Arts* (Chicago, 1958), p. 143.
[47] *Works*, v. 14, 97; xi. 164; xvi. 320–1.

experience of painting, is generalized into a new and revolutionary theory of abstraction. It is an emphasis which is a testimony to the enduring influence of painting in early nineteenth-century critical thought, and yet a testimony which does not at the same time entail support for the decadent pictorialism of the doctrine of *ut pictura poesis*. Only through his attitude to abstraction can we make any sense of his own view of his work as 'the thoughts of a metaphysician expressed by a painter'.

CHAPTER FIVE

Painting and Poetry

> The use of painting to illuminate the essential character
> of poetry—*ut pictura poesis*—so widespread in the
> eighteenth century, almost disappears in the major
> criticism of the romantic period; the comparisons . . .
> that survive are casual. . . . In place of painting, music
> becomes the art frequently pointed to as having a
> profound affinity with poetry.
>
> M. H. ABRAMS, *The Mirror and the Lamp*[1]

1. LITERARY PICTORIALISM: THE ROMANTIC AFTERMATH

HAZLITT's theory of abstraction, important in itself and in
relation to the rest of his work, has other more far-reaching implications, and our awareness of these may alter radically our
response to much of late eighteenth and early nineteenth-century
literary criticism. It suggests caution, for example, in accepting
Abrams's view that 'the use of painting to illuminate the essential
character of poetry . . . almost disappears in the major criticism of
the romantic period'. In so far as this generalization points to the
demise in the early nineteenth century of the eighteenth-century
view of the relation between poetry and painting, the conclusion
is valid. Yet in so far as Abrams is attempting to diminish the
importance of the role played by painting in order to establish his
own thesis of the importance of music, his assertion requires
modification. Painting and vision continued to play the major
analogical role in literary criticism in the Romantic period, but their
role altered from that envisaged by the traditional doctrine of
ut pictura poesis. Once the lessons of the anti-pictorialist school of
Burke, Johnson, Lessing, and Twining had been assimilated by the
English poets and critics, the analogy assumed a new function
which steered between the excessive pictorialism of the traditional
view and the restrictive limitations imposed by Lessing in the

---

[1] Abrams, *The Mirror and the Lamp*, p. 50. Abrams's general conclusion is supported by Hagstrum, *The Sister Arts*, p. 151 and note.

distinction which he drew between the spatial and temporal arts. The latter's delimitation of the sister arts, while salutary within the context of an extreme pictorialism, could never destroy the belief of the early nineteenth century in the essential unity of the poetic.[2] If in considering the literary criticism of this period we regard only the perpetuation of the previous century's reading of the analogy, we shall fail to appreciate the transformation which the analogy underwent. Hazlitt's theory of abstraction and its influence on his literary criticism illustrate this transformation in a quite specific way, and suggest that the priority which Abrams confers upon music as the dominant critical analogy requires modification.

The evidence of a single critic, however, while suggesting caution in accepting such a view, is hardly sufficient to overturn an historical generalization of such magnitude. It suggests the need for a general reappraisal of the whole question of the use of painting as a critical analogy in early nineteenth-century poetic theory, but cannot by itself be held to be conclusive. Nevertheless, the influence of painting on Hazlitt's theory and practice as a critic does help to focus attention on the repeated allusions to painting and comparisons between poetry and painting in the writings of the Romantic critics, allusions and references which recur too often to be dismissed as having little aesthetic significance.

The doctrine of *ut pictura poesis* is one of the most complex problems in the history of aesthetics. Support for the doctrine in the eighteenth century, however, can be resolved into a philosophically naïve preoccupation with that aspect of the analogy now known as literary pictorialism. It is against this background and the transformation of the analogy in the early nineteenth century that the aesthetic implications of Hazlitt's view of abstraction can best be appreciated.[3]

By the middle of the eighteenth century the practice of tracing a formal parallel between the arts of painting and poetry had been established for more than a hundred years. The parallels of Junius, Félibien, De Piles, and Dryden were succeeded in the eighteenth

---

[2] English painters were familiar with Lessing's distinction. See *Lectures on Painting by the Royal Academicians*, ed. R. N. Wornum (London, 1848), pp. 273, 407.

[3] The most extensive treatment of the pictorial tradition in the eighteenth century is to be found in Hagstrum, *The Sister Arts*. Other useful works are C. Hussey, *The Picturesque* (London, 1927), and E. W. Manwaring, *Italian Landscape in Eighteenth Century England* (New York, 1925). See also H. V. S. and M. S. Ogden, *English Taste in Landscape in the Seventeenth Century* (Ann Arbor, 1955).

century by those of Dubos, Batteux, Lamotte, Harris, and Webb. Du Fresnoy's *De Arte Graphica* (1668), however, still remained the most popular and influential, and it was upon this parallel that first De Piles and then Dryden composed their commentaries. In William Mason's translation (1783), published at the height of the cult of the picturesque, Du Fresnoy's use of the Horatian phrase was rendered as: 'True Poetry the Painter's power displays.'[4] James Beattie had warned earlier that Horace's lines could not be generalized in this way,[5] and Sir Joshua Reynolds, who provided the notes to Mason's translation, had already denied in the *Discourses* that one art could be made the measure of success in another.[6] In spite of the growing opposition to pictorialism and the general recognition of the great differences between the two arts within the pictorial tradition itself, the demand for a poetry characterized by an imagery of visual vividness which enabled the reader to 'see' the object as present grew more widespread in the second half of the eighteenth century.[7] Yet within a generation the doctrine had not only declined in popularity but had virtually disappeared. In the criticism of Hazlitt and Coleridge *ut pictura poesis* was no longer a living issue. The emphasis had changed. The resurgence of the doctrine in the latter half of the century had merely served to camouflage a much more important issue—the conflict between art as ideal and art as the minute discrimination of the individual. With the resolution of this conflict in the Romantic theory of art

[4] Reynolds, *Works*, ed. E. Malone (London, 1797), II. 147.

[5] Beattie, *Essays on Poetry and Music*, p. 216.

[6] Reynolds, *Discourses*, p. 240.

[7] Among the painters and critics of painting who adopted a pictorialist viewpoint were J. B. Dubos, *Reflexions Critiques sur la Poësie et sur la Peinture*, I. 267; J. Richardson, *An Account of Some of the Statues, Bas-Reliefs, Drawings and Pictures in Italy* (London, 1722), pp. 92–3; C. Lamotte, *An Essay upon Poetry and Painting* (London, 1730), pp. 45–9; D. Webb, *An Inquiry into the Beauties of Painting* (London, 1760), pp. 198–9; R. A. Bromley, *A Philosophical and Critical History of the Fine Arts* (London, 1793–5), I. 23. Among the literary critics and aestheticians support for the doctrine is to be found in Kames, *Elements of Criticism*, II. 329; Duff, *An Essay on Original Genius*, pp. 157–60; Warton, *An Essay on the Writings and Genius of Pope*, II. 222–3; Blair, *Lectures*, II. 341, 376. The importance attached to vision by philosophy since the time of Descartes exacerbated this tendency. See R. Wellek, *The Rise of English Literary History* (Chapel Hill, 1941), pp. 90–1. While it was natural for empiricists like Hartley, *Observations on Man* (London, 1749), I. 209, 435, to emphasize the visual, even the anti-empiricism of Reid was insufficient to wean him from the views of Addison in this matter, *An Inquiry into the Human Mind* (Edinburgh, 1764), pp. 168–9. Dugald Stewart was one of the few philosophers to dissociate himself from the emphasis on the visual, *Elements* (1843), p. 254.

as the synthesis of the general and particular, pictorialist references to painting declined and the doctrine itself ceased to arouse any critical interest.[8] James Northcote represented the forlorn voice of a reactionary and relatively unimportant minority when he wrote in 1807: 'I have often thought that there is no better way to prove the defects or excellences of a poet . . . than by making a composition for a picture from the images which he raises, and from his own description of his characters and their actions. You by these means put him on his trial; you will detect every deviation from nature; and when his performance is brought to this strict examination, it will sometimes happen, that what in words might seem like a true representation of nature to the poet, to the painter may appear much like the tale of a false witness.'[9] The majority of painters of the late eighteenth and early nineteenth centuries were more cautious, and their increasing circumspection with regard to the analogy was reflected in literature. Leigh Hunt and Thomas Campbell excepted, the Romantic poets and critics viewed the relationship between the two arts in a manner radically opposed to that envisaged by the traditional doctrine of *ut pictura poesis*.

The practice of comparing painting and poetry was too widespread in the eighteenth century to vanish altogether without trace in the nineteenth. However unenlightened many of the applications were to which the doctrine was put, they could never disguise the point made by Barry in opposition to the pictorial and anti-pictorial traditions alike, that both arts were essentially twin facets of a unified poetic experience.[10] In the nineteenth century, Ruskin, hostile to the excesses of pictorialism as well as to the excesses of the reaction which it provoked, made a similar point when he insisted that 'infinite confusion has been introduced into this subject by the careless and illogical custom of opposing painting to poetry, instead of regarding poetry as consisting in a noble use, whether of colours or words. . . . Poetry is the employment of either for the noblest purposes'.[11] In reformulating the relation between the arts in a manner reminiscent of the more cautious of

---

[8] Hussey has pointed out that the cult of the picturesque taught imagination in the late eighteenth century to feel through the eyes. This lesson once learned, overt allusion to painting was unnecessary, *The Picturesque*, p. 4.

[9] J. Northcote, *The Artist*, No. IX (1807), 3–4.   [10] Barry, *Inquiry*, pp. 107–8.

[11] Ruskin, *Works*, v. 31. Cf: 'Do you know . . . what a play is? or what a poem is? or what a novel is? . . . You had better . . . call all the three "poems". . . . All truly imaginative account of man is poetic' (ibid., XVII. 628).

the later eighteenth-century painters, Ruskin was pointing to the new role which painting had begun to play in the literary criticism of the early nineteenth century. A similar view of their relation is to be found in Hazlitt: 'The arts of painting and poetry are conversant with the world of thought within us, and with the world of sense around us—with what we know, and see, and feel intimately. They flow from the sacred shrine of our own breasts, and are kindled at the living lamp of nature' (v. 46).[12] Shelley likewise insisted that 'language, colour, form . . . are all the instruments and materials of poetry',[13] and for Coleridge 'the vehicle alone constitutes the difference'.[14] Schlegel adopted a similar position in Germany when he said that 'poetry, taken in its widest acceptation . . . [is] the power of creating what is beautiful'.[15] No analogy is established, but their essential unity is asserted. For the Romantic poets and critics as for Wallace Stevens today, 'there is a universal poetry that is reflected in everything'.[16] Painting had still important lessons to teach the poet and critic which no previous confusion of the arts could obscure. The very excesses of the traditional doctrine positively encouraged the much more subtle view which emerged after the turn of the century.

If it were true that music replaced painting as the dominant critical analogy in Romantic poetic theory, it would be difficult to account for the ready acceptance of Schlegel's characterization of modern literature as essentially picturesque. In drawing this distinction between classical and modern literature, Schlegel wrote:

> The principal cause of the difference is the plastic spirit of the antique, and the picturesque spirit of the romantic poetry. . . . Painting . . . delights in exhibiting, in a minute manner, along with the principal figures, the surrounding locality and all the secondary objects, and to open to us in the back ground a prospect into a boundless distance.[17]

Hazlitt and Coleridge both accepted this view. In his review of Schlegel's *Lectures* in the *Edinburgh Review* in 1816, Hazlitt summarized the German critic's argument with an enthusiasm which prompted Crabb Robinson to write: 'Hazlitt's review of Schlegel's

[12] Cf. *Works*, x. 10: 'The language of painting and poetry is intelligible enough to mortals; the spirit of both is divine.' See also ibid., viii. 82–3.

[13] Shelley, *Works*, VII. 113.

[14] Coleridge, *Shakespearean Criticism*, ed. T. M. Raysor (London, 1930, 1960), I. 224.

[15] Schlegel, *Lectures*, I. 3.   [16] Stevens, *The Necessary Angel*, p. 160.

[17] Schlegel, *Lectures*, I. 348–9.

lectures on the drama is a capital article, and Hazlitt's own share of the excellent matter is by no means small. He has entered into the sense of the author and evinces a kindred spirit. In reviewing so capital a work he would perhaps have done better if he had attempted to do less.'[18] Something of the 'kindred spirit' that Crabb Robinson remarked is apparent in Hazlitt's paraphrase of Schlegel's distinction between classical and modern literature: 'The one is the poetry of form, the other of effect. The one gives only what is necessarily implied in the subject; the other all that can possibly arise out of it. . . . As, according to our author, the poetry of the Greeks is the same as their sculpture; so, he says, our own more nearly resembles painting,—where the artist can relieve and throw back his figures at pleasure,—use a greater variety of contrasts,—and where light and shade, like the colours of fancy, are reflected on the different objects' (xvi. 63–4). He later made use of the distinction in the *Lectures on the Age of Elizabeth* in distinguishing between classical and modern tragedy.[19] Coleridge in his lectures of 1811–12 also endorsed Schlegel's perception of modern literature as picturesque: 'It is a known but unexplained phenomenon, that among the ancients statuary rose to such a degree of perfection . . . yet painting, at the same period . . . has been proved to be an art of much later growth. . . . The Shakespearean drama and the Greek drama may be compared to statuary and painting.'[20] Yet neither Hazlitt nor Coleridge was a pictorialist. Only by an analysis of the apparent contradiction between their rejection of pictorialism and their view of modern literature as picturesque can we appreciate the nature and extent of the transformation of the traditional analogy between the two arts. The popularity of Schlegel's distinction and of his observation that we can only properly estimate the tragedies of Sophocles before the groups of Niobe or Laocoön[21]—a view which again stresses the

[18] H. C. Robinson on Books and their Writers, I. 182.

[19] *Works*, vi. 347. In *The Complete Works of Lord Macaulay, Essays and Biographies* (London, 1898), I. 136, Macaulay also makes use of Schlegel's distinction. Jeffrey's comparison of Romantic poetry and sculpture is relevant here because the sculpture to which he was referring was a sculpture influenced by painting, *Edinburgh Review*, XVI (1810), 269. The influence of painting on sculpture was also noted by Schlegel, *Lectures*, I. 9.

[20] Coleridge, *Shakespearean Criticism*, II. 121–2. See also ibid., I. 196 and note; *Miscellaneous Criticism*, pp. 7, 190.

[21] Schlegel, *Lectures*, I. 47. Hazlitt, *Works*, xvi. 62, drew attention to this passage in his review.

unity of the arts—indicates that the issue of music versus painting as critical analogy is much more complex than Abrams's analysis seems to suggest.

2. THE AMBIVALENT ANALOGY

Although Hazlitt and Coleridge readily accepted the terms of Schlegel's distinction, their willingness to do so appears to contradict the anti-pictorialist views to be found elsewhere in their writings. This apparent contradiction raises in an acute form the problem of the precise nature of the analogy between poetry and painting in early nineteenth-century poetic theory. There is no simple answer to this problem. Every allusion and comparison, pejorative or otherwise, must be considered first within its specific context, and then in relation to one another. Only by examining a broad cross-section of allusion in this way is it possible to draw conclusions capable of reflecting the complexity of the Romantic response to the problem.

Hazlitt and Coleridge accepted the view, common in eighteenth-century aesthetics, that painting differed from poetry in being essentially imitative.[22] Nevertheless, their manner of expressing it and their application of it to poetic theory was quite distinctive. According to Hazlitt painting was concerned with the object; poetry with the implications of the object. Coleridge, when he complained of the lack of the generic in painting, comparing it unfavourably in this respect with poetry and music,[23] was making a similar point. Painting was the 'intermediate somewhat between a thought and a thing'.[24] Unlike the eighteenth century's use of this distinction, its effect in the work of Hazlitt and Coleridge was to invalidate the doctrine of *ut pictura poesis*. When Hazlitt quoted the lines, 'Oh! who can paint a sun-beam to the blind / Or make

---

[22] For the use which the eighteenth century made of this distinction, see R. De Piles, *The Art of Painting* (London, 1706), p. 3, and *The Principles of Painting* (London, 1743), p. 158; Webb, *Beauties of Painting*, p. ix; A. Gerard, *An Essay on Genius* (London, 1774), p. 334; Blair, *Lectures*, I. 94; Beattie, *Elements*, I. 149; Stewart, *Elements*, (1843), p. 262. Benjamin Robert Haydon in his *Diary*, I. 57, protested strongly against this view. Sir William Jones, 'On the Arts commonly called Imitative', in *Eighteenth-Century Critical Essays*, ed. Elledge, II. 879, argued for painting as expression rather than imitation. See also Macaulay, *Essays*, I. 549–50.

[23] Coleridge, *Notebooks*, II. 1963: 'The generic how superior to the particular illustrated in Music, how infinitely more perfect in passion & its transitions than even Poetry—Poetry than Painting.' Hazlitt's criticism of music was that by emphasizing the generic it neglected the individual altogether, *Works*, v. 296.

[24] Coleridge, *Works*, VI. 296.

him feel a shadow with his mind?' (vi. 237), he was pointing to the intrinsic superiority of language over colour, and to the differences between the two arts which the difference in the medium entailed. To imitate the painter, the poet must relinquish his claim to be a poet: 'I do not mean to give any preference, but it should seem that the argument which has been sometimes set up, that painting must affect the imagination more strongly, because it represents the image more distinctly, is not well founded. . . . Poetry is more poetical than painting. . . . Painting gives the object itself; poetry what it implies. Painting embodies what a thing contains in itself: poetry suggests what exists out of it, in any manner connected with it. But this last is the proper province of the imagination' (v. 10). Such a view clearly contradicts his earlier statement that classical literature is like sculpture because it gives 'only what is necessarily implied in the subject', whilst modern literature more closely resembles painting in that it suggests 'all that can possibly arise out of it'. The contradiction however is once more only apparent. The context is everything. To resolve the conflicting elements in these two statements is to resolve the much wider issue of the early nineteenth century's ambivalent response to the traditional analogy. In the *Lectures on the English Poets* Chaucer is criticized because he does not conform to the distinction which Hazlitt had drawn earlier between poetry and painting. His emphasis on the matter-of-fact, on the object, entails a 'strict parsimony' with the 'poet's materials' (v. 22). He is 'more picturesque . . . than almost any other [poet]' (v. 33). Hazlitt also criticized the early poetry of Shakespeare for the same reasons: 'There is besides a strange attempt to substitute the language of painting for that of poetry, to make us *see* their feelings in the faces of the persons' (iv. 359). Coleridge likewise considered the early poems to be 'as picturesque as language was capable of', suggesting at the same time that this 'was perhaps carried too far'.[25] In these and other passages of a similar import it was the pictorial element, the attempt to rival the painter, to which Hazlitt and Coleridge were objecting. This is most explicit in Hazlitt's criticism of Crabbe:

Thus an admirer of Teniers or Hobbima might think little of the pastoral sketches of Pope or Goldsmith . . . but the adept in Dutch interiors, hovels, and pig-styes must find in Mr. Crabbe a man after his

---

[25] Coleridge, *Shakespearean Criticism*, ii. 64.

own heart. He is the very thing itself; he paints in words, instead of colours: there is no other difference. As Mr. Crabbe is not a painter, only because he does not use a brush and colours, so he is for the most part a poet, only because he writes in lines of ten syllables.

(xi. 166)

According to Alison's associationist theory of the picturesque, the greater familiarity with painting in the late eighteenth century altered the way the ordinary person looked at nature. In Hazlitt's view the same familiarity effected a radical change in the critics' attitude to poetry. The emphasis in criticism altered from art as ideal, as generality, to art as particularity. The critic now read a poem 'with the eye of a connoisseur ... and would turn with double eagerness and relish to the force and precision of individual details'. Hazlitt was prepared to accept painting as the source of the new emphasis upon the individual. He was not prepared to accept an unqualified particularity or the implications of the doctrine of *ut pictura poesis* which the new movement exploited and which conferred upon the new criticism an aura of conservative respectability. In Hazlitt's view Crabbe abandoned the means appropriate to poetry in order to achieve the close imitative effect of an art which, because of its spatial nature, achieved such an effect without relinquishing simultaneity of appearance. By approximating poetry to painting Crabbe renounced the superior advantages accruing to poetry by its use of language. Hazlitt was not alone in making this criticism of Crabbe. Francis Jeffrey made a similar point although the purposes for which it was used were very different: 'In the kindred art of painting, we find that this single consideration has been sufficient to stamp a very high value upon accurate and lively delineations of objects ... and no very inconsiderable part of the pleasure which may be derived from Mr Crabbe's poetry, may be referred to its mere truth and fidelity.' Implicit, however, in this equation of Crabbe's art with the art of the painter is the suggestion that the chief excellence of poetry lies elsewhere. Pictorialism is not enough for Jeffrey: 'The highest delight which poetry produces, does not arise from the mere passive perception of the images or sentiments which it presents to the mind, but from the excitement which is given to its own eternal activity.'[26] In early nineteenth-century literary criticism the superiority of poetry to painting and music is attributed to its

[26] *Edinburgh Review*, XVI (1810), 32; XIV (1809), 2.

medium.[27] It is with words and not with sounds and colours that we shape our reality. In his discussion of the relative merits of poetry and music in the essay, 'Sir Walter Scott, Racine, and Shakespear', Hazlitt wrote:

> Words are the signs which point out and define the objects of the highest import to the human mind; and speech is the habitual, and as it were most *intimate* mode of expressing those signs, and one with which our practical and serious associations are most in unison. . . . A sound expresses, for the most part, nothing but itself; a word expresses a million of sounds. The thought or impression of the moment is one thing, and it may be more or less delightful; but beyond this, it may relate to the fate or events of a whole life, and it is this moral and intellectual perspective that words convey in its full signification and extent. . . . Words are a key to the affections. They not only excite feelings, but they point to the *why* and *wherefore*. They are links in the chain of the universe, and the grappling-irons that bind us to it. . . . They alone answer in any degree to the truth of things.
>
> (xii. 336–7)

In this passage Hazlitt is arguing for the superiority of poetry to music. The same reasoning applies to poetry and painting, 'because the strongest of our recollections relate to feelings, not to faces' (iv. 271). In the introduction to the *Lectures on the English Poets* he confessed that although faces were the best part of a painting, 'even faces are not what we chiefly remember in what interests us most' (v. 10). In this kind of context his allusions to painting are invariably pejorative.

Coleridge's treatment of the analogy is remarkably similar. There is, on the one hand, the acceptance of Schlegel's view of modern literature as picturesque and, on the other, the same anti-pictorial element found in Hazlitt. Coleridge deplored the influence of painting on poetry. He complained, for example, that Erasmus Darwin wrote poetry 'as Painters who of beautiful objects—take—

---

[27] Cf. Shelley, *Works*, VII. 113: 'Language . . . is a more direct representation of the actions and passions of our internal being, and is susceptible of more various and delicate combinations, than colour. . . . For language is arbitrarily produced by the imagination, and has relation to thoughts alone.' Coleridge pointed out that 'the sphere of [words'] action is far wider, the power of giving permanence to them much more certain, and incomparably greater the facility, by which all men . . . may be enabled to derive habitual pleasure and instruction from them', *Shakespearean Criticism*, I. 224. Ruskin, like Hazlitt, stressed the associative power of words which unlike painting bore 'a cloudy companionship of higher or darker meaning', *Works*, XXXIV. 336.

Studies', with the result that his poetry was little more than 'a succession of Landscapes or Paintings'.[28] Hazlitt's specific criticisms of Crabbe are generalized by Coleridge into an indictment of much of late eighteenth and early nineteenth-century poetry: 'The presence of genius is not shown in elaborating a picture: we have had many specimens of this sort of work in modern poems, where all is so dutchified . . . by the most minute touches, that the reader naturally asks why words, and not painting, are used?'[29] The influence of painting in Coleridge's view carried with it an emphasis on the visually vivid and merely particular. Although he thought of the individual as the more important of the two elements of the poetic, he tended in his discussions of the influence of painting on poetry to emphasize only the excesses of unrelated visual detail: 'In the present age the poet . . . seems to propose to himself as his main object, and as that which is the most characteristic of his art, new and striking IMAGES. . . . Both his characters and his descriptions he renders, as much as possible, specific and individual, even to a degree of portraiture.'[30] For Coleridge, as for Burke, a clear idea was synonymous with a little idea; dimness and obscurity are signs of the poet's depth of feeling.[31] Like Hazlitt and Jeffrey, he did not demand the object in all its vivid visual detail, but the object as symbol—created not by observation alone, but by the union of meditation and observation. It is in this sense that the early nineteenth century would subscribe to Wordsworth's view that 'sight is . . . a sad enemy to imagination'.[32] It was not the object but the implications of the object that were important to Coleridge: 'Images taken from nature and accurately described [do] not characterize *the poet*. They must be blended or merged with other images, the offspring of imagination, and blended, besides, with the passions or other pleasurable emotions which contemplation has awakened in the poet himself.'[33] The effectiveness of description

---

[28] Coleridge, *Notebooks*, I. 132.   [29] Coleridge, *Shakespearean Criticism*, II. 134.

[30] Coleridge, *Biographia*, II. 21.

[31] Coleridge, *Notebooks*, I. 921: 'By deep feeling we make our *Ideas dim*.' Later on, ibid., II. 2509, Coleridge wrote: '. . . clear as a pike-staff,—nothing *before* and *nothing behind* . . . having no *root* for then it would have feelings of dimness from growth.' See also *Anima Poetae*, p. 19. Cf. Burke, *A Philosophical Enquiry into the Origin of our Ideas of the Sublime and Beautiful*, ed. J. T. Boulton (London, 1958), pp. 58–64.

[32] Wordsworth, *Prose Works*, ed. A. B. Grosart (London, 1876), III. 89. See also ibid., III. 487.

[33] Coleridge, *Shakespearean Criticism*, II. 64.

in poetry did not rest on the attempt to emulate the painter. To try
to rival within a temporal art the effects achieved within one which
is essentially spatial could only end in failure. It encouraged excessive detail which, without the necessary simultaneity, is anathema
to poetry. Hence Coleridge agreed with Jeffrey that what was
important in poetry was not the image but the 'activity' and
'excitement' of the mind: 'The grandest efforts of poetry are where
the imagination is called forth, not to produce a distinct form, but
a strong working of the mind.'[34] His vehemence on this point
seems to stem from his own early attempts at prose description, the
failure of which he at first ascribed to his ignorance of painting.
He later revised his opinion and aligned himself with the anti-
pictorial tradition of Burke: 'What are deemed fine descriptions,
produce their effects almost purely by a charm of words, with which
& with whose combinations, we associate *feelings* indeed, but no
distinct *Images*.'[35]

Related to Coleridge's view of the inherent inferiority of painting to poetry, and of poetry to music in terms of their limited
generic function,[36] is his belief that, as a visual art concerned
directly with nature as object, painting was peculiarly subject to
subversion by empirical philosophy. In illustrating the consequences for the arts of the rise of empiricism, Coleridge invariably
selected his examples from the history of painting.[37] The decline
of painting since the Renaissance he attributed to the growth of
empirical philosophy from the time of Bacon.[38] This emphasis is
altogether absent from Hazlitt's criticism. Coleridge always remained keenly aware of the natural attraction which detail had for
mankind,[39] as well as the need for the individual in art. What he
criticized in the poetry of his own age was the overgrowth of this
tendency—a tendency aggravated in his view by a tradition of
painting corrupted by empiricism. Modern drama and modern
poetry suffered from a contagion of the real, and Coleridge's
criticism exploited the vocabulary of painting as the most realistic
of the arts to emphasize this and to condemn it. The pejorative use
of artistic imagery and allusion in his criticism of Crabbe, Scott,

[34] Ibid., II. 103. Cf: 'The power of poetry is, by a single word perhaps, to instil
that energy into the mind, which compels the imagination to produce the picture',
ibid., II. 135.

[35] Coleridge, *Letters*, I. 511. Cf. ibid., I. 503.

[36] See above, n. 23.   [37] Coleridge, *Philosophical Lectures*, pp. 193–5.

[38] Coleridge, *Works*, VI. 335.   [39] Coleridge, *Anima Poetae*, p. 128.

and Wordsworth evinces his awareness of the fallacy of the traditional analogy,[40] and reinforces his general position that art was not to be construed on the basis of the real or particular exclusively, but of the ideal as the involution of the individual and the generic.

To argue that the decline of literary pictorialism in the early nineteenth century was paralleled by a corresponding decline in overt allusion to painting is misleading. In spite of the Romantic critics' perception of the limited validity of the doctrine of *ut pictura poesis*, painting, even considered in its negative role, still remained the dominant analogy in the critical writings of the period, and was still employed as illuminative of the essence of poetry. The function of the analogy had changed, however, for while the unity within the arts was still insisted upon, the analogy was now employed to distinguish between the arts of poetry and painting: not to promote but to prevent the extension of eighteenth-century pictorialism. Painting was used negatively to enforce poetry not as object alone, but as object and subject—as ideal—the involution of the general and the individual.

The analogy with painting in Romantic poetic theory also had a more positive function. Only by considering its more positive role can we appreciate the reasons behind the early nineteenth century's acceptance of Schlegel's honorific characterization of modern literature as picturesque. The pejorative use of pictorial allusion operates within a dichotomy set up between poetry and painting. The dichotomy employed in its honorific use, as Schlegel's initial distinction makes clear, is one between painting and sculpture. Hence the apparent discrepancy between Hazlitt's account of painting in the introduction to the *Lectures on the English Poets* and his review of Schlegel's *Lectures*. Sculpture, painting, and poetry for the nineteenth century represented degrees of imitation farther and farther removed from reality.[41] Thus although in relation to poetry painting appeared material and sensible, directly concerned

---

[40] Coleridge, *Biographia*, II. 98, 102–3; *Notebooks*, II. 2599; *Works*, VI. 504. See also his criticism of Darwin, *Notebooks*, I. 132. Coleridge's pejorative use of pictorial allusion is not confined to his criticism of contemporaries but is also to be found in his criticism of Chaucer, *Letters*, III. 30; *Miscellaneous Criticism*, p. 27; Dante, ibid., p. 157; Massinger, ibid., p. 96; and Shakespeare, *Biographia*, II. 19; *Shakespearean Criticism*, II. 29, 53, 96, 99, 129–30.

[41] Addison's view is similar, *The Spectator*, ed. D. F. Bond (Oxford, 1965), III. 559.

with the object, in comparison with sculpture it represented the symbolic nature of all art—bound to the material yet expressive of that which went beyond the merely physical. The Elgin Marbles excepted, sculpture remained a comparatively unpopular art form. Its three-dimensional representation of reality symbolized the abstract, the general, the universal divorced from the particular. By contrast painting achieved a seemingly perfect involution. Coleridge considered that 'the very essence of statuary is a high degree of abstraction'.[42] For De Quincey 'painting is sensuous and concrete; sculpture abstract'.[43] Hazlitt's antipathy to sculpture is marked. Its abstraction was a 'cold abstraction' (x. 163).

As it became clear that the eighteenth-century pictorialist tradition had pursued the analogy between poetry and painting in a manner incompatible with the nature of language as the medium of poetry, it became equally clear that a parallel confusion had occurred in their view of the relation between painting and sculpture. Commenting on this confusion in 1806, Sir Charles Bell wrote:

> In the infancy of their art, sculptors did not venture to give to their figures either animation or character; they did not even open the eyelids, or raise the arm from the side. A stillness and simplicity of composition is thus the characteristic of ancient sculpture. . . . Among the most striking marks of excellency which distinguish the Grecian artists, the first and most admirable is this noble simplicity; this sedate grandeur of expression; and the prevailing tranquillity of soul. . . . Unfortunately this style of composing has been perverted into an additional authority for rejecting powerful expression and character even from the canvass. But we must never forget the distinction between statuary and painting. . . . There is an essential and important difference between the principle of composition in painting and in sculpture.[44]

Bell, not Hazlitt, was the first to attack the ideal theory of art in a full-scale way,[45] anticipating almost all of Hazlitt's major criticisms. Bell's criticism of the eighteenth-century theory of art as ideal was the consequence of his perception of it as an improper transference

---

[42] Coleridge, *Shakespearean Criticism*, II. 122.

[43] *The Collected Writings of Thomas De Quincey*, ed. D. Masson (Edinburgh, 1889–90), XI. 196 n.

[44] C. Bell, *Essays on the Anatomy of Expression in Painting* (London, 1806), pp. 4–5. Bell was greatly admired by Haydon who lent copies of his works to friends, *Diary*, I. 34, 94, 130. Bell's volume of essays was enthusiastically reviewed by Jeffrey, *Edinburgh Review*, VIII (1806), 365–78.

[45] Hagstrum, *The Sister Arts*, p. 142, suggests that Hazlitt was the first to attack the ideal theory.

of principles from one art to another: the intrusion into the
aesthetic and practice of painting, as a result of the eighteenth
century's exaggerated admiration of Graeco-Roman sculpture, of
a theory generalized from the principles of sculpture. Its effect on
painting, as Bell and later critics were to point out, was almost
entirely pernicious. The correctness of his analysis is validated by
Winckelmann's earlier injunction to painters to imitate the
ancients.[46] In the absence of any examples of Greek painting, this
injunction can only refer to sculpture. Hazlitt was also aware of the
improper transference of principles involved in postulating sculpture as the model for the painter. He was convinced, for example,
that Michelangelo had taken his ideas of painting from sculpture
and that Reynolds in his theory and practice had been unduly
influenced by Michelangelo's example.[47] Hence his view of
Reynolds's ideal theory of art that it 'accounts for nothing but the
beauty of the common Antique, and hardly for that' (viii. 144).
Moreover, in criticizing painting which he considered to be executed in accordance with the ideal theory, Hazlitt frequently re-
sorted to sculpture for purposes of comparison.[48] By contrasting
sculpture unfavourably with painting, and the abstraction of the
one with the ideal involution achieved by the other, the early
nineteenth century was rejecting the earlier aesthetic based upon
this confusion.

This view is quite clearly implied by Schlegel's characterization
of modern literature as picturesque. The 'statuesque' is the abstract;
the 'picturesque' the individual out of which the general is created:

> We compared the antique tragedy to a group in sculpture. . . . But the
> romantic drama must be viewed as a large picture. . . . In the representa-
> tion of the figure, painting cannot compete with sculpture . . . but, on
> the other hand, it communicates more life to its imitations, by colours
> which are made to express the finest gradations of mental expression in
> the countenance . . . [and] enables us in painting to read much deeper in
> the mind, and to perceive its lightest movements . . . to see in bodily
> objects what is least corporeal.[49]

[46] J. Winckelmann, *Reflections on the Painting and Sculpture of the Greeks*, tr.
H. Fuseli (London, 1765), p. 2. For confirmation of Bell's view that sculpture
influenced painting, see Reynolds, *Discourses*, p. 45.
[47] *Works*, xviii. 83 n: 'Michael Angelo took his ideas of painting from sculpture,
and Sir Joshua from Michael Angelo.'
[48] *Works*, x. 30; xii. 332; xviii. 49, 68, 88, 139.
[49] Schlegel, *Lectures*, ii. 99–100.

The concluding line of this passage—'to see in bodily objects what is least corporeal'—is all-important to an understanding of the function of the analogy in its new, non-pejorative capacity. Allusions to painting in this context meant more than the mere particularity which they served to symbolize elsewhere. For Coleridge, for example, painting by its 'balance, counteraction, inter-modifications, and final harmony of differents',[50] by its ability through light and shade to reveal the internal through the external, symbolized the 'complexity, variety, and symbolical character' of all modern art.[51] Even at his most anti-pictorial Coleridge nowhere denied painting to be ideal, since to have done so would have been to admit it as being a copy and not an imitation. It is simply a question of the degree of ideality within a given context. Exactly the same balance between the pejorative and non-pejorative is to be found in Hazlitt's handling of the analogy: on the one hand a strong anti-pictorial element, and on the other a view of painting as a 'revelation of the workings of the mind within . . . a language pointing to something beyond, and full of this ultimate import' (xvii. 145). In the greatest paintings the object is no longer object but, as Coleridge expressed it, 'a divine something corresponding to [something] within, which no image can exhaust'.[52] Much as Hazlitt admired Hogarth, his ultimate objection was that he 'conformed' to the world and the object; he in no way 'transformed' it (vi. 146). Sculpture deviated from this fusion of the individual and universal because of its generic excess.

The decline in the popularity of the traditional pictorial view of the relation between painting and poetry in no way diminished the potency of the analogy itself as a source of allusions and comparisons illuminative of the essence of poetry. The anti-pictorialism of the early nineteenth century, while still permitting an extensive reference to painting designed to isolate the specific differences between the two arts, was modified by its awareness of the important point of contact between them—their symbolic function and the necessity in both for an involution of the individual or sensible in the universal or spiritual. So manifestly sensible and material, painting

---

[50] Coleridge, *Miscellaneous Criticism*, p. 190. See also *Shakespearean Criticism*, I. 157, 196; II. 213.

[51] Ibid., p. 7. Coleridge's use of pictorial allusion is expressive of his view of poetry as ideal. It exhibits one of the important ways in which his criticism is intimately related to his aesthetic theory.

[52] Coleridge, *Philosophical Lectures*, p. 194.

yet partook of the divine, the spiritual, the infinite, defying any merely scientific interpretation of it as copy. Viewed in this way, painting acquired an altogether new significance which Hazlitt summed up when he wrote:

> A fine gallery of pictures is a sort of illustration of Berkeley's Theory of Matter and Spirit. It is like a palace of thought—another universe, built of air, of shadows, of colours. . . . Substances turn to shadows by the painter's arch-chemic touch; shadows harden into substances. . . . The material is in some sense embodied in the immaterial.
>
> (x. 19)

3. PAINTING AND THE IDEAL

To concentrate exclusively upon specific instances in which the analogy with painting was quite overt, although in a form differing radically from that envisaged by the doctrine of *ut pictura poesis*, is to run the risk of overlooking more general considerations, the neglect of which can result only in the failure to perceive the overall pattern in which these specific instances play an integral part. Even although the analogy between poetry and painting in its new guise remained the dominant critical analogy, it is still necessary to explain the comparatively sudden transition from the pictorialism of the late eighteenth century to the ambivalent transformation effected by the major critics of the Romantic period.

In the absence of a non-empirical philosophy able to counter effectively the threat to the imaginative life of man posed by the growing dominance of empirical philosophy, literature in the early nineteenth century took upon itself the task of drawing and maintaining a strict division between poetry and science. It is clear, however, that in carrying this out the Romantics did not consider themselves in any way indebted to the poetry and criticism of the eighteenth century. The contempt felt by Coleridge and Carlyle for the period 1760–1800 results from their sense that somehow literature in the second half of the eighteenth century had surrendered its spiritual aspirations in the face of the growing threat from the new materialism.[53] Yet coinciding with this period of decline in English poetry, English painting, for so long the butt of continental speculation concerning the effect of climatic conditions on the vigour of the fine arts, underwent a transformation. The

---

[53] R. F. Brinkley, *Coleridge on the Seventeenth Century* (Durham, N. C., 1955), p. xxiii; Carlyle, *Essays*, I. 68, 262–3. See also Macaulay, *Essays*, I. 550–1.

period from 1760 to 1820 embraces almost every great name in English art: Hogarth, Reynolds, Gainsborough, Romney, Raeburn, Crome, Girtin, Cozens, Blake, Wilkie, Constable, Turner, and Bonington. Moreover the ideal theory which constituted the dominant aesthetic, whether it is viewed as essentially neo-Platonic or otherwise, interpreted the art of painting in a manner designed to elevate it above the empirical and sensible, and to place it in fundamental opposition to the eighteenth-century empirical epistemology. Opie in his lectures to the Royal Academy remarked on this opposition:

As the most fashionable and approved metaphysicians of the present day seem inclined to deny the existence of general ideas, I shall not contend for the propriety of applying that term to ideas formed on the principles I have been mentioning; but, under whatever denomination they may be classed, it cannot be denied that they are the true and genuine object of the highest style of painting. . . . They are born, bred, and reside in the human imagination only.[54]

Coleridge adopted a similar position. In spite of his rejection of the ideal theory on the grounds that 'the *essence* must be mastered', and that 'nothing *lives* or is *real*, but as definite and particular', his admiration for Reynolds is the result of his awareness that the theory itself represented a direct challenge to the growth of empirical philosophy:

This was the real state of the arts during the predominance of that kind of philosophy. But at length what was the mark of a better taste . . . arose with Sir Joshua Reynolds; and it is no slight confirmation of my opinion that it is recorded that in evil days, and with every obstacle around him, he had drunk deeply of Platonism, at least of what is best of all the vital feelings of Platonism, in his early youth [and] since that time. And now I am happy to see and feel that men are craving for a better diet than the wretched trash they have been fed with for the last century; that they will be taught that what is sound must come out of themselves . . . that they will not discover them in the crucible or bring them out of a machine, but must look into the living soul which God has made His image, in order to learn, even in fragments, what that power is by which we are to execute the delegated power entrusted to us by Him.[55]

In spite of the opposition to the ideal theory even within the

---

[54] *Lectures on Painting by the Royal Academicians*, p. 246.
[55] Coleridge, *Philosophical Lectures*, pp. 194–5.

eighteenth century,[56] and its outright rejection by the major critics of the nineteenth, there was an awareness, seldom as explicit or articulate as in Coleridge, that its ultimate import was to impress upon the world that painting—with its material medium—and art in general were yet expressive of the divinity within man.[57] It was precisely this aspect which the dominant speculative philosophy was incapable of taking into account.

Although the ideal theory has been traditionally regarded as essentially neo-Platonic, it seems clear that, as expressed by Reynolds, it has a greater affinity with Locke's conceptualist theory of abstract ideas.[58] In Reynolds the ideal is not a synthetic *a priori* intuited by the artist, but an *a posteriori* idea generalized from his own experience. Like Locke's view of abstraction, the ideal theory was construed as a pledge of man's intellectual and spiritual maturity: the culmination of his development as a rational being. Among its supporters one painting was to be preferred to another, and one kind of painting to another, in proportion to its appeal to man's rational nature and its ability to make him 'think'.[59] At the same time the ideal theory, by postulating that the artist addressed the mind through the transference to canvas of an abstract image, ruled out any empirical attempt to interpret the art of the painter as a process of copying. In his knowledge of man's spiritual nature the painter was a philosopher. In *A Treatise on Ancient Painting*

[56] Barry, *Inquiry*, pp. 134–5, argued that the ideal was not incompatible with an emphasis on the individual. See also G. Campbell, *The Philosophy of Rhetoric*, II. 88–9, and W. Blake, *Complete Writings*, ed. G. Keynes (London, 1966), pp. 445–79. The ideal theory was rejected in the early nineteenth century by Bell, Richard Payne Knight, Schlegel, Coleridge, Hazlitt, Ruskin, and Constable. For a little-known defence of Reynolds and a criticism of Hazlitt, see [G. Darley], 'Painting and the Fine Arts', *Athenaeum* (14, 21, 28 July 1838).

[57] See Reynolds, *Discourses*, p. 244.

[58] The neo-Platonic interpretation of the eighteenth century's theory of art as ideal is accepted by Croce, *Aesthetic*, p. 262, E. H. Gombrich, *Art and Illusion*, pp. 133–4, W. P. Ker, *Essays of John Dryden* (Oxford, 1900), I. lxviii, and R. Wellek, *The Rise of English Literary History*, p. 52. Wellek and Gombrich both allude to Reynolds as a Platonist, a view not shared by R. R. Wark, for whom the influence of Aristotle is equally potent, *Discourses*, p. xx. Wark and Hagstrum, *The Sister Arts*, p. 142, insist on the strong empirical bias. Hagstrum denies a neo-Platonic reading altogether. Reynolds's theory is Platonic in a weak or non-doctrinal sense as any isomorphic theory would be which postulates a one-for-one relationship between idea and work of art. It is perhaps in this sense that Coleridge referred to his 'semi-Platonism', *Letters*, IV. 759.

[59] That a painting should make the spectator 'think' is insisted upon by A. R. Mengs, *Works* (London, 1796), II. 95; Reynolds, *Discourses*, p. 50; Winckelmann, *Reflections*, p. 57; and Quatremère de Quincy, *Essay*, pp. 204–5.

(1740), George Turnbull suggested that historical painting in particular was a branch of moral philosophy.[60] Unfortunately, in establishing itself in opposition to eighteenth-century empiricism, the ideal theory carried with it less welcome implications. By its emphasis on art as addressed to the reason and as something known rather than to the imagination and as something felt and seen, and by its emphasis on the general nature of the imitation rather than the generality of its significance, the theory fostered a rigid stratification among kinds of painting and an undue insistence on the intrinsic importance of certain subjects.[61] Landscape painting, the appreciation of which was perhaps the most significant single development in the painting of this period, was ignored almost completely by Winckelmann, Reynolds, Mengs, and Quatremère de Quincy.[62] The allegorical and the historical occupy the foreground in all eighteenth-century discussion of art. Looking back on the period in 1833, Bulwer-Lytton attributed the growth and popularity of landscape painting to this lack of 'academic dictation'.[63]

Nevertheless, the formulation of an aesthetic for painting in terms of the ideal indicated the way in which the existential or imaginative element in art could be safeguarded from the encroachments of empirical philosophy, and thereby provided a model for the literary critics of the early nineteenth century. At the same time the efflorescence of painting in England during this period and its

[60] G. Turnbull, *A Treatise on Ancient Painting* (London, 1740), p. 145. Reynolds, *Discourses*, pp. 117–18, and Mengs, *Works*, I. 119, also compared the task of the painter to that of the philosopher.

[61] Hazlitt's theory of abstract ideas is important in relation to the development of the 'innocent eye' which was to find its greatest support in the paintings of Constable and the art criticism of Ruskin. Hazlitt was a severe critic of the subject approach to painting: 'We have a great respect for *high* art, and an anxiety for its advancement and cultivation; but we have a greater still for the advancement and encouragement of *true* art. . . . The perception of beauty and power, in whatever objects or in whatever degree they subsist. . . . The principle is the same in painting an archangel's or a butterfly's wing' (xvi. 206). See also *Works*, viii. 219–20; x. 25–6, 45–6. Cf. Croce, *Aesthetic*, p. 321.

[62] Winckelmann accepted the view that in landscape painting 'the artist . . . thinks but very little; and the connoisseur, in considering them, thinks no more', *Reflections*, p. 190. Barry, *Inquiry*, p. 124, suggests that in landscape the genius of the painter 'had little or nothing to employ itself upon'. There was a general insistence that landscape should include figures. See Dubos, *Reflexions Critiques sur la Poësie et sur la Peinture*, I. 49. See also Manwaring, *Italian Landscape*, pp. 23–4, for other examples of this demand.

[63] Bulwer, *England and the English*, II. 217–18.

increasing popularity provided an even more influential model. They reinforced the imaginative import of the ideal theory while denying some of its less welcome implications.[64] The growing emphasis on the individual and the minute discrimination of the particular were no longer seen as compromising the imaginative nature of art. A theory of undiluted generality which was flatly contradicted by the paintings themselves was no longer necessary to defend the art of painting as one of imitation rather than of copying. In the transition from a theory of art as ideal to a theory of art as essentially individual, painting was literature's most potent ally. In the late eighteenth century, however, this emphasis was directly related to its source in painting by means of the traditional pictorial theory. The early nineteenth century's denial of the pictorial implications of the analogy tended to obscure the origin of the Romantics' insistence on the individual. Once the transition from the general to the particular had been successfully effected the doctrine of *ut pictura poesis*, which had previously served to cloak the new emphasis in eighteenth-century critical thought, could be discarded. But as Hazlitt's essay on Crabbe in *The Spirit of the Age* (xi. 164–9) reveals, the decline in overt allusion did not render the analogy with painting any the less potent. This essay is an excellent example of the Romantic transformation of the pictorial theory. It criticized Crabbe's attempt to emulate the painter by emphasizing the particular. Yet it recognized the important role played by painting in stimulating awareness of the significance of the individual in the Romantic aesthetic. While stressing the unity of the poetic in the mastery of the individual, it warned against the attempt to rival in one art the unique effects of another achieved by virtue of its medium.

Painting influenced nineteenth-century criticism by emphasizing the individual. Romantic poetic theory, however, did not dwell on the general or individual exclusively but insisted on their successful involution. This insistence and their perception of the differences entailed by the different media rendered the Romantic critics' attitude to painting ambivalent. Herein lies the source of the tension between the pejorative and non-pejorative uses of pictorial allusion. Whatever form the allusion took it was still an

[64] Hussey, *The Picturesque*, p. 51, suggests that the advantages derived by literature from the influence of painting in the late eighteenth century were largely nullified by the materialism of Victorian England.

allusion to painting which in spite of the decline of literary pictorialism remained the dominant and most potent analogy in the critical vocabulary of the Romantic period.

Painting also influenced poetry in other more general but less tangible ways. Any conclusions therefore about the precise nature of the influence at this general level must remain tentative and somewhat speculative.

Painters and art critics never lost sight of the Old Masters in the same way that literary critics of the seventeenth and eighteenth centuries came to neglect the poets and dramatists of the Elizabethan and Jacobean periods. There were fashions in the discussion as in the purchase of paintings, but there was never any air of superiority, real or affected, to the painters of the past. To discuss painting was to discuss the work of Raphael, Michelangelo, Titian, and Correggio. Critical discussion was much more closely related to the great past and tended as a result to be less susceptible of neo-classical cliché. Homer and Virgil, Aristotle and Horace had no counterparts in the history of painting. This advantage was offset to some extent by the compulsion felt by some art critics to introduce comparisons with sculpture and drama, thereby allowing greater scope for reference to classical example and precept. In spite of this the demand of the art critic throughout the seventeenth and eighteenth centuries was that the painter should 'express the sentiment' of the work and of the individuals and groups comprising the whole.[65] Quite apart from its demand for the concrete particular which necessitated a radical alteration in the prevailing aesthetic, painting by its emphasis on expression, sentiment, and the great tradition provided a standard of comparison that was increasingly difficult for critics of poetry to ignore.

As an art of enactment rather than of statement, painting also taught a new generation of poets and critics to interpret all art as a revelation of reality. This, the least tangible of painting's wider influence, is perhaps the most significant. Paintings, Hazlitt wrote, are 'the bright consummate essences of things' (viii. 173); they are 'a sort of *revelation* of the subjects' (x. 44). Although concerned

---

[65] The demand for the 'expression of the sentiment' is the one critical criterion which Roger Fry sees as a serious rival to his own claims for 'significant form'. He also draws attention to its long history in art criticism, *Transformations* (London, 1926), p. 105.

with sensible objects and individual details the painter, by giving these significance as symbols extending beyond the physical and temporal, 'revealed' their essential character and through colour expressed the highest values of human life. As non-pejorative the analogy with painting alluded to the infinite, the invisible, the evanescent, the fleeting and transient, the complex and varied. To convey these the painter relied upon expression. The moralistic fallacy, the consequence of viewing art as knowledge, as something to be interrogated directly, is confined, as Roger Fry has observed, almost entirely to literature and critics of literature.[66] Yet it is a fallacy conspicuously absent from the literary criticism of the early nineteenth century. It does not seem unreasonable to conjecture that painting contributed more than just a little to this development.[67]

[66] Fry, *Transformations*, pp. 41–2.
[67] Quatremère de Quincy attributed the Romantic rejection of poetic diction to the influence of painting, *Essay*, p. 104.

CHAPTER SIX

The Painter as Critic

> In the theatre, a knowledge of anatomy is the
> foundation of true criticism.
>
> BELL, *Essays*

1. PAINTING AND DRAMA: THE POINT OF TRANSITION

HAZLITT was twenty when he first visited the Orleans Gallery
in the spring of 1799. The significance of this visit in terms of his
subsequent intellectual development cannot be exaggerated. Looking back on the event more than twenty years later, he captured
something of its initial impact in the essay 'On the Pleasure of
Painting':

> My first initiation in the mysteries of the art was at the Orleans
> Gallery: it was there I formed my taste, such as it is. . . . I was staggered
> when I saw the works there collected, and looked at them with wondering
> and with longing eyes. A mist passed away from my sight: the scales fell
> off. A new sense came upon me, a new heaven and a new earth stood
> before me. I saw the soul speaking in the face. . . . We had all heard the
> names of Titian, Raphael, Guido, Domenichino, the Caracci—but to see
> them face to face, to be in the same room with their deathless productions,
> was like breaking some mighty spell—was almost an effect of necro-
> mancy! From that time I lived in a world of pictures.
>
> (viii. 14)

It is clear from this passage that Hazlitt did not intend his account
of the visit to be regarded merely as an evocation of a jejune
adolescent enthusiasm for a famous collection of Old Masters, or
as an exercise in romantic nostalgia. His first acquaintance with
painters, like his first acquaintance with poets, was much more
significant. It had become, in his own words, an 'expressive
symbol' linking the past with the future. His visit to the exhibition
changed the course of his life and exercised the profoundest
influence on his subsequent career as a literary critic.

Hazlitt received his only formal lessons in painting from his
brother John who had studied under Sir Joshua Reynolds. In 1802
he visited Paris where, according to his own account, he spent most

of his time painting and sketching in the Louvre. In his catalogue of Hazlitt's paintings P. P. Howe lists fourteen portraits painted between 1800 and 1812, and suggests that, as well as the landscapes known to have been executed during this period, Hazlitt must have completed many more portraits of which no record exists.[1] Although he finally abandoned painting as a career in 1811 or 1812, Hazlitt continued to paint at intervals throughout his life. He wrote a great deal of formal art criticism; many of his essays were the result of his lifelong preoccupation with painting; and between 1824 and his death in 1830 he published three books devoted almost exclusively to the subject of painting.[2] His first piece of literary criticism appeared in the *Morning Chronicle* in September 1813 and led to his appointment as the newspaper's drama critic.[3] His early dramatic notices were later collected and published as *A View of the English Stage* in 1818. The painter and philosopher had at last turned critic. The terms of this transition, however, are almost as important as the fact of transition itself. That Hazlitt the painter should begin his critical career specifically as a critic of drama assumes a certain significance in the light of the close relationship between painting and drama postulated by late eighteenth-century critical thought. The analogy between the art of painting and that of stage presentation is central to an appreciation of his mature handling of pictorial allusion.

With the decline of the Augustan ideal critical attention focused increasingly on the drama. The gradual eclipse of the epic and the emergence of drama as the supreme form of poetic art coincided with the growing popularity of painting in the second half of the century. In an age dominated by the doctrine of *ut pictura poesis* it was inevitable that, among the innumerable equivalences established between the sister arts, historical painting as the highest form of pictorial art should be seen as correlative to drama. Dryden had already outlined a parallel between tragedy and historical painting,[4] and it was frequently suggested that the neo-classical rules of drama were equally applicable to this form of painting.[5] The pictorialists'

---

[1] P. P. Howe, *The Life of William Hazlitt*, ed. F. Swinnerton (London, 1947), p. 395.
[2] *Sketches of the Principal Picture-Galleries in England* (1824); *Notes on a Journey through France and Italy* (1826); *Conversations of James Northcote* (1830).
[3] Rptd. in *Works*, iv. 10–14; xx. 1–12.
[4] Dryden, *Essays*, II. 130–1. See also Hagstrum, *The Sister Arts*, p. 186.
[5] [W. Gilpin], *An Essay upon Prints* (London, 1768), pp. 3–4; Barry, *Inquiry*, p. 107.

high regard for drama wrought a transformation in the traditional doctrine. *Ut pictura poesis* became *ut poesis pictura*, and in accordance with this reformulation Daniel Webb could define history painting in terms of theatrical representation: 'A History Painting is the representation of a momentary drama: We may therefore, in treating of composition, borrow our ideas from the stage; and divide it into two parts, the scenery, and the drama.'[6] Kames equated an historical painting with a single act in a play,[7] and in Walpole's *Anecdotes* a parallel was established between kinds of painting and kinds of drama.[8] The eighteenth-century reverence for Raphael was in many cases a reverence for the great dramatist.

Even within the anti-pictorialist tradition which attempted to discriminate among the senses in which poetry and painting could be said to be arts of imitation, drama, and in particular the stage presentation of drama, was the sole exception to the otherwise general condemnation of the analogy between the two arts.[9] In 1807 Henry Pye, the Poet Laureate, writing in *The Artist*, suggested that painters would do well to learn from the stage production of drama since 'the Drama exhibited on the stage, exceed[s] every species of imitation short of actual deception'.[10] The attraction of the stage for the painters of the late eighteenth and early nineteenth centuries was already sufficiently widespread, however, to render Pye's injunction unnecessary. Earlier that year, James Northcote, writing in the same periodical, had rejected the doctrine of *ut poesis pictura*: 'It is, surely, not the province of one art to imitate another. . . . To paint, therefore, the passions from the exhibitions of them on the stage . . . is to remove yourself one degree farther from truth. . . . Not one of those pictures [in the Shakespeare Gallery] . . . gained the smallest degree of intrinsic worth from the genius of Shakespere.'[11] The common bond between the two arts, as Northcote's criticism indicates, was their ability to express the passions through form and colour. The superiority of the stage and

---

[6] Webb, *Beauties of Painting*, p. 136. See also ibid., p. 144.

[7] Kames, *Elements of Criticism*, II. 414.

[8] H. Walpole, *Anecdotes of Painting in England*, ed. R. N. Wornum (London, 1849), III. 721–2. See Beattie, *Elements*, II. 600, for a similar comparison.

[9] See Burke, *The Sublime and Beautiful*, pp. 172–3, and Twining, *Eighteenth-Century Critical Essays*, ed. Elledge, II. 994.

[10] H. J. P[ye], *The Artist*, No. XVIII (1807), 7.

[11] J. Northcote, *The Artist*, No. IX (1807), 5–6. For the views of Barry and Opie on the subject of drama, see *Lectures on Painting by the Royal Academicians*, pp. 116, 246. See also Quatremère de Quincy, *Essay*, p. 33.

its attraction for the artist lay in its control of movement, its ability to capture the transient and evanescent expression of successive passions. Dramatic performance thus fulfilled a role comparable to the gymnastic exercises of ancient Greece. It was a school for the study of expression and was considered by Sir Charles Bell to be much more effective than the academy figure: 'The study of the academy figure is . . . most essential, but unless conducted with some regard to science, it necessarily leads to error. . . . The academy figure can give us no aid in the study of the countenance. Here the lessons of anatomy, taken along with the descriptions of the great poets . . . afford the only resource.'[12] In Bell, however, the relationship between the two was interpreted in terms of interaction. Stage performance assisted the painter; the knowledge of the painter, on the other hand, assisted in the proper appreciation of the stage performance. This knowledge 'in the theatre . . . is the foundation of true criticism'.[13] In the light of Bell's view of the close connection between painting and drama, Hazlitt's transition from painting to theatrical criticism becomes much more meaningful.

The decline of pictorialism in the early nineteenth century did not witness any significant alteration in the analogy between painting and the stage presentation of drama. Schlegel's characterization of modern literature as picturesque, for example, was made with specific reference to Elizabethan and Shakespearean drama. Modern or romantic drama in this sense was to be viewed as a 'large picture', its theatrical performance as a 'living' one.[14] Expression of feeling was their unifying element. Drama was like painting because like painting it expressed 'the finest gradations of mental expression in the countenance . . . [and] enables us . . . to read much deeper in the mind, and to perceive its lightest movements'.[15] By accepting Schlegel's argument, Hazlitt and Coleridge were giving their assent to the proposition implicit in Schlegel and Bell that the essential link between painting and drama was their common basis in expression.[16] Hazlitt's experience as a painter is crucially important in explaining the suddenness of his emergence

---

[12] Bell, *Essays*, p. 8.
[13] Ibid., p. 19.
[14] Schlegel, *Lectures*, II. 99; I. 37.
[15] Ibid., II. 100.
[16] According to Mengs, *Works*, III. 53, expression in painting was sufficient to place the art on a par with poetry.

as a critic of major importance and the maturity of his critical achievement. That his earliest critical efforts should have been directed towards the drama cannot be accepted as entirely fortuitous. The relationship traditionally thought to exist between painting and drama, and the basis of both in expression, renders his belated emergence as a critic of drama much more significant. Stage performance, because of its affinities with painting, eased his transition from the one to the other and ensured that the special talents which he had acquired as a painter would not be altogether useless in his new role as drama critic. Bell's view of the special relationship between the two arts was not an isolated one. For Lessing too, 'the art of the actor here stands midway between the plastic arts and poetry'.[17] To some extent painting can be said to have determined the area of literature in which Hazlitt first exercised his critical talents. It also determined the emphases within that field and their mode of expression. Dramatic criticism and the criticism of dramatic literature constitute more than two-thirds of his critical output, and within that body of work pictorial allusion figures much more prominently than in the rest of his critical writings. 'There is a tone', as he once remarked apropos of Kean, 'in acting, as well as in painting, which is the chief and master excellence' (v. 184). This 'tone' is intimately bound up with their common basis in expression.

Hazlitt's criticism of the acting of Kean confirms this analysis. In Hazlitt's view Kean's greatness as an actor was not the result of external or physical attributes of appearance or vocal technique. Defective in both, Kean triumphed by his command of facial and bodily expression. Having witnessed one of his performances from a seat in the boxes, Hazlitt was unable at first to explain his disappointment. The reason he concluded was that from this unusual angle:

> . . . the expression of his face is quite lost, and only the harsh and grating tones of his voice produce their full effect on the ear. . . . The varieties and finer modulations are lost in their passage over the pit. . . . All you discover is an abstraction of his defects, both of person, voice, and manner. . . . The accompaniment of expression is absolutely necessary to explain his tones and gestures: and the outline . . . requires to be filled up and modified by all the details of execution. Without seeing the workings of his face, through which you read the movements of his

[17] Lessing, *Selected Prose Works*, ed. E. Bell (London, 1879), p. 247.

soul . . . it is impossible to understand or feel pleasure in the part. All strong expression, deprived of its gradations and connecting motives, unavoidably degenerates into caricature.

(v. 284–5)

Hazlitt was seldom disappointed by any of Kean's performances. In general, he considered Kean, 'in the picturesque expression of passion, by outward action', to be unrivalled (v. 344). The pictorial allusion in these and other passages is unobtrusive. His references to 'outline', 'details of execution', 'gradations', 'expression', 'caricature', and 'picturesque', do not draw attention to themselves, and his handling of them here and elsewhere always evinces his respect for the differences as well as for the similarities between the two arts. His use of pictorial imagery is seldom confused or employed indiscriminately but is always controlled by his conception of kinds of gusto. The subtlety and incisiveness of his analysis of a dramatic role derives from his pictorial stance. The profusion of pictorial images constantly betrays the painter as dramatic critic. Even when he criticized Kean for 'the extreme elaboration of the parts [which] injures the broad and massy effect' (v. 184), or praised Mrs. Siddons because she 'combined the utmost grandeur and force with every variety of expression and excellence: her transitions were rapid and extreme, but were massed into unity and breadth' (xviii. 408), the language is that of a painter looking at drama in accordance with Schlegel's view of it as a 'living' picture. The terminology of art criticism is often just sufficient to establish the latent presence of the analogy and the unique posture of the critic. It gives a valid support to his criticism without stretching the analogy beyond its limits.

This technique of sub-insinuation is occasionally replaced by quite explicit iconographic attempts to paint or capture some static or fleeting moment in one of Kean's more famous roles. Of Kean's performance as Lear, he wrote: 'He threw himself on his knees; lifted up his arms like withered stumps; threw his head quite back, and in that position, as if severed from all that held him to society, breathed a heart-struck prayer, like the figure of a man obtruncated!' (xviii. 333). The effect of such a passage is to frame the sequence of events for the reader, transforming succession into the simultaneity of a static vision. Occasionally, as in the passage above, he will deliberately draw the reader's attention to the technique by remarking of the acting that 'it would have done for Titian to paint' (v. 182), or that there was 'a flexibility and indefiniteness of outline about it, like a figure with a landscape back-ground' (xviii. 377). There can be little doubt that the success of his early reviews of Kean were due in no small measure to the fact that, as a painter, he was uniquely equipped to judge the peculiar merits of Kean's talents as an actor and to convey his appreciation of them to the public at large. He went to the theatre as a painter and found an actor, making his first appearance in London, who could 'furnish studies to the painter or anatomist' (xviii. 302). The distinction which he drew between the 'picturesque' character of Kean's performances and the 'statuesque' quality of Kemble's, a distinction which recurs again and again in his dramatic criticism, is an important early manifestation of the non-pejorative use of pictorial allusion, and is one which governed his entire approach to the stage presentation of drama. His description of Kean's achievement in Shakespeare might well stand, in the history of dramatic criticism, as a just portrayal of his own achievement: 'Mr. Kean's acting . . . presents a perpetual succession of striking pictures. He bids fair to supply us with the best Shakespear Gallery we have had!' (v. 184).

Hazlitt's reliance on the analogy with painting and his use of pictorial allusion require some modification of the view that painting ceased to be the dominant analogy in early nineteenth-century critical thought. Inevitably, however, as a result of the transitional nature of his early dramatic criticism, there is little indication that his use of the analogy was in any sense illuminative of the essence of poetry. Nevertheless, it does throw a great deal of light on his conception of acting, and if we accept Lessing's view that acting stands midway between painting and poetry, it is still important in considering the development of his mature handling of pictorial imagery. It establishes the significant role which the analogy played in his early criticism; it indicates a use of the analogy radically different from that envisaged by the traditional pictorial theory; and it illustrates that his employment of pictorial allusion was seldom confused or undiscriminating. Far from diminishing as he left his career in painting further and further behind, his manner of exploiting the analogy grew more refined and complex. The examples that follow indicate some of the ways in which painting became the most important of Hazlitt's critical metaphors:

(*i*)   The beauty of these writers in general was, that they gave every kind and gradation of character ... because their portraits were taken from life. ... Their refinement consisted in working out the parts, not in leaving a vague outline. They painted human nature as it was, and as they saw it with individual character and circumstance (xx. 7–8). [of Restoration Comedy].

(*ii*)   We have fine studies of heads, a piece of richly-coloured drapery ... but the groups are ill disposed, nor are the figures proportioned to each other or the size of the canvas (vi. 215). [of Middleton's *Women Beware Women*].

(*iii*)   There is the least colour possible used; the pencil drags; the canvas is almost seen through: but then, what precision of outline, what truth and purity of tone, what firmness of hand, what marking of character! ... We seem to see the gestures, and to hear the tone with which they are accompanied (vi. 237). [of Massinger's *A New Way to Pay Old Debts*].

(*iv*)   Chaucer's characters are ... like portraits or physiognomical studies, with the distinguishing features marked with inconceivable truth and precision, but that preserve the same unaltered air and attitude. Shakspeare's are historical figures ... put into action (v. 50–1).

(*v*)   It is a real tragedy; a sound historical painting. ... It presents a succession of pictures. We might suppose each scene almost to be copied from a beautiful bas-relief, or to have formed a group on some antique vase (xviii. 345–6). [of Sheridan Knowles's *Virginius*].

(*vi*)   They were buried in it for want of grouping and relief, like the colours of a well-drawn picture sunk in the canvass (vi. 164). [of Sheridan's *School for Scandal*].

(*vii*)   We judge of [Shakespeare's] characters ... as we do of the likeness of a particular friend, which must have not only the general outline but the minute details and the exact expression to come up to our expectations (ix. 90).

2. GUSTO

(i) *The Correlation of Kinds*

'Gusto' is the most obvious of Hazlitt's borrowings from the vocabulary of the painter and art critic. Its presence in his critical terminology, his unique use of it, and its source in art criticism, have frequently been commented upon. Nevertheless, the part which it plays in his more general use of pictorial allusion has never fully been appreciated. 'Gusto' epitomizes the experiential nature of his view of the poetic, and underlines his indebtedness to painting for the power to express it. As a critical concept 'gusto' symbolizes the fusion of the philosopher and painter in the literary critic. It emphasizes the way in which his experience as a painter enabled him, by means of a theory of abstract ideas, to achieve the fully mature experiential position characteristic of his greatest work, while at the same time providing him with the perfect instrument for its expression in criticism.

According to Hazlitt's theory of abstract ideas there are no two leaves, no two grains of sand in the world exactly alike. In a very general way gusto may be said to be the expression of this unique quality of objects in the work of art. The work of art, or the dramatic performance of a role which succeeds in expressing this characteristic excellence, this essence of the individual, has gusto. Gusto or expression, whether in painting, acting, or poetry, is in some sense the revelation of the significance of man's relationship to the world. Hazlitt described gusto as 'the extreme beauty and power of an impression with all its accompaniments, or the very intensity and truth of feeling, that pushes the poet over the verge of matter-of-fact, and justifies him in resorting to the licence of fiction to express what . . . must have remained for ever untold' (xx. 211).[18] Two preliminary points require to be made. His notion of gusto, like Coleridge's view of the imagination, has a dual reference. It has an ontological as well as a psychological significance. It relates to his theory of poetry as symbol as well as to his account of the psychological functioning of the imagination in the process of artistic creation. The psychological component of gusto is much less important than its ontological implications, although critical discussion by emphasizing the former has tended to suggest the converse to be the case. In the present instance, gusto is treated in relation to poetic value, not poetic effect or poetic creation. The second point is that gusto, although a single concept, is susceptible of the greatest flexibility in its formulation and application. There is a gusto in Burke, a gusto in Milton, and a gusto in Shakespeare, each differing from the other. Its formulation varies in accordance with the 'kind' involved. Criticism is not only concerned with 'settling the standard of excellence', but the standard 'both as to degree and kind' (vi. 108). To recognize this, and to appreciate Hazlitt's use of pejorative and non-pejorative pictorial allusion, is to acknowledge that Abrams's criticism of his 'confused' imagery,

---

[18] Cf. Hazlitt, *Works*, iv. 77: '[Gusto] is in giving this truth of character from the truth of feeling.'

at least in so far as it relates to pictorial imagery, is not well-founded.[19]

In formulating his demand for gusto in this flexible way, according to whether the work under discussion is a poem, a play, or a piece of prose, Hazlitt was not being wilfully idiosyncratic. His use of the concept is perfectly consistent with, and is validated by, the best practice of seventeenth and eighteenth-century art criticism. De Piles a century earlier had recognized 'kinds' of gusto, or a gusto of 'kinds', when he said that 'the Painter, to be perfect, must design correctly with a good Gusto, and a different Stile, sometimes Heroic, sometimes Pastoral, according to the Character of the Figures he introduces. . . . Besides, Nature differing in all her Productions requires that the Painter should have an answerable Variety in his'.[20] In every branch of painting, in design, colouring, chiaroscuro, there was also an appropriate gusto. Even at the risk of anticipating some of the issues to be raised later, it is important to appreciate from the outset the experiential nature of De Piles' view of gusto, and of Hazlitt's use of the same concept as it occurs, for example, in his criticism of prose style. Of Burke's prose style, Hazlitt observed:

Burke's style . . . never loses sight of the subject; nay, is always in contact with, and derives its increased or varying impulse from it. . . . It is all the same to him, so that he loses no particle of the exact, characteristic, extreme expression of the thing he writes about. . . . Burke's execution, like that of all good prose, savours of the texture of what he describes, and his pen slides or drags over the ground of his subject, like the painter's pencil.

(xii. 10, 12)

A passage of prose which successfully conveys 'the extreme impression of the thing' possesses the gusto appropriate to prose. Unlike Burke, Dr. Johnson had 'no style, that is, no scale of words answering to the differences of his subject' (iv. 371). In the *Lectures on the English Comic Writers*, Hazlitt criticized Johnson's style, as

---

[19] Abrams, *The Mirror and the Lamp*, p. 52, writes of Hazlitt's 'wealth of sometimes confused imagery'.

[20] De Piles, *The Art of Painting*, p. 3. Cf. Hazlitt, *Works*, iv. 77: 'It is not so difficult to explain this term in what relates to expression (of which it may be said to be the highest degree) as in what relates to things without expression, to the natural appearances of objects, as mere colour or form. . . . It is in giving this truth of character . . . whether in the highest or lowest degree, but always in the highest degree of which the subject is capable, that gusto consists.'

De Piles would have criticized the style of a bad painter, as having 'little fitness to the variety of things. . . . It destroys all shades of difference' (vi. 101–2). The effect of his prose style is to put a 'mask on the face of nature' (vii. 310). His criticism of Bolingbroke and Sidney is similar. Their prose 'veils', 'hides', or 'disguises' the individual reality of the objects described. Bolingbroke achieved this effect by a 'parade of words' (vi. 168), and Sidney by a 'systematic interpolation of the wit, learning, ingenuity, wisdom . . . of the writer, so as to disguise the object, instead of displaying it in its true colours and real proportions' (vi. 320). His criticism in every instance is a criticism of abstraction. Burke's freedom from abstraction constituted his greatness as a prose writer. In Burke, 'words are the most like things' (vii. 309). Hazlitt's repeated attempts to characterize the gusto of Burke's prose, which he admired more than any other, are the result of a desire to express experientially that which was in itself experiential; or, to express it another way, to present in non-abstract prose the essence of a prose style which was supremely non-abstract. The best general introduction to his criticism of individual prose writers is the essay 'On Familiar Style' (viii. 242–8). The refusal of women to be 'implicated in theories' and their propensity to 'judge of objects more from their immediate and involuntary impression on the mind' likewise resulted in a non-abstract prose style in which they expressed themselves 'according to the impression which things make upon them' (viii. 77; iv. 371–2). Hazlitt's fondness for representative metre is another aspect of his concern that words should answer to 'the variety of things'. The imagery of appearance and reality, used to criticize the abstraction of Johnson, Bolingbroke, and Sidney, was not peculiar to Hazlitt. Shelley in the *Defence*, for example, criticized the religious abstraction of Dante, Calderon, and Milton in similar terms. Their preconceptions and language 'mask', 'disguise', 'envelop', and 'distort' the reality they attempted to portray. Unlike Shelley, however, Hazlitt's criticism of abstraction was operative through his conception of gusto and was expressed in a language which was both directly and indirectly derivative from painting. In emphasizing the concrete particularity of things it was indirectly derivative, a consequence of his theory of abstract ideas which he explicitly acknowledged to be generalized from his experience of painting.

The gusto which he required of the prose-writer was not the

gusto he required of Shakespeare or Milton. It was always a gusto
appropriate to the branch of literature under consideration. As a
single concept gusto emphasized the unity of the poetic; in its
flexibility of formulation, it answered to the differences within that
unity. His systematic and coherent use of pictorial allusion was the
result of the specific manner in which he formulated each of his
demands for gusto at its appropriate level. He always demanded the
gusto appropriate to the branch of literature he was discussing, and
the pictorial imagery which he employed in making this demand
approximated to the terminology of the painter and art critic
considering a comparable branch of painting. Implicit in all his
literary criticism are equivalences between kinds of painting and
kinds of literature—a correlation which excluded pictorialism. An
obvious example of this occurs in his frequent attempts to illuminate the characteristic excellence of a particular poet by reference to
a painter. The poetry of Spenser, for example, is assimilated to the
painting of Rubens (x. 71-2), Milton to Poussin (viii. 169), Restoration Comedy to Watteau (vi. 70), Crabbe to Teniers (xi. 166), and
Wordsworth to Rembrandt. Of the relation between Wordsworth
and Rembrandt, Hazlitt commented: '[Wordsworth's] eye also
does justice to Rembrandt's fine and masterly effects. In the way in
which that artist works something out of nothing, and transforms
the stump of a tree, a common figure into an *ideal* object, by the
gorgeous light and shade thrown upon it, he perceives an analogy
to his own mode of investing the minute details of nature with an
atmosphere of sentiment' (xi. 93). Among the eighteenth-century
pictorialists, the practice of assimilating poetry and painting in this
manner was part of the current critical cliché. Hazlitt's use of the
equivalence, on the other hand, has none of the glibness and superficiality of eighteenth-century pictorialism. He always remained
aware of the limits of the two arts, and partly because of this, his
use of it was almost always significant. By comparison, Leigh
Hunt's attempt to exploit the equivalence in this way in 'A New
Gallery of Pictures' (1833), reverted to the crude, uncritical naïveté
characteristic of the previous century.

Another danger inherent in this type of equivalence, and indeed
in the correlation of kinds generally, is the tendency to identify a
poet with one kind of gusto only. Hazlitt succeeded in avoiding
this temptation. The correlation of kinds always remained an
instrument of his own intuitive grasp of the variety and differences

to be found in the work of individual poets. It was never rigidly applied as a preconceived formula regardless of the individual poem or poet under discussion. He characterized the gusto of Crabbe, Cowper, and Bloomfield as the gusto of still-life painting, and the terms in which he discussed their poetry directly and indirectly alluded to this equivalence.[21] Cowper was more 'picturesque' than Thomson because he was more concerned with the minutiae of objects.[22] Chaucer, on the other hand, the most 'picturesque' of the English poets in this respect, also possessed a higher gusto. Of his gusto as a painter of still-life, Hazlitt observed that he always 'speaks of what he wishes to describe with the accuracy, the discrimination of one who relates what has happened to himself. . . . The strokes of his pencil always tell. . . . His descriptions have a sort of tangible character' (v. 21-2). When he came to characterize Chaucer's gusto as a landscape painter the terms of his formulation were correspondingly different: 'Chaucer's descriptions of natural scenery possess the same sort of characteristic excellence, or what might be termed *gusto*. They have a local truth and freshness, which gives the very feeling of the air, the coolness or moisture of the ground' (v. 26-7). The gusto implicit in the first differs from the gusto explicitly referred to in the second. The former, if we compare it with his criticism of Burke's prose style, is more akin to the gusto of good prose. In both cases, his discrimination of the appropriate gusto is framed by his unobtrusive control of pictorial allusion. In neither of his criticisms of Chaucer is there any obvious allusion to an equivalence in the field of painting. Such a correlation nevertheless exists. The terms used to describe Chaucer's gusto in natural description are the same terms used to describe a similar quality in the great landscape painters. The highest compliment he could pay to such painters was that 'in looking at them we breath the very air which the scene inspires, and feel the genius of the place present to us. . . . There is all the cool freshness of a misty spring morning: the sky, the water, the dim horizon all convey the same feeling. . . . It conveys not only the image, but the feeling of nature, and excites a new interest unborrowed from the eye' (xviii. 24-5).[23] His criticism of Thomson's *The Seasons* cannot fully

[21] Hazlitt, *Works*, v. 91 ff.

[22] Ibid., v. 87.

[23] Cf. Coleridge, *Biographia*, II. 237: 'The true compliment to the picture was made by a lady . . . who declared . . . that she never stood before that landscape without seeming to feel the breeze blow out of it upon her.' See also Hazlitt's

be appreciated unless we are aware, in spite of the absence of any overt pictorial imagery, of his invocation of the gusto of the great landscape painters:

> Nature in his descriptions is seen growing around us, fresh and lusty as in itself. We feel the effect of the atmosphere, its humidity or clearness, its heat or cold, the glow of summer. . . . We hear the snow drifting against the broken casement without, and see the fire blazing on the hearth within. . . . In a word, he describes not to the eye alone, but to the other senses.

(v. 87)[24]

(ii) *Dramatic Gusto: The Final Formulation*

In view of the almost disproportionate emphasis on drama in Hazlitt's critical writings, the most important of his formulations of gusto is that of dramatic gusto or expression. It was not the task of the dramatist to convey the absolute character of the object, or the feeling of the atmosphere. Still-life, Dutch painting, and landscape were no longer adequate analogies. Only historical painting could fulfil this role satisfactorily. This correlation between drama and historical painting is made quite explicitly in a variety of ways in numerous contexts.[25] It is not sufficient merely to point out that his response to Middleton's *Women Beware Women* and Massinger's *A New Way to Pay Old Debts* was conveyed in pictorial terms. The specific terms are those of the eighteenth-century art critic of historical painting. Even in these somewhat extreme examples, however, Hazlitt was not subscribing to a pictorialist viewpoint. The correlation of kinds was independent of the doctrine of *ut pictura poesis*. He was not arguing that drama should conform to the principles of its correlative genre in painting. His use of pictorial equivalences is descriptive, rather than prescriptive, and whether

---

praise of Wordsworth's taste in landscape: 'He would not give a rush for any landscape that did not express the time of day, the climate, the period of the world it was meant to illustrate' (xi. 93).

[24] Hazlitt introduced this passage in the following way: 'The colours with which [Thomson] paints seem yet wet and breathing' (v. 87). The gusto of the prose writer is primarily concerned with the absolute character of objects. When these are the objects of landscape, Hazlitt's language approximated the gusto of prose to that of natural description in poetry: '[Cobbett] will describe you to the life a turnip-field with the green sprouts glittering in the sun, the turnips frozen to a mere clod, the breath of the oxen steaming near that are biting it. . . . Who does it . . . with richer gusto?' (xix. 96–7).

[25] See above, p. 145. For specific correlations of drama and historical painting, see v. 51; vi. 151, 240, 265; xviii. 345.

latent or overt, effectively evoke a cumulative series of resonances which act as important unifying factors in his criticism. By means of a system of pictorial equivalences, Hazlitt exploited the language of painting, quintessentially the experiential art, to convey his own conviction of the experiential nature of poetry and of the poetic generally.

Since the means of poetry are not the means of painting, and since poetry owes its superiority to the nature of its medium which 'alone answers in any degree to the truth of things', the analogy between drama and historical painting is not exact. On Hazlitt's own admission, however, there is a further difference between poetry and painting which appears to cast doubt on the validity even of the most inexact analogy. Painting, according to Hazlitt, is concerned primarily with objects. Drama, on the other hand, is concerned with events. An equivalence between a static and a kinetic art consequently seems singularly unfruitful and suggests a tendentious strain damaging to his own experiential position. Fortunately, his view of painting as an art preoccupied with objects is not as limiting as it appears at first sight. He did concede that painting in so far 'as it relates to passion' was also concerned with events (v. 10), and this concession enables historical painting and drama to be balanced more evenly in his correlation of kinds. Nevertheless, the spatial and non-temporal nature of painting still appears to present an insurmountable obstacle to the establishment of any meaningful or illuminating equivalence. Hazlitt drew attention to this distinction in his first piece of literary criticism in September 1813:

[Drama] represents not only looks, but motion and speech. The painter gives only the former, looks without action or speech, and the mere writer only the latter, words without looks or action. . . . [Drama] brings them into action, obtrudes them on the sight, embodies them in habits, in gestures, in dress, in circumstances, and in speech. It renders every thing overt and ostensible, and presents human nature not in its elementary principles . . . but exhibits its essential quality in all their variety of combinations.

(xx. 9–10)

When he compared the characters of Shakespeare to the figures in an historical painting, the comparison was limited by his qualification that in Shakespeare the figures were 'put into action' (v. 51). The important question is how any equivalence at this level is possible, if an essential point of his formulation of dramatic gusto involves a reference to movement as well as to events.

The solution of this problem is comparable to the solution of the problem posed by the pejorative and non-pejorative use of pictorial allusion. In both cases, the context is all-important. If we allow the two poles of the present equivalence, drama and historical painting, to dominate, and insist on viewing historical painting only in relation to drama, the obstacles to the establishment of a meaningful correlation are insuperable. If, on the other hand, we emphasize the eighteenth-century view of historical painting as the highest form of pictorial art, and perceive that as an equivalence both poles must first be established in relation to the different branches of their respective arts, it becomes clear that, in relation to other forms of painting, historical painting was supremely the kinetic branch of the art. Its superiority to portraiture was precisely its ability to capture movement and to convey this by implication. Portrait-painting was the static branch of painting: 'It is easier to paint a portrait than an historical face, because the head *sits* for the first, but the expression will hardly *sit* for the last' (xviii. 162). The whole question of action and movement in painting is relative: 'A portrait is to history what still-life is to portraiture: that is, the whole remains the same while you are doing it. . . . The face in its most ordinary state is continually varying and in action' (ibid.). Hazlitt did not believe that the head *sat* for the portrait painter, although in relation to historical painting this might appear to be the case: 'The human face is not one thing . . . nor does it remain always the same. It has infinite varieties. . . . Not only the light and shade upon it do not continue for two minutes the same: the position of the head constantly varies . . . each feature is in motion every moment' (xii. 287). The highest praise which he could bestow on an historical painting was to say that 'the scene moves before you' (xviii. 161), or that 'the business of the scene never stand[s] still' (iv. 28). The kinetic superiority of drama over historical painting does not render the equivalence abortive or forced. Action and movement form the very basis of the correlation. Within the context of painting, Hazlitt's discussion of historical painting invariably alluded to the kinetic nature of this branch of the art. In doing so he was being consistent with his own view that '*the historical is nature in action*. . . . Every feature, limb, figure, group, is instinct with life and motion. . . . There is a continual and complete action and reaction of one variable part upon another. . . . The action of any one part, the contraction or relaxation of any one muscle, extends . . . to every other' (xviii. 160–1).

Hazlitt's final formulation of gusto as dramatic has a number of features in common with his previous formulations. In many cases, for example, it is expressed in terms so unobtrusive as almost to escape detection altogether. To anyone conversant with his art criticism, however, or with the art criticism of the eighteenth century, it is clear that the vocabulary of action and movement employed in elaborating dramatic gusto is the vocabulary of the painter and art critic discussing the gusto of historical painting. In other cases, as in his criticism of Chaucer, Thomson, and Burke, it found expression within a context of overt pictorial allusion. Throughout, the kinetic terminology of dramatic gusto, like the terminology of the other equivalences, harmonized perfectly with the vocabulary of particularity derived from his theory of abstract ideas. Although these characteristics are common to all forms of gusto, dramatic gusto has a greater affinity with the gusto of prose. Like 'prosaic' gusto it has greater flexibility of application. Both operate within much less restricted fields than, for example, the gusto of a poetry limited to the description of objects or external nature, where there is not the same need to exploit an extensive vocabulary of terms all pointing in the same direction. Nevertheless, his predilection for drama required a kinetic terminology which, in its range and variety, far exceeded the vocabulary necessary to convey an appreciation of the prose writer's ability to capture the 'absolute' or 'essential' character of his subject. Consequently, while the terms 'action' and 'reaction' established the kinetic nature of the final formulation, they were insufficient by themselves to express the full implications of his demand for a gusto which was dramatic. His kinetic vocabulary comprises a vast network of synonymous and cognate terms all expressive of the need for action and movement: motion, life, workings, fluctuations, play, flexibility, malleability, movement, inflection, undulation, wrestling, writhing, yielding, varying, transient, evanescent, fleeting, momentary, passing. These terms, in turn, are related to others which emphasized the infinite variety and complexity of life: a complexity and variety which must on no account be diminished by the imposition of a conceptual framework or indeed any form of abstraction. The introduction of the ideas of action and reaction only served to heighten and increase the complexity and variety to which these terms contrived to draw specific attention: modulation, modification, involution, combination, connection. Drama's inherent kinetic superiority over historical painting, however, entailed the use of certain epithets which, characteristic of his discussion of dramatic literature, occur less frequently in his criticism of historical painting. These included such terms as: strife, struggle, conflict, collision, contention, combat. The weakness of the equivalence at this point serves to remind us that the analogy is only an analogy, that the means of poetry are not the means of painting. It is an acknowledgment of Hazlitt's own view of the superiority of poetry to painting, and of the dramatic principle in the one to the historical principle in the other.

Hazlitt's final formulation of gusto as dramatic appears to confirm, in a limited but specific way, the suggestion that painting played an important part in effecting the transition from the eighteenth-century view of art as knowledge and as something stated, to art as revelation and as something expressed. His emphasis on action and reaction, on the involution and expression of the passions, was essentially a demand for drama to enact its values. Poetry does not state truths; it expresses significant human values which the reader re-creates by submitting to the poet's original vision. They cannot be formulated outside the work of art in non-poetic discourse. They can only be expressed in all their complexity and variety in the work itself. They cannot be intuited as ideas. The poetic muse, in Hazlitt's view, was not concerned with abstraction, scientific, philosophical or religious. On the contrary, the experiential and revelatory nature of art prompted him to exploit a terminology which attempted to draw attention to its non-abstract nature. Art, therefore, is said to reveal, unfold, show, present, lay bare, express, display. The work of art itself is an emanation, expression, effusion, or distillation of enduring human values. The revelation is thus in the widest sense a moral revelation: 'We apprehend that morality is little more than truth. . . . We do not think . . . that the only instruction to be derived from the drama is, not from the insight it gives us into the nature of human character and passion, but from some artificial piece of patchwork morality tacked to the end' (v. 288). By 'insight' Hazlitt does not mean 'psychological and moral truths' of human nature. The work which possesses dramatic gusto has a 'natural' or 'dramatic' morality (ix. 39; viii. 77): 'The morality of Shakespear in this way is great; but it is not to be found in the four last lines of his plays, in the form of extreme unction' (xx. 84).[26] This emerges clearly from his comparison between the plays of Byron and Webster in the essay 'On Reason and Imagination'. The extract that follows is given at length because, more than any other, it represents the quintessence of his critical achievement. It embodies almost all his major aesthetic preoccupations, and the 'vocabularies' isolated in the previous discussion for the purposes of analysis are now seen to form a unified critical terminology. The philosopher and painter are involved in the literary critic. It is also one of the best examples of fruitful generalization from the consideration of an individual work in the nineteenth century:

It is not merely the fashion among philosophers—the poets also have got into a way of scouting individuality as beneath the sublimity of their pretensions, and the universality of their genius. . . . Modern tragedy, in particular, is no longer like a vessel making the voyage of life, and tossed about by the winds and waves of passion, but is converted into a handsomely-constructed steam-boat, that is moved by the sole expansive power of words. Lord Byron has launched several of these ventures lately. . . . We have not now a number of *dramatis personae* affected by particular incidents and speaking according to their feelings, or as the occasion suggests, but each mounting the rostrum, and delivering his opinion on fate, fortune, and the entire consummation of things. The individual is not of sufficient importance to occupy his own thoughts or the thoughts of others. The poet fills his page with *grandes pensées*. He covers the face of nature with the beauty of his sentiments and the brilliancy of his paradoxes. We have the subtleties of the head, instead of the workings of the heart, and possible justifications instead of the actual motives of conduct. This all seems to proceed on a false estimate of individual nature and the value of human life. . . . As an instance of the opposite style of dramatic dialogue . . . I will give, by way of illustration, a passage from an old tragedy, in which a brother has just caused his sister to be put to a violent death.

> 'Bosola. Fix your eye here.
> Ferdinand. Constantly.
> Bosola. Do you not weep?

[26] This explains the apparent contradiction in Hazlitt's view that Shakespeare was the most moral (xi. 267) and the least moral (v. 283) of writers: 'The most moral writers, after all, are those who do not pretend to inculcate any moral' (vi. 107). His non-abstract approach scorned the didactic as 'an insult offered to its free-will' (iv. 154).

Other sins only speak; murther shrieks out:
The element of water moistens the earth;
But blood flies upwards, and bedews the heavens.
  Ferdinand. Cover her face: mine eyes dazzle; she died
                                        [young.

  Bosola. I think not so: her infelicity
Seem'd to have years too many.
  Ferdinand. She and I were twins:
And should I die this instant, I had lived
Her time to a minute.'
                          DUCHESS OF MALFY, Act IV. Scene 2.

How fine is the constancy with which he first fixes his eye on the dead
body, with a forced courage, and then, as his resolution wavers, how
natural is his turning his face away, and the reflection that strikes him on
her youth and beauty and untimely death, and the thought that they
were twins, and his measuring his life by hers up to the present period, as
if all that was to come of it were nothing! Now, I would fain ask whether
there is not in this contemplation of the interval that separates the
beginning from the end of life, of a life too so varied from good to ill,
and of the pitiable termination of which the person speaking has been
the wilful and guilty cause, enough to 'give the mind pause?' Is not that
revelation as it were of the whole extent of our being which is made by
the flashes of passion and stroke of calamity, a subject sufficiently stagger-
ing to have place in legitimate tragedy? Are not the struggles of the will
with untoward events and the adverse passions of others as interesting
and instructive in the representation as reflections on the mutability of
fortune or inevitableness of destiny, or on the passions of men in general?
The tragic Muse does not merely utter muffled sounds: but we see the
paleness on the cheek, and the life-blood gushing from the heart! The
interest we take in our own lives, in our successes or disappointments,
and the *home* feelings that arise out of these, when well described, are the
clearest and truest mirror in which we can see the image of human
nature. For in this sense each man is a microcosm. What he is, the rest
are—whatever his joys and sorrows are composed of, theirs are the same
—no more, no less.
              'One touch of nature makes the whole world kin.'
But it must be the genuine touch of nature, not the outward flourishes
and varnish of art. The spouting, oracular, didactic figure of the poet no
more answers to the living man, than the lay-figure of the painter does.
We may well say to such a one,
          'Thou hast no speculation in those eyes
          That thou dost glare with: thy bones are marrowless,
          Thy blood is cold!'

Man is (so to speak) an endless and infinitely varied repetition: and if we know what one man feels, we so far know what a thousand feel in the sanctuary of their being. Our feeling of general humanity is at once an aggregate of a thousand different truths, and it is also the same truth a thousand times told. As is our perception of this original truth, the root of our imagination, so will the force and richness of the general impression proceeding from it be. The boundary of our sympathy is a circle which enlarges itself according to its propulsion from the centre—the heart. If we are imbued with a deep sense of individual weal or woe, we shall be awe-struck at the idea of humanity in general. If we know little of it but its abstract and common properties, without their particular application, their force or degrees, we shall care just as little as we know either about the whole or the individuals. If we understand the texture and vital feeling, we then can fill up the outline, but we cannot supply the former from having the latter given. Moral and poetical truth is like expression in a picture—the one is not to be attained by smearing over a large canvas, nor the other by bestriding a vague topic. . . . I defy any great tragic writer to despise that nature which he understands, or that heart which he has probed, with all its rich bleeding materials of joy and sorrow. The subject may not be a source of much triumph to him, from its alternate light and shade, but it can never become one of supercilious indifference.

(xii. 53–5)

When Hazlitt and Coleridge say that they 'hear', 'see', and 'feel' the characters, events, or situations, it is not that they are treating art as life. It is an attempt to characterize phenomenologically their own vital response to the work under discussion as revealing in some way the significance of human existence. For Hazlitt, the dialogue between Bosola and Ferdinand is not 'the bandying of idle words and rhetorical commonplaces, but the writhing and conflict, and the sublime colloquy of man's nature with itself' (vi. 246). Only through the enactment of values can the poet achieve the highest form of gusto and morality. Gusto, in all its variety of formulations, epitomizes Hazlitt's experiential view of the poetic, and at the same time emphasizes his indebtedness to painting for its adequate expression in criticism.

PART III

The Critic

The formed and disciplined critic tends to ask the same questions about one work after another; to find, recurrently, similar grounds for praise or condemnation; and to a greater or lesser extent, to record his findings in a recurrent terminology.... To the degree that a critic ... repeatedly asks the same question of the works he discusses, repeatedly brings forward similar findings as matters of prime interest, and repeatedly does so in the same vocabulary, there is, implicit in what he writes, a more or less definite idea of the *real nature of a literary work*. There is an 'ulterior conception' of what a work must be *to be literature*. The critic may not have formulated this idea explicitly to himself. He may even be the better critic for not doing so. For all that, it is there, and it controls what he does.

JOHN HOLLOWAY, *The Story of the Night*, pp. 9–10

CHAPTER SEVEN

The Abstract Muse

I say what I think: I think what I feel.
HAZLITT, *A View of the English Stage*, v. 175

1. SINCERITY OF FEELING: THE ANALOGY WITH MORALITY

HAZLITT'S distrust of abstraction, scientific or philosophical, empirical or idealist, clearly distinguishes his response to the existential from the responses of Bentham and Coleridge. He recognized the existence but refused to acknowledge the exclusive validity of the contemporary opposition between empiricism and idealism, mechanism and dynamism, which modern critics have since made central to an understanding of the Romantic period. Conscious of the authenticity of the existential or imaginative realm, he has, of course, much more in common with Coleridge than with Bentham. This similarity however, which is far from being unimportant, must not be allowed to disguise the fundamental conflict between their respective philosophies. To emphasize the importance of painting in the evolution of his distrust of abstraction helps to clarify the precise nature of this opposition. Painting afforded him insights which, as a philosopher, he was able to appreciate and develop in the context of poetry. It provided him with a terminology, sufficiently flexible and diversified, with which to express not only his general philosophical and aesthetic conclusions, but also his specific insights as a literary critic. It only remains to show the manner in which his experiential view of poetry as self-authenticating is operative at the level of his practical criticism, and to convey some sense of the unique way in which this basic attitude modifies his response to criticism, literary history, and the whole tradition of English literature.

In developing his view of the non-abstract nature of poetry Hazlitt laid particular stress on three elements: the poet's openness to the whole of human experience; his 'truth to nature', or fidelity to the infinite particularity and complexity of that experience; and the poetic sensitivity which alone could make these possible. Sometimes, as in 'The Indian Jugglers', all three elements are present at once: 'The unravelling this mysterious web of thought and feeling is alone in the Muse's gift, namely, in the power of that trembling sensibility which is awake to every change and every modification of its ever-varying impressions' (viii. 83). Philosophers, on the other hand, were insufficiently poetical: 'They are determined upon something beforehand. This gives a hardness and rigidity to their understandings, and takes away that tremulous sensibility to every slight and wandering impression which is necessary to complete the fine balance of the mind, and enable us to follow all the infinite fluctuations of thought through their nicest distinctions' (ii. 261). All three elements, openness, truth to nature, and feeling, are again present. On other occasions, as in 'The Spirit of Philosophy', explicit reference to two of the components serves to evoke the third more effectively: 'The phenomena are infinite, obscure, and intricately inwoven together, so that it is only by being always alive to their tacit and varying influences, that we can hope to seize on the power that guides and binds them together' (xx. 373). In this instance, however, the element of feeling is deliberately suppressed so that its introduction and elaboration later in the essay is doubly effective. By emphasizing 'the fine balance of the mind' and 'the power that guides and binds', and by insisting in others that the discrimination of the particular 'mounts up to a mighty sum in the end, which is an essential part of an important whole' (viii. 39), Hazlitt was calling attention to the fact that the particularity he required was not unqualified, that unity, wholeness, and generality, were important factors in his conception of poetry.

His objection to abstraction was not an objection to generality and theories in themselves. Theories and theorizing play an important part in determining our response to the world. They categorize our responses, conditioning us to regard certain things in a certain way. Consequently, their correct formulation and mode of operation are matters of some importance. In his criticism Hazlitt often appears contemptuous of all theories: 'I cannot give up my partiality to [Hogarth and Fielding] for the fag-end of a theory' (xii. 322), or 'No idle theories . . . should hinder us from greeting [beauty] with rapture' (xi. 162), or even 'And shall we cut ourselves off from beauties like these with a theory?' (v. 79). His objection in these passages is not to generality as such, but to vagueness or inadequately supported generality. The general must arise out of as exhaustive an assimilation as possible of the complexity of human experience: 'No theory is good for any thing that is not founded on general observation and experience; and, where this is the case, it *must* hold good generally as a guide or rule to direct our decisions or expectations. . . . A vague theory that does not rest on the efficient and essential principles of things, will indeed necessarily deceive us' (xix. 220). The same is true of poetry: 'Any general results . . . must be from the aggregate of well-founded particulars: to embody an abstract theory, as if it were a given part of actual nature, is an impertinence' (xii. 246). Shakespeare exemplified this ideal perfectly. He remained 'exquisitely alive to the slightest impulses and most evanescent shades of character and feeling' (v. 204); he did not 'tamper with nature or warp her to his own purposes', but ' "knew all qualities with a learned spirit", instead of judging of them by his own predilections' (viii. 42). To attain this ideal the poet must rely on feeling. Feeling alone guarantees the non-abstract nature of the work of art and hence the possibility of escape from the empirical/idealist duality in philosophy. The openness necessary to the poet, philosopher, and critic is a function of his affective nature. Man, for Hazlitt, is essentially a poetical and therefore an affective animal.

Hazlitt's early interest in philosophy influenced his later work in a variety of ways. It enabled him to interpret his experience of painting in a manner applicable to all art, thereby facilitating the transference and application to literature of the skills and insights of the painter. Its influence, however, was also much more direct. The *Essay on the Principles of Human Action*, although an early work whose basic issues had preoccupied him since 1795, embodied a psychology and ontology of moral action that remained fundamentally the same throughout his life. Its key terms, sympathy, imagination, sincerity, disinterestedness, feeling, sensibility, are the terms familiar to every reader of his essays and criticism. They are the terms employed in his discussion of the imaginative life of man, moral and aesthetic, for they relate not only to the psychology and ontology of moral action but also to the psychology and ontology of poetry and poetic creation. Recent critical discussion has tended to concentrate on the psychological component of his critical theory. Hazlitt's handling of imagination and sympathy, which are especially susceptible of a purely psychological interpretation, has been emphasized at the expense of sensibility and feeling. It would be equally mistaken to reverse this situation by emphasizing the latter at the expense of the former. Sensibility, feeling, imagination, and sympathy have psychological as well as ontological implications. In the early *Essay* imagination in particular plays an important role, being defined as the faculty that 'must carry me out of myself into the feelings of others' (i. 1). His psychological account of its mode of operation plays a vital part in the development of his early moral theory. Nevertheless, the significance of imagination and its sympathetic function is not exhausted by a purely psychological interpretation. If we compare this early view of the imaginative faculty with that occurring in the essay 'On Genius and Common Sense', it becomes clear that in both cases the primacy must be accorded to feeling rather than to imagination and sympathy: 'Imagination is, more properly, the power of carrying on a given feeling into other situations, which must be done best according to the hold which the feeling itself has taken of the mind. . . . There can be no sympathy, where there is no passion. . . . In general the strength and consistency of the imagination will be in proportion to the strength and depth of feeling' (viii. 42). Imagination's sympathetic function, its ability to transcend the self, makes moral as distinct from selfish action possible. It is a psychological means to a philosophical or moral end. Without feeling, however, no moral agency selfish or otherwise is possible. Feeling and not imagination is the irreducible datum of human experience. As sensibility, feeling relates to the agent's sensitivity to his own feeling. It is 'an acute . . . feeling of all that relate[s] to his own impressions' (iv. 88). As imagination, feeling relates to his sensitivity to the feelings of others. Imagination is only possible on the basis of personal feeling: 'But to sympathise with passion, a greater fund of sensibility is demanded in proportion to the strength or tenderness of the passion' (xviii. 162).

Feeling, therefore, is the most important single factor in Hazlitt's distrust of abstraction. His response to the imaginative element in life was determined principally by his view of the part played by feeling in human experience. Openness to the truth of nature is dependent upon the poet's or philosopher's powers of sensibility. The injunction to remain 'open', or 'alive', or 'awake' to the complexity of nature is addressed to the sensibility and not to the imagination. This is confirmed by his criticism of Dr. Johnson. What debarred Johnson from being a good critic of Shakespeare was not his attempt to subordinate imagination to reason, but his inherent deficiency of feeling: 'He was not only without any particular fineness of organic sensibility, alive to all the "mighty world of ear and eye" ... but without that intenseness of passion, which, seeking to exaggerate whatever excites the feelings of pleasure or power in the mind, and moulding the impressions of natural objects according to the impulses of imagination, produces a genius and a taste for poetry' (iv. 176). Feeling, passion, or sensibility, in art as in moral action, guarantee the openness essential to the experiential response. Dogmas, creeds, and systems, by diminishing the 'tremulous sensibility', diminish the 'openness'. Feeling and only feeling, in Hazlitt's view, could capture the evanescent complexity of nature and art: 'In art, in taste, in life ... you decide from feeling, and not from reason' (viii. 31). The aesthetic judgement like the moral judgement was both rational and affective. Feeling directs thought: 'I say what I think: I think what I feel' (v. 175).[1]

More than any other age, the Romantic age emphasized the difference between experience which could be verbalized and experience which, although intensely felt, could only be articulated with difficulty. Hazlitt frequently drew attention to this and was praised by contemporaries for his ability, as a moral psychologist, to provide reasons for some of the more puzzling instances.[2] Nevertheless, he always insisted that rational explanation, once effected, could never legislate *a priori* with regard to our own responses. Rules are always posterior to the expression of feeling and are by their nature general and limiting. Feeling, on the other hand, and the expression of feeling, are infinite. We judge from feeling and not from rules because 'there is nothing like feeling *but* feeling' (xii. 335).[3] There are no rules for the expression of feeling in art because human feeling is infinitely complex and hypothetical.

---

[1] Cf. his criticism of Sheridan Knowles: 'His heart dictates to his head. ... He instinctively obeys the impulses of natural feeling, and produces a perfect work of art' (xi. 184).

[2] *Leigh Hunt's Dramatic Criticism, 1808–31*, ed. L. H. and C. W. Houtchens (New York, 1949), p. 168; [John Scott], *London Magazine*, II (1820), 636.

[3] Hazlitt's most important general statement of the relationship between feeling and reason is to be found in his long two-part essay, 'On Genius and Common Sense' (viii. 31–41, 42–50).

The poet is constantly concerned with 'new and unknown combinations' (viii. 42), with 'every variety of untried being' (iv. 23):

> We know the meaning of certain looks, and we feel how they modify one another in conjunction. But we cannot have a separate rule to judge of all their combinations in different degrees and circumstances, without foreseeing all those combinations, which is impossible.
>
> (viii. 40)

In the *Lectures on the English Poets* he compared the creative task of Shakespeare in this respect to that of the alchemist: 'In Shakspeare there is a continual composition and decomposition of its elements, a fermentation of every particle in the whole mass. . . . Till the experiment is tried, we do not know the result. . . . The passions are in a state of projection' (v. 51). Only feeling is sufficiently sensitive to support such a view of poetry, although without the sympathetic function of the imagination the conception of dramatic poetry which this particular passage embodies would not be possible. Feeling is necessary but is not by itself sufficient to sustain Hazlitt's conception either of dramatic poetry or of moral action. This can best be seen if we compare his views on the psychology of dramatic creation with his account of the psychology of moral action set out in the *Essay*. The terms of both are remarkably similar. The role of feeling in both is of the utmost importance.

According to John Stuart Mill 'the motive has nothing to do with the morality of the action, though much with the worth of the agent'.[4] In Hazlitt's view, on the other hand, and in the opinion of the majority of his contemporaries, sincerity or the good will was the essence of moral action. The early *Essay* had attempted to develop a psychology of moral action designed to confute psychological egoism and to show how sincerity or the absence of selfish motives was possible. If man were purely egoistic, then moral or right action was not possible. Psychological egoism excluded the possibility of moral action by excluding the possibility of impartiality. The openness guaranteed by feeling is circumscribed in such cases by an awareness of the external only as it affects the agent. Thus, in the *Essay*, he writes: 'The idea of self habitually clings to the mind of every man . . . deadening it's discriminating powers' (i. 3). The importance of imagination in his moral theory rests on its sympathetic function. Sympathy enables the agent to

---

[4] Mill, *Utilitarianism*, p. 17.

judge of a situation not only in relation to his own feelings but in relation to the feelings of others: 'This is the true imagination, to put yourself in the place of others, and to feel and speak for them' (xviii. 345). Only in this way can the agent, in judging or acting morally, be said to be sincere or disinterested. Imagination is correlative to sincerity or loss of self. The self is transcended in the contemplation of the action, and to judge or act according to first impressions—a favourite phrase of Hazlitt's—is to act and judge in accordance with the demands of the situation without reference to our own selfish purposes or preconceptions.

Hazlitt, unlike Coleridge, employed a single concept of imagination in his discussion of the moral and aesthetic aspects of the existential. In so doing he emphasized the importance in both spheres of feeling/passion and self-transcendence as necessary pre-requisites for the achievement of an experiential openness. In the sphere of morality this condition is termed moral sincerity. In the sphere of art it is an imaginative sincerity, the term 'imagina-tive' being synonymous with 'poetic' or 'aesthetic'. Imagination itself is the basis of both forms of sincerity. In the essay 'Madame Pasta and Mademoiselle Mars', in which he attempted to dis-criminate the relative merits of the two actresses, he wrote:

Madame Pasta thinks no more of the audience than Nina herself would. . . . She gives herself entirely up to the impression of the part, loses her power over herself . . . and is transformed into the very being she represents. She does not act the character—she *is* it, looks it, breathes it. She does not study for an effect, but strives to possess herself of the feeling which should dictate what she is to do. . . . The French leave *sincerity* out of their nature (not moral but imaginative sincerity).

(xii. 326, 328)[5]

This passage is important for several reasons. It is the only passage in which Hazlitt attempted to characterize the concept precisely as

[5] Cf. Hazlitt's criticism of the acting of Mrs. Siddons: 'Feeling is in fact the scale that weighs the truth of all original conceptions. When Mrs. Siddons played the part of Mrs. Beverley in the Gamester, and on Stukely's abrupt declaration of his unprincipled passion at the moment of her husband's imprisonment, threw into her face that noble succession of varying emotions, first seeming not to understand him, then, as her doubt is removed, rising into sudden indignation, then turning to pity, and ending in a burst of hysteric scorn and laughter, was this the effect of stratagem or forethought as a painter arranges a number of colours on his palette? No—but by placing herself amply in the situation of her heroine, and entering into all the circumstances, and feeling the dignity of insulted virtue and misfortune, that wonderful display of keen and high-wrought expressions burst from her involuntarily at the same moment' (xii. 298–9).

imaginative sincerity. By distinguishing it from moral sincerity he established a parallel between moral and poetic value and between moral action and poetic creation. By relating poetic openness to self-transcendence and sincerity of feeling he also drew attention to the crucial role played by feeling in his distrust of abstraction. Imaginative sincerity performs a function in his literary criticism analogous to Keats's concept of negative capability. Its significance extends far beyond his discussion of individual dramatic perform-ances and is central to an appreciation of his entire critical achieve-ment: 'The art of writing may be said to consist in thinking of nothing but one's subject' (xvi. 300).

Hazlitt nowhere alluded explicitly to the concept of sincerity as imaginative sincerity of feeling. Only on one occasion does he even refer to imaginative sincerity. He was content for the most part to commend a writer for his sincerity or to praise a work as being sincere. In using this abbreviated formulation he left himself open to serious misinterpretation. To praise or blame on the grounds of sincerity or lack of sincerity is in most cases a dubious critical practice that raises a number of important aesthetic issues. It is important, therefore, to appreciate that his use of the term does not conform to conventional usage. To interpret sincerity as it occurs in his critical writings as imaginative sincerity of feeling emphasizes this fact and helps to avoid irrelevant aesthetic objec-tions. In his general essays he frequently employed sincerity in its conventional sense to mean 'real', 'true', 'genuine', 'without pretence'. More often, however, it was used to indicate moral sincerity. In this sense it corresponds to Kant's good will and is synonymous with disinterestedness. As imaginative sincerity, the term signifies absence of the self, and is thus intimately related to the concept of gusto. Moral sincerity or disinterestedness relates to the agent's ability to divest himself of personal predilections and interests, to consider the situation in relation to others as well as to himself, and to remain open to all possible nuances of the situation. Imaginative sincerity, on the other hand, relates to poetic value. Its significance is experiential. A work of art which is sincere in this sense does not entail a correspondence between the work and the author's thoughts and sentiments. A work of art is sincere only if the writer has allowed his thoughts to evolve out of his feelings. Sincerity marks a relation between thought and feeling. To be sincere in this sense is to think what we feel. Thus, while a poet might be a sincere Christian and his poetry adequately reflect his religious beliefs and experience, he is not sincere in Hazlitt's sense of the word. He still lacks imaginative sincerity. Openness, self-transcendence, contemplation of the subject, judgement in accordance with first impressions, which are essential to his conception of sincerity, depend upon feeling directing thought.[6] In abstraction, philosophical and religious, the converse is true. Thought directs feeling. Feeling is distorted and the existential nature of man is falsified. Explicit scientific criteria are rejected, but are reintroduced in the form of non-natural facts. The openness of feeling is circumscribed by the intrusion of an element in a manner analogous to the intrusion of self-interest in the moral sphere. Hazlitt frequently refers to abstraction as a 'personal' intrusion. It acts as a barrier between the subject and the reader as well as the subject and the author, and sincerity as a consequence is lost.

Imaginative sincerity of feeling, gusto, and the distrust of abstraction represent so many facets of Hazlitt's experiential view of poetry. They give a unity to his criticism of English literature different from the unity of any of his contemporaries. This is most obvious in his criticism of contemporary literature where abstraction and hence insincerity were the chief characteristics of the spirit of the age. It is equally true, however, of his criticism of the poetry and drama of the past, where the emphasis on sincerity and gusto are to be found together. Thomson's *The Seasons*, for example, has the gusto appropriate to a poetry descriptive of natural scenery. But he also possesses imaginative sincerity: 'All that is admirable in the Seasons, is the emanation of a fine natural genius, and sincere love of his subject, unforced, unstudied, that comes uncalled for. . . . He puts his heart into his subject, [and] writes as he feels' (v. 86–7). The same is true of his criticism of Chaucer. The gusto of his poetry is matched by the poet's own sincerity of feeling: 'He does not affect to shew his power over the reader's mind, but the power which his subject has over his own. The readers of Chaucer's poetry feel more nearly what the persons he describes must have felt, than perhaps those of any other poet. . . . There is . . . a sincerity of feeling, which never relaxes' (v. 22). There is in both these

---

[6] Cf: 'Objects, on our first acquaintance with them, have that singleness and integrity of impression that it seems as if nothing could destroy or obliterate them, so firmly are they stamped and rivetted on the brain' (xvii. 196).

cases the same emphasis on the absence of self, the importance of the subject, and the primacy of feeling. His criticism of Milton on the other hand is markedly different. He admired the gusto of Milton's poetry (iv. 38, 79–80), but only in his discussion of the sonnets did he comment upon the poet's sincerity (viii. 176). Imaginative sincerity of feeling cannot be characteristic of a poet who was supremely a Christian-poet:

Shakspeare discovers in his writings little religious enthusiasm . . . he had none of the bigotry of his age. . . . In these respects, as well as in every other, he formed a direct contrast to Milton . . . [who] had his thoughts constantly fixed on the contemplation of the Hebrew theo-cracy . . . and he seized the pen with a hand just warm from the touch of the ark of faith. His religious zeal infused its character into his imagina-tion. . . . The spirit of the poet . . . and the prophet vied with each other in his breast.

(v. 56–7)[7]

His view of Milton did not change, and several years later, in the *Lec-tures on the Age of Elizabeth*, he could still say that 'in reading Milton's Comus, and most of his other works, we seem to be entering a lofty dome raised over our heads and ascending to the skies, and as if nature and every thing in it were but a temple and an image consecrated by the poet's art to the worship of virtue and pure religion' (vi. 256). Hazlitt's reservation in this passage is significant. He clearly did not accept Milton's Christian interpretation of human experience. The phrase 'as if' conveys at once his reluctance to disagree openly with a poet whom he admired as second only to Shakespeare, and his refusal to accept religious abstraction in poetry. The problem raised by the dissociation of sincerity and gusto in his discussion of Milton's poetry is considered later.

The muted nature of his objection to religious dogma in Milton helps to clarify his criticism of Spenser. The strategy in both cases is in some respects similar. He observed of the *Faerie Queene* and its critics that 'if they do not meddle with the allegory, the allegory will not meddle with them. . . . It might as well be pretended that, we cannot see Poussin's pictures for the allegory, as that the allegory prevents us from understanding Spenser' (v. 38). His regard for Spenser's poetry led him to couple his name with those of Chaucer,

---

[7] Cf. Wordsworth's view that the absence of religious sentiment constituted Shakespeare's greatest defect, *Prose Works*, II. 488.

Shakespeare, and Milton as the four greatest English poets. But like most of his contemporaries he disliked allegory. His problem was to reconcile his reverence of Spenser with his dislike of the allegorical mode, and this he did by denying the significance of the allegorical nature of the poem. Coleridge's attitude was similar: 'If the allegoric personage be strongly individualized so as to interest us, we cease to think of it as allegory; and if it does not interest us, it had better be away.'[8] They both viewed allegory as a form of translation. Allegory, according to Coleridge, was 'but a translation of abstract notions into a picture-language, which is itself nothing but an abstraction from objects of the senses; the principal being more worthless even than its phantom proxy, both alike unsubstantial, and the former shapeless to boot'.[9] Here the similarity ends. Coleridge rejected allegory in favour of symbol, preferring a complete instantiation of moral and religious truths in the individual or particular to a crude and imperfect translation. His objection to allegory was not that it conveyed truths but that it conveyed them badly. Hazlitt's objection to allegory, on the other hand, was not that it was an ineffectual mode of conveying truths poetically, but that it attempted to convey truths at all. His isomorphic conception of allegory was incompatible with his demand for imaginative sincerity. By minimizing the significance of the allegory, he avoided the necessity of criticizing the poem for its moral abstraction. He contented himself with the observation that Spenser was 'very apt to pry into mysteries which do not belong to the Muses' (iv. 110). He could not ignore the religious

---

[8] Coleridge, *Miscellaneous Criticism*, p. 31. Coleridge went on to say that 'the dullest and most defective parts of Spenser are those in which we are compelled to think of his agents as allegories . . . but in that admirable allegory, the first Part of *Pilgrim's Progress* . . . the interest is so great that [in] spite of all the writer's attempts to force the allegoric purpose on the reader's mind by his strange names . . . his piety was baffled by his genius, and the Bunyan of Parnassus had the better of Bunyan of the conventicle' (ibid.).

[9] Coleridge, *Works*, I. 437. Allegory for Coleridge is neither a poetry of statement nor a poetry of symbol. It is not ideal, but a half-way house—'the proper intermedium between person and personification', *Miscellaneous Criticism*, p. 32. The two elements are present, but their relation is not a unified one. Allegory operates on the basis of this disjunction and its perception by the reader. Consequently, it is inferior to symbol which is characterized 'by a translucence of the special in the individual, or of the general in the special . . . above all by the translucence of the eternal through and in the temporal. It always partakes of the reality which it renders intelligible', *Works*, I. 437. Whatever success Spenser or Bunyan may have in conveying their religious and moral views is the consequence not of the allegorical mode but of its transition into the symbolic.

abstraction in Milton's poetry, however much he chose to under-state it. In the case of Spenser, however, he could disengage from his own critical criteria by diminishing the relevance of an allegor-ical interpretation. The ambivalence of his reponse to the poetry of Spenser and Milton was never as explicit as Shelley's in his criticism of Milton and Dante: 'The distorted notions of invisible things which Dante and his rival Milton have idealised, are merely the mask and the mantle in which these great poets walk through eternity enveloped and disguised.'[10] Nevertheless, this ambivalence, vacillating between an admiration for the poetry and a muted criticism of the poet's attempt to subvert what Hazlitt considered to be the essence of poetry, is perhaps the most significant general feature of his criticisms of these two poets. To criticize the Roman-tics for misconceiving the nature of allegorical writing would be altogether too easy. What is important was their refusal to allow their appreciation to be circumscribed by such an inadequate con-ception. In this respect they prepared the way for the more fruitful new approaches to allegory characteristic of modern criticism.

Hazlitt's criticism of Spenser and Milton is unusual. In the majority of cases he was not prepared to compromise on the issue of abstraction. He was much more aggressive in his criticism of poets whose talents he did not estimate quite so highly. His criticism of Sidney and Donne is a good example of this. In dealing with a writer like Montaigne who did fulfil his experiential ideal of imaginative sincerity, he was equally uncompromising in his general but non-specific rejection of moral and religious ab-straction:

The great merit of Montaigne then was, that he may be said to have been the first who had the courage to say as an author what he felt as a man. . . . He had the power of looking at things for himself, or as they really were, instead of blindly trusting to . . . what others told him that they were. . . . In taking up his pen he did not set up for a philosopher, wit, orator, or moralist, but he became all these by merely daring to tell us whatever passed through his mind, in its naked simplicity and force. . . . He was neither a pedant nor a bigot. He neither supposed that he was bound to know all things, nor that all things were bound to conform to what he had fancied. . . . In treating of men and manners, he spoke of them as he found them, not according to preconceived notions and abstract dogmas. . . . In criticising books he did not compare them with

[10] Shelley, *Works*, VII. 129.

rules and systems. .... [He] wrote not to make converts of others to established creeds and prejudices, but to satisfy his own mind of the truth of things. .... There is an inexpressible frankness and sincerity, as well as power, in what he writes.

(vi. 92–3)[11]

The qualities which he attributes to Montaigne in this passage represent an ideal which Hazlitt himself strove constantly to achieve both as an essayist and critic. They are also qualities which, as far as he achieved them in his own writings, he associated with his experience of painting (viii. 10). His criticism of Montaigne is important for a number of reasons. Its open hostility to abstraction is entirely characteristic. The deference shown to Spenser and Milton in spite of their abstraction is thus exceptional. It also employs certain significant terms and phrases which are easily overlooked but which recur throughout his criticism. These serve to alert us on those occasions when he invokes the concept of imaginative sincerity without referring to it explicitly. They may appear trite and commonplace and to have little critical relevance. In Hazlitt's criticism, however, they derive additional resonance from their repeated use in certain significant contexts. The terms 'moralist', 'philosopher', 'bigot', 'pedant', 'orator', 'creed', 'abstract dogma', 'system', are not terms he used lightly. In the context of imaginative sincerity a moralist is one who 'almost unavoidably degenerates into the partisan of a system' (vi. 107). A philosopher, on the other hand, is 'too apt to warp the evidence to his own purpose' (ibid.). In most cases these remain as implications to be inferred by the reader. His criticism of Montaigne's sincerity is as important as his criticism of Burke's gusto. They represent differing but complementary aspects of his experiential response to the poetic.

His account of Sidney's *Arcadia* gives some indication of the way in which he attempted to fuse the concepts of gusto and sincerity and their respective vocabularies in a criticism of an abstraction which was neither moral nor religious but intellectual:

Out of five hundred folio pages, there are hardly, I conceive, half a dozen sentences expressed simply and directly, with the sincere desire to convey the image implied, and without a systematic interpolation of the

[11] Hazlitt's affinities with Montaigne are discussed by C. Dédéyan, 'Le Fils d'Alliance: William Hazlitt', in his *Montaigne dans le Romantisme Anglo-Saxon et ses Prolongements Victoriens* (Paris, [1946]), pp. 170–82.

wit, learning, ingenuity, wisdom ... so as to disguise the object, instead of displaying it in its true colours and real proportions. .... He writes a court-hand, with flourishes like a schoolmaster; his figures are wrought in chain-stitch. All his thoughts are forced and painful births, and may be said to be delivered by the Caesarean operation ... cramped and twisted and swaddled into lifelessness and deformity. .... [It] is spun with great labour out of the author's brains, and hangs like a huge cobweb over the face of nature! ... He must officiously and gratuitously interpose between you and the subject as the Cicerone of Nature.... The moving spring of his mind is not sensibility or imagination, but dry, literal, unceasing craving after intellectual excitement. ... [It is] an artificial excrescence transferred from logic and rhetoric to poetry.

(vi. 320–2)

He later criticized the same work as 'a riddle, a rebus, an acrostic in folio' (vi. 325), and elsewhere censured Sidney's sonnets for being 'more like riddles than sonnets' (viii. 175). By introducing allusions to 'riddles' and 'Caesarean births' Hazlitt was calling attention to the specifically intellectual nature of this particular deviation from his experiential ideal. His criticism of Donne and the metaphysical poets is very similar. In both cases, his concern for sincerity and gusto, although never explicitly referred to, gives rise to a terminology which is at once critical of abstraction in general and of intellectual abstraction in particular. It is against this background that his acceptance of Dr. Johnson's verdict on the Metaphysicals must be assessed. There is a superficial similarity between the views expressed by both critics. But the grounds of Hazlitt's adverse judgement and his terminology are radically different. The metaphysical poets, like Sidney, do not express 'the natural impression of things'. They 'distort the immediate feeling', 'twisting and torturing almost every subject ... to the mould of their self-opinion and the previous fabrications of their own fancy, like those who pen acrostics'. Many of their poems read 'like riddles or an allegory', and instead of being 'conversant with the face of nature ... [they were] lost in the labyrinths of intellectual abstraction' (vi. 49–51). His accusation that they distorted reality in due course elicits the image of the Caesarean birth: '[Donne's] Muse suffers continual pangs and throes. His thoughts are delivered by the Caesarean operation. The sentiments, profound and tender as they often are, are stifled in the expression; and "heaved pantingly forth", are "buried quick again" under the ruins and rubbish of analytical distinctions' (vi. 51). He preferred Cowley's prose to his poetry, characterizing the latter as a poetry of 'verbal generalities' (vi. 58).

His criticism of Cowley has little intrinsic importance. The criteria and terminology are the same as in his criticism of Montaigne, Sidney, and Donne. It does, however, possess a certain significance in relation to his sense of literary history. Cowley was the last of the poets prior to those of the late eighteenth and early nineteenth centuries whom he discussed in these terms. Thomson is an exception to this. With the poetry of the Augustans Hazlitt's criteria and terminology altered. The relevance of sincerity and gusto, designed to emphasize feeling and the dangers of abstraction, was greatly diminished. The reason for this is clear. Cowley's poetry marked the transition from a poetry of nature to one of artifice. However much he might criticize the element of artificiality in the poetry of Sidney, Jonson, Donne and Cowley, he always regarded them as part of the great natural tradition of Chaucer, Spenser, Shakespeare, and Milton. Their poetry was natural in the sense that 'the more ethereal, evanescent, more refined and sublime part of art is the seeing nature through the medium of sentiment and passion' (viii. 82–3). Sidney and Donne represented a falling-off from this tradition. Natural poetry in this sense, however, was not the whole of poetry, only the 'more refined and sublime part of art'. The poetry of Dryden and Pope was of a different kind, requiring different criteria. A poetry of artifice was not a poetry of feeling. Consequently, Hazlitt's experiential criteria, indissolubly linked to feeling, were largely inoperative. His criticism of Augustan prose is an altogether different matter. Sincerity and gusto still remain his major criteria. There is thus a continuity between his criticism of the prose of Montaigne, Sidney, and Burke, and the prose of Addison, Steele, Bolingbroke, Goldsmith, and Johnson.

Hazlitt's criticism of English drama follows a similar pattern in many respects. There are differences in emphasis; certain key words and phrases recur more frequently; imagination becomes much more important. Abstraction, however, remains his constant concern here as elsewhere. Imaginative sincerity of feeling, a concept first coined in the context of dramatic performance, assumes an even greater significance in his criticism of dramatic writing. His criticism of Steele's comedies gives some indication of the way in which it continued to dominate his critical thought:

It is almost a misnomer to call them comedies; they are rather homilies in dialogue, in which . . . [men] discuss the fashionable topics of gaming, of duelling, of seduction, of scandal, &c . . . [Real drama] translates morality from the language of theory into that of practice. But Steele, by introducing the artificial mechanism of morals on the stage, and making his characters act, not from individual motives and existing circumstances . . . but from vague topics and general rules . . . takes away from it its best grace, the grace of sincerity.

(vi. 156–7)

The abstraction to which he objected in Steele's comedies is one of commonplace moralism in which once again feeling, instead of directing thought, is directed and consequently distorted by thought. The remedy he proposed is entirely characteristic: 'The comic writer . . . ought to open the volume of nature and the world for his living materials, and not take them out of his ethical common-place book' (vi. 157). Steele's essays, unlike his comedies, had none of these deficiencies. But whether he was criticizing the comedies or praising the essays, Hazlitt's criterion in both cases was the same. He preferred the essays of Steele to those of Addison because they had 'more of the original spirit, more of the freshness and stamp of nature. The indications of character and strokes of humour are more true and frequent, the reflections that suggest themselves arise more from the occasion, and are less spun out into regular dissertations' (iv. 8).

In tracing the decline of English tragedy from the age of Elizabeth to the sentimental drama of domestic life in the eighteenth century, Hazlitt chose to criticize the plays of Beaumont and Fletcher as the first major departure from the great Elizabethan tradition: 'They thought less of their subject, and more of themselves. . . . With respect to most of the writers of this age, their subject was their master. . . . But Beaumont and Fletcher were the first who made a plaything of it, or a convenient vehicle for the display of their own powers' (vi. 248). By criticizing them in this way Hazlitt was in effect criticizing them for their insincerity, and at the same time attributing the decline of English drama to abstraction. This emerges quite clearly later in the same lecture, where he accuses them of 'swelling out ordinary and unmeaning topics to certain preconceived . . . standards' (vi. 251). In Shakespeare's plays, on the other hand, the characters and incidents have no appearance of premeditation: 'There is no set purpose, no

straining at a point' (iv. 233). Shakespeare the poet was more vulnerable than Shakespeare the dramatist. Hazlitt's only query about
his sincerity occurs in his criticism of the poetry: 'The author seems
all the time to be thinking of his verses, and not of his subject'
(iv. 358). In the plays themselves the sincerity of the dramatist is
evidenced by the unstudied, unforced, and unconscious naturalness,
as well as by the variety, complexity, and particularity which his
command over feeling entailed. The distinction which Hazlitt
drew between the characters of Shakespeare's plays and those of
Massinger's serves to make the same point. In Massinger 'the
passion is . . . wound up to its height at once. . . . It does not gradually arise out of previous circumstances, nor is it modified by other
passions. . . . Shakespear's characters act from mixed motives. . . .
Massinger's characters act from single motives. . . . [Massinger] endeavoured to embody an abstract principle' (vi. 269 n).[12] Ford's
plays by their 'naked declaration of passions' offended in another
and equally damaging way (vi. 268).

Hazlitt's approach to Restoration Comedy, which he considered
the golden age of comedy (vi. 68), and to the eighteenth-century
novel, conforms in the main to the same general pattern. In his
first essay in literary criticism in 1813 he cited the novelists and
dramatists in support of his contention that poetry was not philosophy, that there was a difference between 'laboured analysis' and
'intuitive perception', between 'general truth' and 'individual observation' (xx. 9). Wycherley, Congreve, Fielding, Richardson,
and Sterne are important to him because of their sincerity and
freedom from abstraction. If poetry is 'intuitive perception' then
they were poets: 'The beauty of these writers in general was, that
they gave every kind and gradation of character, and they did this,
because their portraits were taken from life. They were true to
nature, full of meaning, perfectly understood and executed in every
part. . . . They painted human nature as it was, and as they saw it
with individual character and circumstances, not human nature in
general, abstracted from time, place and circumstance' (xx. 7–8).

2. HAZLITT'S THEORY OF GENIUS

Sincerity of feeling performs a function in Hazlitt's poetic theory
analogous to its role in his moral theory. The analogy however is

[12] Hazlitt criticized the plays of Joanna Baillie as 'heresies in the dramatic art'
for their attempt to isolate a single overmastering passion (v. 147). For his praise
of Webster's variety, see *Works*, vi. 240.

not complete. He himself alluded to this when he chose to differentiate between imaginative or poetic sincerity and moral sincerity. In both spheres the imagination, operating on the basis of personal feeling, enables the poet or moral agent to transcend his own interests. But although there is a similarity in their mode of operation there is an important difference in their respective roles. Self-interest or insincerity in moral action necessarily precludes rightness. Poetic insincerity, on the other hand, does not preclude poetic value. Sincerity is not the sole test of poetic value in the work of art. Were this the case, Hazlitt's range of critical sympathies would be as limited and exclusive as the previous pages have perhaps tended to suggest. The emphasis on abstraction and sincerity in his practice as a critic is a necessary one, but it is not without its dangers. It focused attention on the close relationship between his critical theory and practice; it emphasized the unity and coherence of his criticism of English literature; it illustrated that abstraction was as important for his view of English literary history as the opposition between mechanism and dynamism was for Coleridge. Certain other factors however must be taken into account for this interpretation to reflect adequately the complexity of his critical achievement. The principal danger inherent in thus stressing the significance of imaginative sincerity is to convey an impression of Hazlitt as a rigid, unsympathetic, and exclusive critic. Such a view would be unfair as well as misleading. His experiential criteria are severe but they are not inflexible or incapable of modification. Their severity was tempered in a variety of ways. The most important of these was his theory of genius.

Hazlitt posited two kinds of genius. The first of these, protean or universal genius, is best exemplified by Shakespeare. A genius of this kind fully satisfied his demand for imaginative sincerity at the highest level of expression or dramatic gusto. Indeed, without sincerity, gusto as expression or dramatic morality is inconceivable. The notion of protean genius, however, has only a limited value as a tool of critical analysis. It is singularly unilluminating in approaching critically a literature which boasts few Shakespeares. Hazlitt's own view of criticism as the discrimination and appreciation of all kinds and degrees of poetic excellence fortunately prevented its indiscriminate application as a criterion of poetic value. His conception of the critic's role required a second, less protean, more exclusive form of genius. Shakespeare may have been 'the Proteus of human intellect', but 'genius in ordinary is a more obstinate and less versatile thing. It is sufficiently exclusive and self-willed, quaint and peculiar. It does some one thing by virtue of doing nothing else: it excels in some one pursuit by being blind to all excellence but its own' (viii. 42–3). His theory of genius therefore is in effect a theory of non-protean genius. In his development of it he relied heavily on his theory of abstract ideas. Viewing abstraction as a process of individuation rather than of generalization, he postulated an infinite divisibility of mind and matter that depended for its validity on a conception of the human mind as creative. He illustrated his view of abstraction by frequent references to painters and painting. Consequently, painting and the notion of creativity play an important part in his discussion of genius. This is best exemplified by his essay 'On Genius and Common Sense', in which he moves from a brief statement of the nature of abstract ideas to a discussion of genius that is elaborated in terms of painting:

> Nature has a thousand aspects, and one man can only draw out one of them. Whoever does this, is a man of genius. One displays her force, another her refinement, one her power of harmony, another her suddenness of contrast, one her beauty of form, another her splendour of colour. Each does that for which he is best fitted by his particular genius, that is to say, by some quality of mind in which the quality of the object sinks deepest.
>
> (viii. 47)

In another essay, 'The Outlines of Taste', the same elements are present in a discussion of abstract ideas, but the emphasis is correspondingly different: 'Nature contains an infinite variety of parts, with their relations and significations, and different artists take these, and altogether do not give the whole. Thus Titian coloured, Raphael designed, Rubens gave the florid hue and motions, Rembrandt *chiaro-scuro*, &c' (xx. 391). Hazlitt's theory of genius is the inevitable consequence of his theory of abstract ideas.

In developing his theory of abstract ideas Hazlitt constantly emphasized the complexity and variety of nature. To be true to nature was to be open or alive to this complexity and variety. Truth to nature was dependent upon feeling, for only feeling commanded the necessary openness. According to his theory of genius only the poet possessed the requisite 'organic sensibility'

(iv. 176) to appreciate and convey this truth. Genius, therefore, in so far as it related to the 'more refined and sublime part of art' was dependent upon feeling. When he describes genius as 'some quality of mind' answering to and bringing out a corresponding quality in nature, it is clear that he considered this quality to be essentially affective. In the essay 'On Genius and Common Sense' he developed this idea on an analogy with magnetism: 'The imagination gives out what it has first absorbed by congeniality of temperament, what it has attracted and moulded into itself by elective affinity, as the loadstone draws and impregnates iron' (viii. 47). In the same essay he discussed the genius of Rembrandt in terms of 'congeniality' and explicitly related it to feeling: 'He was led to adopt this style . . . from its congeniality to his own feelings. . . . Originality is then nothing but nature and feeling working in the mind. . . . His eye seemed to come in contact with [colour] as a feeling' (viii. 43). This raises a problem, however, for if feeling is exclusive how can it be open or non-exclusive? If abstraction restricts the poet's range of impressions, then genius likewise circumscribes his response to certain aspects of nature. Why isn't genius which is dependent upon exclusiveness of feeling treated as a form of genial abstraction? How can the exclusive genius ever achieve imaginative sincerity? To answer these questions is to grasp something of the way in which Hazlitt tempered the severity of his criterion of imaginative sincerity. Imaginative sincerity is of the greatest importance in his critical thought. But to estimate its significance correctly it must be seen in relation to his perception of kinds and varieties of gusto and genius. This can best be done by considering the relationship between sincerity of feeling and gusto.

Keats's remark that the mind should be 'a thoroughfare for all thoughts [and] not a select party'[13] helps to clarify the position. Like the concept of imaginative sincerity, Keats's observation appears to contradict Hazlitt's view of the exclusive, selective nature of genius. The conflict, however, is more apparent than real. His principal objection was not to the fact that the thoughts were limited in number but to the abstract principle operative in their selection. This becomes clearer when he writes later in the same passage: 'They never begin upon a subject they have not pre-resolved on.' The selection is determined by an ulterior purpose or 'palpable design' which in turn is related to personal theories or

13 Keats, *Letters*, II. 213.

systems of belief. Hazlitt's notion of protean genius fulfils Keats's demand for negative capability. As ideals, negative capability and imaginative sincerity have serious limitations. They are altogether too inflexible and monolithic for a practising critic engaged in discriminating the unique particularity and variety of individual works of art. To do justice to this uniqueness and variety, Hazlitt introduced the notion of poetic genius as exclusive. His theory marks an advance on Keats's position while remaining compatible with their mutual distrust of abstraction. The reason is that the selectivity or exclusiveness of the poet of genius is dependent upon feeling, not upon abstract thought. Thomson did not 'choose' to write a poetry descriptive of natural scenery any more than Rembrandt 'chose' to excel in chiaroscuro. The characteristic excellence of the painter or poet is determined by his genius. His exclusiveness is not 'selfish', for the feeling on which genius is dependent for its existence still governs thought. Feeling is still open or alive to impressions within the limited range established by the exclusive nature of his genius. The poetic genius is *susceptible* of a 'certain class of impressions, or of a certain kind of beauty or power; and this peculiar strength, congeniality, truth of imagination, or command over a certain part of nature, is ... genius' (xx. 299). The feeling responsible for the poet's exclusiveness is still operative to secure the most complete susceptibility compatible with the kind of gusto characteristic of his poetry.

According to Hazlitt's notion of genius, a lyric or dramatic poet will have much in common with other lyric or dramatic poets. Their poetry can be discussed in terms of the same kind of gusto. In addition, however, each poet possesses an individual, peculiar, or characteristic genius. Because of its dependence upon feeling, genius is related to gusto: 'Nature presents an endless variety of aspects, of which the mind seldom takes in more than a part or than one view at a time; and it is in seizing on this unexplored variety, and giving some one of these new but easily recognized features, in its characteristic essence, and according to the peculiar bent and force of the artist's genius, that true originality consists' (xx. 297). In this passage he is once again discussing genius in terms of painting. Since painting is essentially imitative, concerned with objects, gusto is interpreted in a very specific manner as a gusto of 'characteristic essence'. What is important is not the specific characterization of gusto, but the general relationship which is established between genius/feeling and gusto. The gusto of a work is dependent upon the intensity and not upon the sincerity of feeling. Abstraction distorts feeling. It need not, although it frequently does, diminish its intensity. Insincerity of feeling only precludes gusto at the highest level of dramatic gusto. But equally the sincerity of a Shakespeare may dissipate the intensity of feeling necessary to convey the 'characteristic essence' or gusto of objects. Milton's insincerity, on the other hand, does not prevent him 'grappling' with his subject and succeeding where sincere poets have failed (iv. 79).

The relationship between sincerity of feeling and gusto, therefore, is not a simple but a complex and variable one designed to reflect the complexity of his own response to the uniqueness and variety of poetic genius. Three factors are involved: sincerity, feeling, and gusto. The correctness or otherwise of the preceding analysis can best be tested against Hazlitt's criticism of individual poets. He censured Sidney, Donne, and Cowley for their intellectual abstraction. The terms of his criticism implied that their work was deficient in gusto. He did not deny them feeling. Donne's sentiments were 'profound and tender' (vi. 51). Sidney and Cowley had 'more truth and feeling' than 'a host of insipid and merely natural writers' (xvi. 43). It would appear from this that insincerity not only distorted the feeling, but diminished its intensity and thus impaired the gusto of their work.

His criticism of Milton affords another example of the variable nature of the relationship between sincerity of feeling and gusto. The genius of Milton, like that of Chaucer and Thomson, is an exclusive one. As natural poets the genius of all three was dependent upon feeling. Milton, however, lacked the imaginative sincerity characteristic of Chaucer and Thomson. His exclusiveness was the consequence of religious belief rather than of feeling. It is a 'selfish' or 'partisan' exclusiveness in which abstract thought dictated the area within which Milton excelled as a poet. Unlike the intellectual abstraction of the metaphysical poets, Milton's preoccupation with religion did not impair the intensity of feeling. Feeling is distorted by thought, but its intensity is enhanced. Consequently, Milton's gusto is a constant theme of Hazlitt's criticism of the poetry. Religious abstraction relates to the ontological status of the poetic object, not to the poet's ability to convey his sense of that object. By remarking of his poetry that it was 'as if nature . . . were but a temple . . . consecrated by the poet's art to the worship of . . .

pure religion', Hazlitt was indicating his disapproval of the distortion of feeling resulting from Milton's religious zeal, while at the same time recognizing that his very intensity of feeling was dependent on the abstraction to which he was objecting. He recognized that Milton's poetry and religion could not be dissociated. For the purposes of his criticism however he chose like Shelley to distinguish between them, and to emphasize the intensity and gusto rather than the distortion and abstraction, the poetry rather than the theology.

His criticism of Sidney, Donne, and Milton illustrates two of the more important ways in which he was prepared to vary the relationship between sincerity, feeling, and gusto. A third and equally important formulation is to be found in his criticism of Rousseau and Wordsworth. Hazlitt greatly admired both writers. Rousseau was 'the father of sentiment' (xvii. 133), while Wordsworth opened a 'finer and deeper vein of thought and feeling than any poet in modern times' (v. 156). Both owed their power to 'sentiment': 'We see no other difference between them, than that the one wrote in prose and the other in poetry' (iv. 92). The precise nature of their affinity is established once again in terms of feeling and sincerity. Both were egotists. Neither possessed imaginative sincerity. They confirmed his view that 'the personal interest may in some cases oppress and circumscribe the imaginative faculty' (viii. 42). The egotism of Wordsworth and Rousseau performed a similar function to Milton's religious enthusiasm, giving to their work its special character which Hazlitt termed 'sentiment': 'Both create an interest out of nothing, or rather out of their own feelings; both weave numberless recollections into one sentiment; both wind their own being round whatever object occurs to them' (iv. 92). Their gusto is a gusto of sentiment where the poet's feeling is turned inward upon itself and 'the heart reposes almost entirely upon itself' (iv. 331). Intensity of feeling is less important. Sentiment is more a brooding pressure or habitual working of some one self-involuted but powerful feeling.

The parallel with Milton is instructive in another way. The work of every good poet has its own characteristic gusto. In many cases however Hazlitt also tended to assimilate a poet's gusto to its general 'kind'. Thomson's gusto, for example, is the gusto of a poetry descriptive of natural scenery. In his discussion of *The Seasons* this generality was further emphasized by a critical vocabulary which invoked the correlative gusto of landscape painting. Fleeting references to individual painters in such instances only serve to reinforce the idea of a 'kind' of gusto. His criticism of Wordsworth and Milton is an exception to this. Their originality is such that he could not assimilate the gusto of their poetry to a more general gusto without distorting his perception of their uniqueness. Milton's epic gusto was Miltonic, Wordsworth's gusto of sentiment Wordsworthian. Hazlitt's criticism concentrated almost exclusively on this individuality. Consequently, his comparisons are not general but particular. He invoked the names of specific writers and painters to illustrate his analysis. The gusto of Wordsworth's poetry is said to have affinities with that of Rousseau's prose or Rembrandt's paintings: '[Wordsworth's] eye also does justice to Rembrandt's fine and masterly effects. In the way in which that artist works something out of nothing, and transforms the stump of a tree, a common figure into an *ideal* object, by the gorgeous light and shade thrown upon it, he perceives an analogy to his own mode of investing the minute details of nature with an atmosphere of sentiment' (xi. 93). Poussin and Dante perform a similar function in his criticism of Milton. Dante is the 'only one of the moderns with whom he has anything in common' (iv. 37).

In view of Hazlitt's admiration of Boccaccio's power of sentiment—'he carried sentiment of every kind to its very highest purity and perfection' (iv. 331)—it may seem surprising that he nowhere alluded to him in his criticism of Wordsworth and Rousseau. The reason is that in Boccaccio the relationship between gusto, sincerity, and feeling, is of an entirely different kind. Although Hazlitt invariably praised him in terms of sentiment, Boccaccio was also characterized by imaginative sincerity. He was always in 'full possession of his subject' (iv. 162). The sentiment of Wordsworth and Rousseau is self-involved. Boccaccio's on the other hand is not his own. The gusto of his stories is the result of his ability to dramatize the sentiment of others. It is not so much a power *of* sentiment as a power *over* sentiment.

However rigorously Hazlitt applied the concept of imaginative sincerity in his attempt to detect and eradicate all forms of abstraction in poetry, it was never employed quite as inflexibly as the corresponding concept of moral sincerity. He had two principal aims as a critic: the first was to isolate and characterize the 'peculiar', 'original', or 'characteristic' nature of the work of art in relation to the strength and weakness of the poet's individual genius;[14] the second was to discriminate kinds and degrees of poetic excellence. It was never his intention merely to exhibit the variety of ways in which individual poets failed to measure up to his own conception of poetry. The importance of his views on genius is twofold. They emphasize once again the significance he attributed to feeling. They are also the theoretical foundation of a critical response to literature of the most catholic and flexible kind.

3. THE POWER AND THE IMPOTENCE

Hazlitt's critical theory accommodated the exclusiveness of poetic genius without much difficulty. Egotism, vanity, artificiality, convention, abstraction even, were reconciled in a theory which attempted to discriminate all kinds and degrees of poetic excellence. One form of exclusiveness he was not prepared to accept, however, was a one-sided emphasis on human pain and suffering. Writers of this kind in Hazlitt's view were incapable of expressing adequately even the limited range of experience to which they were confined by the nature of their genius. Poetic openness is circumscribed by their pessimism as well as by their exclusiveness. The sincere poet must acknowledge the power as well as the impotence of man:

> The philosopher in painting the dark side of human nature may have reason on his side, and a moral lesson or remedy in view. The tragic poet, who shows the sad vicissitudes of things and the disappointments of the passions, at least strengthens our yearnings after imaginary good. . . . But Mr. Crabbe does neither. He gives us discoloured paintings of life; helpless, repining, unprofitable, unedifying distress. . . . Nor does he give us the *pros* and *cons* of . . . Nature. . . . He does not weave the web of their lives of a mingled yarn, good and ill together. . . . He blocks out all possibility of good, cancels the hope . . . disables all his adversary's white pieces, and leaves none but black ones on the board.
>
> (xi. 167)

Crabbe's emphasis on human misery and degradation is clearly a form of abstraction. What concerned Hazlitt in his criticism of Crabbe, Jonson, Butler, Defoe, and Dr. Johnson was less the fact of abstraction and more the precise nature of the view of human life which it expressed. His criticism utilized not only poetic but moral

[14] For examples of his emphasis on the 'peculiar', 'characteristic', and 'original' features of a writer's work, see *Works*, iv. 172, 227, 284, 294; v. 47, 79, 106, 111; vi. 34, 39, 71, 120, 123, 209, 214, 267 n, 270, 326; vii. 245, 302; ix. 48, 234, 243; xi. 96, 131, 177; xii. 226; xvi. 64, 65, 138, 403; xix. 96; xx. 39.

criteria. In denying them truth to nature he was compelled to justify himself by relating his denial to his own conception of the *summum bonum*. It is against the background of his view of sentiment (outlined in Chapter II) that we must assess his criticism of these writers. The close relationship between his moral and poetic theories is more explicit here than anywhere else in his writings.

Life for Hazlitt was a 'splendid boon' (xvii. 191), a precious gift to be cherished by man: 'Life is indeed a strange gift, and its privileges are most miraculous' (ibid.). It was not an unmixed blessing, however, and even in the midst of a rhapsody on the wonders of living in the essay 'On the Feeling of Immortality in Youth', he remained aware of the disappointments and distresses of life: 'To see the golden sun and the azure sky, the outstretched ocean, to walk upon the green earth . . . to feel heat and cold, pleasure and pain, right and wrong, truth and falsehood . . . to be and to do all this, and then in a moment to be nothing' (xvii. 192–3). The duality of life, its mixture of good and evil, pleasure and pain, corresponded to the dual nature of man himself. Hence his frequent use of the quotation, 'The web of our life is of a mingled yarn, good and ill together'. The egoistic theories of Hobbes, Mandeville, Rochefoucauld, and Helvétius ignored the complexity of human life and human motivation. Man was not purely selfish. Human nature was not and could not be wholly evil. What Hazlitt did was to insist that, however exclusive a poet's genius might be, whatever limited range of impressions he was susceptible of, his poetry must acknowledge this complexity. His own essays fulfilled this demand perfectly. They criticize and embody certain values. They are at once destructive and constructive, satirical and creative. As Leigh Hunt wrote: 'His regard for human nature, and his power to love truth and loveliness in their humblest shapes, survived his subtlest detections of human pride and folly.'[15]

Hazlitt preferred a work of art which conferred dignity upon human nature to one which degraded it (ix. 198). The representation of brutality and coarseness, he argued, was less desirable than the representation of the opposite qualities (xx. 275). This did not entail support for what he contemptuously referred to as '*do-me-good*' or '*baby-house*' poetry (v. 147). He strongly supported Lamb's criticism of 'the insipid levelling morality' of the contemporary theatre.[16] His criticism of Crabbe therefore was not an

---

[15] Hunt, *Literary Criticism*, p. 277.   [16] Quoted by Hazlitt (xviii. 213).

attempt to legislate an area of human experience out of existence. What he required was that evil and suffering be somehow rendered meaningful in terms of human experience. This point emerges clearly in his comparison of the suffering endured by Crabbe's characters and the sufferings of the tragic hero. The comparison here with tragedy is not fortuitous. The attraction of tragedy for Hazlitt lay in its ability to 'resolve the sense of pain or suffering into the sense of *power*' (xx. 274). Tragedy was an expression of man's power as well as of his impotence. He is not judging Crabbe by the standards of tragedy. Tragedy merely illustrates one of the ways in which evil and suffering can be rendered meaningful:

> Tragic poetry . . . loses the sense of present suffering . . . exhausts the terror or pity . . . [and] lifts us from the depths of woe to the highest contemplations on human life. . . . In proportion as it sharpens the edge of calamity and disappointment, it strengthens the desire of good. It enhances our consciousness of the blessing. . . . The keenness of immediate suffering only gives us a more intense aspiration after, and a more intimate participation with the antagonist world of good.
>
> (v. 5–6)

Matthew Arnold faced the same problem later in the century when he attempted to justify the omission of 'Empedocles on Etna' from the *Poems* of 1853. He too saw the significance of tragedy in this context: 'In presence of the most tragic circumstances, represented in a work of art, the feeling of enjoyment, as is well known, may still subsist; the representation of the most utter calamity, of the liveliest anguish, is not sufficient to destroy it; the more tragic the situation, the deeper becomes the enjoyment.' His criticism of 'Empedocles on Etna' is substantially the same as Hazlitt's criticism of Crabbe's poetry as one of 'helpless, repining, unprofitable, unedifying distress'. Arnold saw his early poem as one 'in which a continuous state of mental distress is prolonged, unrelieved by incident, hope, or resistance; in which there is everything to be endured, nothing to be done'.[17] Crabbe's poetry did not express the dual nature of man and life. It neglected the duality in favour of a biased emphasis in favour of human pain and suffering.

[17] Arnold, *Prose Works*, I. 2–3. Cf. Hazlitt's criticism of O'Neill in the role of Elwina in Hannah More's *Percy*: 'We did not approve of her dying scene at all. It was a mere convulsive struggle for breath . . . one of those agonies of human nature, which, as they do not appeal to the imagination, should not certainly be obtruded on the senses' (v. 258). See also his criticism of *Roderick Random* (vi. 116).

Hazlitt's dislike of his poetry was further aggravated by his conviction that the poet was not only guilty but guilty with malice prepense. The element of imaginative sincerity is still operative even although the major emphasis lies elsewhere.

His criticism of this allegedly distorted view of human life was not confined to Crabbe's poetry. Crabbe was a particularly good example from Hazlitt's point of view. He was not only a popular contemporary poet but one whom the *Edinburgh Review* had defended from the common complaint that he had 'represented human nature under too unfavourable an aspect'.[18] By criticizing Crabbe at length in this way in lectures and articles,[19] Hazlitt was taking advantage of a controversial issue of topical interest in order to make his own position clear. His criticism of eighteenth-century domestic tragedy is very similar to his criticism of Crabbe. The comparison with tragedy is more appropriate in a discussion of the dramas of Moore and Lillo, but its function is the same here as elsewhere: 'The tragedies of Moore and Lillo ... however affecting at the time, oppress and lie like a dead weight upon the mind, a load of misery which it is unable to throw off: the tragedy of Shakespeare ... stirs our inmost affections; abstracts evil from itself ... and rouses the whole man within us' (v. 6). When he has Northcote say that we prefer *Paradise Lost* to *Hudibras* because it raises our idea of human worth and dignity (xi. 201), he was deliberately overstating his own position. Nevertheless, *Hudibras* was in Hazlitt's view a classic example of the one-sided view of human nature: 'The vulgarity and meanness of sentiment which Butler complains of in the Presbyterians, seems at last from long familiarity and close contemplation to have tainted his own mind. Their worst vices appear to have taken root in his imagination. Nothing but what was selfish and groveling sunk into his memory.... He has, indeed, carried his private grudge too far into his general speculations' (vi. 66). The poem's inadequacy in this respect reflects the poet's own inadequate response to life.

This criterion plays an important part in determining Hazlitt's critical likes and dislikes. Northcote praised the novels of Cervantes,

---

[18] *Edinburgh Review*, XVI (1810), 36.

[19] *Works*, v. 96–8; x. 200; xix. 51–62. Views similar to Hazlitt's were expressed by Wordsworth, *The Critical Opinions of William Wordsworth*, ed. M. L. Peacock (Baltimore, 1950), pp. 235–7, and Crabb Robinson, *On Books and their Writers*, I. 150, 234. See also Coleridge's complaint that 'there is an absolute defect of the high imagination; he gives me little or no pleasure', *Miscellaneous Criticism*, p. 433.

Richardson, and Scott because they had 'raised the idea of human nature' (xi. 280). Hazlitt did not disagree, for in spite of the critical naïveté of the observation it calls attention to an important element in his own criticism not only of Cervantes and Scott, but of Le Sage, Fielding, Sterne, Smollett, and Goldsmith. His affection for characters like Don Quixote, Sir Roger de Coverley, Parson Adams, Uncle Toby, Dr. Primrose, and John Buncle indicates an appreciation of comedy far removed from the theories of Aristotle and Hobbes. Defoe's novels, on the other hand, simplified and distorted the complexity of life by overemphasizing one element. This distortion he attributes to the novelist's Puritanism:

> According to our author's overstrained Puritanical notions, there were but two choices, God or the Devil—Sinners and Saints. . . . All Defoe's characters . . . are of the worst and lowest description—the refuse of the prisons and the stews—thieves, prostitutes, vagabonds, and pirates. . . . There is no sentiment, no atmosphere of imagination, no 'purple light' thrown round virtue or vice;—all is either physical grati-fication on the one hand, or a selfish calculation of consequences on the other.
>
> (xvi. 388–9)

His criticism of Defoe is like his criticism of Butler. Neither did justice to nature. Yet where they failed, Gay, with the same materials, succeeded. Hazlitt's objections to *Hudibras* and *Moll Flanders* are in no way comparable to the eighteenth century's dis-like of 'low' or 'vulgar' subjects. He was not attempting to erect a subject approach to poetry. His criteria are not extra-literary. His critical position is not determined by pressures from a latent moralism, but by his emphasis on sincerity, truth to nature, and sensibility.

His criticism of *The Beggar's Opera* is important in this respect, revealing as it does that his objection is not aimed at legislating 'thieves, prostitutes, vagabonds and pirates' out of poetry. In Gay's work 'the scenes, characters, and incidents are, in themselves, of the lowest and most disgusting kind: but, by the sentiments and reflections . . . Gay has turned the tables on the critics; and . . . has enabled himself to *do justice to nature*, that is, to give all the force, truth, and locality of real feeling to the thoughts and expressions' (v. 107). *The Beggar's Opera* fulfilled his demand that the evil must be seen in relation to the good. It confirmed his belief that ' "There

is some soul of goodness in things evil" ' (v, 108). Swift also succeeded where Crabbe and Butler had failed. Hazlitt's preoccupation
with certain fundamental human values did not blind him to the
subtleties of Swiftian irony. Alone of the Romantic critics he
refused to accept Jeffrey's view that 'in all his writings . . . there is
nothing to raise or exalt our notions of human nature,—but every
thing to vilify and degrade'.[20] Swift, unlike Crabbe, distorts and
overemphasizes for a satirical purpose: 'I cannot see the harm, the
misanthropy, the immoral and degrading tendency of this. The
moral lesson is as fine as the intellectual exhibition is amusing. . . .
It is, indeed, the way with our quacks in morality to preach up the
dignity of human nature . . . but it was not Swift's way to cant
morality, or any thing else' (v. 111). He could find no extenuating
circumstances for Johnson's *Rasselas* which he condemned sum-
marily as 'the most melancholy and debilitating moral speculation
that ever was put forth' (vi. 102).

Hazlitt's insistence that 'the web of our life is of a mingled yarn,
good and ill together', is of the greatest consequence in the appreciation of his work as an essayist and critic. Too often the emphasis
(even during his own lifetime) has been placed on his antipathies,
his scorn, anger, malevolence, and misanthropy. Crabb Robinson,
who confessed that he read almost everything of Hazlitt's with
enjoyment, could still compare him unfavourably with Leigh
Hunt: 'Hunt seems, the very opposite of Hazlitt, to love everything. He catches the sunny side of everything, and . . . finds everything beautiful.'[21] The *Quarterly Review* criticized him for his
dominantly satirical vein,[22] and De Quincey on the evidence of his
essays accused him of an ignoble misanthropy.[23] In his reply to the
Quarterly Hazlitt drew attention to the duality in his essays: 'You
reproach me with the cynical turn of many of my Essays, which are
in fact prose-satires; but when you say I hate every thing . . . you
forget what you had before said that I was a great imitator of
Addison, and wrote much about "poetry and painting, and music
and *gusto*". You make no mention of my character of Rousseau,

[20] *Edinburgh Review*, XXVII (1816), 45. Cf. Hazlitt's criticism of Swift with the
unfavourable views of Coleridge, *Miscellaneous Criticism*, pp. 128–30; De Quincey,
Collected Writings, XI. 14; Hunt, L. Landré, *Leigh Hunt: Contribution à l'Histoire du
Romantisme Anglais* (Paris, 1935–6), II. 713.

[21] *H. C. Robinson on Books and their Writers*, I. 255.

[22] *Quarterly Review*, XVII (1817), 158.

[23] *New Essays by De Quincey*, ed. S. M. Tave (Princeton, 1966), p. 193.

or of the paper on Actors and Acting. You also forget my praise of John Buncle!' (ix. 30).[24] He might almost have been replying to De Quincey when he wrote that 'true misanthropy consists not in pointing out the faults and follies of men, but in encouraging them in the pursuit. They who wish well to their fellow-creatures are angry at their vices and sore at their mishaps' (xx. 339).

[24] Hunt drew attention to the apparent discrepancy between the satirical spirit of many of Hazlitt's essays and his enthusiastic regard for certain fictional characters (iv. 366, n. 9).

CHAPTER EIGHT

The Critical Perception

> The 'thing itself' with which one is here dealing,—the
> critical perception of poetic truth,—is of all things the
> most volatile, elusive, and evanescent; by even pres-
> sing too impetuously after it, one runs the risk of
> losing it. The critic of poetry should have the finest
> tact, the nicest moderation, the most free, flexible, and
> elastic spirit imaginable; he should be indeed the
> 'ondoyant et divers', the *undulating and diverse* being of
> Montaigne.
>
> ARNOLD, *On Translating Homer*[1]

WHILE Hazlitt was prepared to accommodate and even to welcome exclusiveness in the poet as the inevitable outcome of 'genius
in ordinary', he was unwilling to extend the same privilege to the
critic of poetry. The gravest threat to the intellectual and imaginative life of the early nineteenth century was not the predominance
of an empirical philosophy. The growth of empiricism was only
one aspect of a more serious and complex issue. The besetting sin
of the English mind was its exclusiveness. Many of the essays deal
in one way or another with the diverse contemporary manifestations of this exclusive spirit. One of the spheres in which Hazlitt
was determined it should not flourish was in the field of literary
criticism.[2] His rejection of the exclusive mind—of sects, parties,
creeds, systems, and dogmas—anticipates some of the major
emphases in the writings of Matthew Arnold. But whereas Arnold
sought to break down the opposition of the Victorian middle-
classes to a free play of ideas by cultivating a style designed to
charm and persuade,[3] Hazlitt in advocating an affective openness

---

[1] Arnold, *Prose Works*, I. 174.

[2] The most important of Hazlitt's essays on the subject of criticism are, 'On
Criticism' (viii. 214–26), 'Thoughts on Taste' (xvii. 57–66), and 'The Exclusionists
in Taste' (xx. 262–3).

[3] *Letters of Matthew Arnold, 1848–1888*, ed. G. W. E. Russell (London, 1895),
I. 201.

could seldom conceal his irritation and sense of grievance. In some essays, 'On People with One Idea', 'On People of Sense', 'On the Jealousy and the Spleen of Party', 'On Public Opinion', 'The Exclusionists in Taste', 'Sects and Parties', and 'Our National Theatres',[4] the overall impression is of an essayist writing against the grain of his audience.

Hazlitt's view of the function of criticism is the logical outcome of his view of art. In his criticism of *The Excursion* he complained of the absence in the later Wordsworth of that 'frankness and sincerity of opinion, which is a paramount obligation in all questions of intellect' (iv. 116). He exacted the same demand of the literary critic. The critic is always protean, never exclusive. The protean/exclusive distinction in poetry does not extend to the criticism of poetry. Few poets could measure up to his conception of protean genius, and in so far as their own poetry was concerned he did not expect them to do so. As a result, however, the exclusive poet, who 'excels in some one pursuit by being blind to all excellence but its own', is seldom the best critic of poetry. The limitations imposed on the critical sensibility by the exclusive cast of his genius disqualified him as a critic who must by definition be 'open to the general impressions of things' and not blind to them: 'Men of the greatest genius and originality are not always persons of the most liberal and unprejudiced taste; they have a strong bias to certain qualities themselves, are for reducing others to their own standard, and lie less open to the general impressions of things. This exclusive preference of their own peculiar excellencies to those of others . . . may sometimes be seen mounting up to a degree of bigotry and intolerance, little short of insanity' (xvii. 65).[5] In addition, the poet or artist was too often immersed in the technical minutiae of his art to make a good critic (iv. 76). Sincerity and openness, therefore, assume an even greater importance in his discussion of literary criticism. Critical exclusiveness has none of the redeeming features of poetic exclusiveness and is viewed strictly as a form of abstraction. Whereas the exclusive poet is often a great poet, the exclusive critic is a contradiction in terms. Hazlitt, for example, could appreciate the critical powers of Lamb, but was compelled to criticize the exclusiveness that circumscribed the range of his

---

[4] *Works*, viii. 59–69; xii. 242–52, 365–82; xvii. 303–8; xx. 262–3, 264–7, 287–8.

[5] Similar views are to be found elsewhere in his writings, *Works*, iv. 175–6; viii. 224; xii. 101–2.

sympathies and limited the value of his achievement. The exclusiveness of Wordsworth or Thomson, however, he accepted as an inescapable fact. In criticizing the critic Hazlitt returned to the vocabulary of protean genius. The critic's greatest virtues are his sincerity, disinterestedness, humility, and humanity; his openness, universality, catholicity, and liberality.[6]

Hazlitt reviewed Schlegel's *Course of Lectures on Dramatic Art and Literature* for the *Edinburgh Review* in 1815. One of the passages to which he drew his readers' attention was the German critic's description of the ideal critic:

> No man can be a true critic or connoisseur, who does not possess a universality of mind,—who does not possess that flexibility which, throwing aside all personal predilections and blind habits, enables him to transport himself into the peculiarities of other ages and nations,—to feel them as it were from their proper and central point,—and to recognize and respect whatever is beautiful and grand.
>
> (Quoted by Hazlitt, xvi. 59)

The similarity between this and Hazlitt's view of the critic's function is striking. Both emphasize the same qualities: universality, flexibility, freedom from prejudices and theories, and the ability to transcend the self in the contemplation of the work. In Hazlitt's writings these general critical ideals are given particular significance and individual resonance by their relation to the concept of imaginative sincerity of feeling and the theory of abstract ideas. They can be achieved only by the critic who says what he thinks, and thinks what he feels, who has endeavoured 'to feel what was good, and to "give a reason for the faith that was in [him]" ' (vi. 302), whose imagination while operative on the basis of personal feeling is not circumscribed in any way. The critic in this respect is like the actor. The actor does not analyse his role in terms of rules and formulae. Instead, he grasps the central feeling behind the character that alone determines the weight to be given to particular aspects of its portrayal. Like the actor, the critic must eliminate the personal in grasping the dominant feeling of the work as a whole. The critic and moralist are akin to the poet in this respect, for the critical judgement like the moral judgement is an 'intuitive perception' of the feelings or heart. Unlike the majority of poets, however, they must make their judgements, moral and aesthetic, in a manner that takes account of the whole of human experience:

---

[6] *Works*, viii. 223–5; xi. 115; xvi. 164, 223; xx. 270, 284.

'Taste is the highest degree of sensibility, or the impression made on . . . minds, as genius is the result of the highest powers both of feeling and invention' (xvii. 47–8). The critic must be able to judge not just one kind but all kinds and degrees of poetic excellence. The poet is master of some one aspect of nature. The greater the gusto in expressing this, the greater the poetry. The task of the critic is threefold: first, to isolate the peculiar quality that constitutes the poetic genius of individual poets, and to convey his sense of its uniqueness; to relate this quality and its characteristic gusto, wherever possible and however tenuously, to similar qualities in the work of other poets; and finally, to estimate its value relative to other poetic achievements of a similar nature. Taste, according to Hazlitt, is 'nothing but sensibility to the different degrees and kinds of excellence in the works of art or nature. . . . I would . . . estimate every one's pretensions to taste by the degree of their sensibility to the highest and most various excellence' (xvii. 57, 61).

Hazlitt refused to modify the severity of his experiential criteria in his discussion of the function of criticism. The critic, therefore, unlike the poet, has two difficulties to overcome. He must not only avoid the abstraction of systems, rules, theories and the like, in which thought controls feeling; he must also avoid the abstraction resulting from his sensitivity to one particular kind of poetic excellence. His critical responsiveness to certain aspects of poetry must not legislate his response to others. He must remain open to the truth of nature expressed in the work of art whatever its kind or degree. He is 'open to all impressions alike'. A critic whose reliance on feeling is circumscribed by personal idiosyncrasy and egotism is only slightly less blameworthy than one who relies on rules.

The emphasis on feeling represents only one aspect of his hostility to the exclusive critic. His theory of abstract ideas plays an equally important part and, as in his conception of poetry, is intimately related to the affective emphasis. In criticism, as in poetry, there is no limit to the infinite variety of impressions. It is not that there is 'some one thing in the world which we have found out to be good, and that mankind are fools for admiring anything else, but that there is an endless variety of excellence nearly equal in different ways, if we had but the sense and spirit to enter properly into it' (xx. 263). He is not criticizing the utility of comparative evaluation in literary criticism, but is objecting instead to the exclusive critic's misapplication of the comparative method. Comparisons are too often used to establish a 'dogmatic or bigoted standard of taste, like a formula of faith' (xx. 386). In the hands of the exclusive critic, comparisons become the instruments of abstraction designed to diminish the complexity and variety of experience. Their function is exclusive rather than differential or relational: 'Comparisons are odious, because they reduce every one to a standard he ought not to be tried by, or leave us in possession only of those claims which we can set up, to the entire exclusion of others' (ix. 201). Hazlitt himself frequently used comparisons to elicit the essential difference between two poets, two poems, or two characters in a play. It is a vital critical tool in the discrimination of kinds and degrees of poetic excellence. Confronted by the early nineteenth century's revulsion from the classicism of the eighteenth century, he found ample opportunity to reaffirm this principle of his critical faith. He did not share Mr. Crotchet's naïve belief that a victory for classicism or romanticism was possible or even desirable: 'Both are founded in essential and indestructible principles of human nature. We may prefer the one to the other, as we chuse, but to set up an arbitrary and bigotted standard of excellence in consequence of this preference, and to exclude either one or the other from poetry or art, is to deny the existence of the first principles of the human mind' (vi. 348).[7]

Hazlitt criticized the critics with the same criteria that he employed in his criticism of the poets, novelists, and dramatists. There are two significant differences however. First, he applied them with greater rigour. He refused to acknowledge the validity of an exclusive critical sensibility. Secondly, feeling or critical responsiveness is more important than the ability to articulate reasons for one's critical faith. He had a greater respect for the critic who felt more than he could say than for the critic who, circumscribed in his feelings, could say all that he felt. He set a high value on the critic's powers of expression except where this was achieved at the expense of feeling:

A man may be dextrous and able in explaining the grounds of his opinions, and yet may be a mere sophist, because he only sees one half

---

[7] Peacock, *Crotchet Castle*, Chapter II: 'The sentimental against the rational, the intuitive against the inductive, the ornamental against the useful, the intense against the tranquil, the romantic against the classical; these are great and interesting controversies, which I should like, before I die, to see satisfactorily settled.'

of a subject. Another may feel the whole weight of a question, nothing
relating to it may be lost upon him, and yet he may be able to give no
account of the manner in which it affects him, or to drag his reasons
from their silent lurking-places. . . . Goldsmith was a fool to Dr. Johnson
in argument; that is, in assigning the specific grounds of his opinions:
Dr. Johnson was a fool to Goldsmith in the fine tact, the airy, intuitive
faculty with which he skimmed the surfaces of things.

(viii. 31–2)

He preferred Steele's criticism to Addison's for similar reasons. The
significance which he attached to critical sensitivity led him to
choose the little-known Joseph Fawcett as the embodiment of his
critical ideal. Fawcett, a Unitarian clergyman and friend of his
youth and early manhood, published no works of literary criticism.
Yet Hazlitt chose him in preference to Dryden, Addison, or Johnson, to convey his sense of the critic's function. His eulogy of
Fawcett in the essay 'On Criticism' is an expression of his three
conditions of criticism. The critic must be non-exclusive; he must
appreciate the infinite variety of excellence; he must judge from
feeling:

He had a masterly perception of all styles and of every kind and degree
of excellence, sublime or beautiful, from Milton's Paradise Lost to
Shenstone's Pastoral Ballad, from Butler's Analogy down to Humphry
Clinker. . . . 'That is the most delicious feeling of all', I have heard him
exclaim, 'to like what is excellent, no matter whose it is. . . .' He was
incapable of harbouring a sinister motive, and judged only from what
he felt. There was no flaw or mist in the clear mirror of his mind. He
was as open to impressions as he was strenuous in maintaining them. . . .
[Some critics] like Gil Blas, but can see nothing to laugh at in Don
Quixote: they adore Richardson, but are disgusted with Fielding.
Fawcett had a taste accommodated to all these. He was not exceptious.
He gave a cordial welcome to all sorts, provided they were the best in
their kind. . . . His own style was laboured and artificial to a fault. . . .
He has made me feel (by contrast) the want of genuine sincerity and
generous sentiment in some that I have listened to since, and convinced
me . . . of the truth of that text of Scripture—'That had I all knowledge
and could speak with the tongues of angels, yet without charity I were
nothing!' I would rather be a man of disinterested taste and liberal
feeling, to see and acknowledge truth and beauty wherever I found it,
than a man of greater and more original genius, to hate, envy, and deny
all excellence but my own.

(viii. 224–5)[8]

[8] Hazlitt refers to Fawcett's critical powers elsewhere, *Works*, iii. 171 n; xvii. 65.

Recognizing kinds and degrees of poetic genius, Hazlitt did not require poets to satisfy the conditions of protean genius. In his criticism of the critics this is precisely what he demanded.

His criticism of Dryden is a good illustration of this duality. In Dryden's poetry nature is not seen 'through the medium of sentiment and passion'. His was not a 'natural' poetry dependent upon feeling, but an 'artificial' poetry which had to be judged on its own terms and without reference to 'natural' criteria. His reverence of Wordsworth did not diminish his capacity to appreciate the poetic genius of Dryden. Dryden and Pope, each in their different ways, achieved the highest degree of poetic excellence of which their kind of poetry was susceptible. Only when the issue of kind and degree is settled can the question of relative value be discussed. To reverse the procedure is to incur the risk of exclusiveness. Arnold made this mistake when he said that Dryden and Pope were classics of our prose not of our poetry.[9] The theory of touchstones, by ignoring the diversity of kinds, fosters an exclusive spirit. On the basis of a comparison of one line of Goldsmith and one line of Shakespeare, Arnold criticized the artificiality of eighteenth-century poetic diction. The judgement itself and the assumptions on which it rests betray a monolithic exclusiveness which Hazlitt would not have appreciated. He refused to concern himself with the contemporary debate as to whether or not Pope was a poet. The terms of the dispute were unacceptable to him. Pope was a poet. The important question was what kind of poetry did he write, and how good was he as a poet of artificial life? He dismissed the early nineteenth-century attempt to deny Pope the status of a poet: 'The question whether Pope was a poet, has hardly yet been settled, and is hardly worth settling; for if he was not a great poet, he must have been a great prose writer, that is, he was a great writer of some sort' (xx. 89).

While Hazlitt could appreciate the poetry of Dryden as one differing in kind from a poetry of feeling (whether of passion or sentiment), the same concession was not available to him as a critic. Dryden's poetry was not to be censured because it was not the poetry of Shakespeare or Wordsworth. The absence of feeling did not entail that it was defective, only that it was different. Criticism without sensibility on the other hand is bad criticism. The critic, unlike the poet, must be protean. His criticism must operate from

[9] Arnold, 'The Study of Poetry', in the second series of *Essays in Criticism*.

a foundation in feeling. According to Hazlitt, Dryden, except in his criticism of Ovid, Chaucer, and Shakespeare, failed to meet these requirements. Rather than trust to feeling he relied too heavily on abstract rules:

> Neither are we less removed at present from the dry and meagre mode of dissecting the skeletons of works, instead of transfusing their living principles, which prevailed in Dryden's Prefaces. . . . A genuine criticism should, as I take it, reflect the colours, the light and shade, the soul and body of a work:—here we have nothing but its superficial plan and elevation, as if a poem were a piece of formal architecture. We are told something of the plot or fable, of the moral, and of the observance or violation of the three unities of time, place, and action; and perhaps a word or two is added on the dignity of the persons or the baldness of the style: but we no more know, after reading one of these complacent *tirades*, what the essence of the work is, what passion has been touched, or how skilfully, what tone and movement the author's mind imparts to his subject or receives from it, than if we had been reading a homily or a gazette. That is, we are left quite in the dark as to the feelings of pleasure or pain to be derived from the genius of the performance or the manner in which it appeals to the imagination. . . . We know every thing about the work, and nothing of it.
>
> (viii. 217–18)

Dryden's deficiencies as a critic he attributed to the influence of the French critical tradition 'which always seeks for excellence in the external image, and never in the internal power and feeling' (xvi. 41). The English critical tradition initiated by Dryden therefore was flawed by a defect potentially subversive of the independent nature of poetry. In the criticism of Addison, Dryden's immediate successor, the abstraction assumed a different guise. The one relied on rules, the other on 'straight-laced' or 'fine-spun' theories (vi. 22; iv. 9). The neglect of 'the internal power and feeling', however, is common to both. Hazlitt compared Addison's bias to the theoretical unfavourably with the critical practice of Steele: 'His critical essays we do not think quite so good. We prefer Steele's occasional selection of beautiful poetical passages, without any affectation of analysing their beauties, to Addison's fine-spun theories. The best criticism in the *Spectator*, that on the *Cartoons* of Raphael, is by Steele' (iv. 9).

Dr. Johnson represented a much more serious threat than either Dryden or Addison to Hazlitt's conception of the function of criticism. His authority as a critic, although not unquestioned, was nevertheless a potent factor in the formation of public attitudes to poetry in the late eighteenth and early nineteenth centuries. His position as 'literary oracle' of the age prompted Percival Stockdale's intemperate and ineffectual outburst in his *Lectures on the Truly Eminent English Poets* (1807). Leigh Hunt's criticisms of Johnson in the early numbers of the *Theatrical Examiner* were similarly motivated. He wanted to convince his readers of Johnson's 'absolute unfitness for poetical criticism, at least with regard to works of a higher order'.[10] His strictures were less effective than they might have been, confined as they were to periodical skirmishes. Hazlitt, on the other hand, nowhere alludes to Johnson in his early dramatic reviews. The references to Johnson in his discussion of Shakespeare's plays are few and fleeting. It was impossible to ignore Johnson but, equally, it was impossible to lessen his authority by piecemeal criticism. In the preface to the *Characters of Shakespear's Plays*, therefore, Hazlitt, like Coleridge, concentrated his criticism of Johnson as a critic of Shakespeare into a single sustained attack. The object of the preface being to diminish Johnson's authority, the first stage is denigration by omission. It opens with a quotation from Pope's Preface to his 1725 edition of Shakespeare, praises Whately's *Remarks on Some of the Characters of Shakespere*, refers to Richardson's *Essays on Shakespeare's Dramatic Characters*, and quotes extensively from Schlegel's *Lectures*. Johnson's Preface and notes are studiously ignored. This deliberate omission renders the criticism of Johnson that follows all the more effective. The desultory collocation of quotations and references to noteworthy critics of Shakespeare in the opening pages is in marked contrast with the cutting incisiveness of the subsequent analysis of Johnson —an incisiveness only surpassed by some of the portraits in *The Spirit of the Age*.

Hazlitt's objections to Johnson in the preface (iv. 174–8) are wholly characteristic. Johnson sinned against all his critical criteria. His was an exclusive, rational, generalizing mind directly contrary to Hazlitt's ideal of the non-abstract, protean sensibility.[11] First, he was a poet himself and confirmed Hazlitt's more general claim that

[10] Hunt, *Dramatic Criticism*, p. 65.
[11] Cf. his view of Pope as a critic: 'His feelings as to poetry, are certainly rather liberal than exclusive; and his scale of excellence has a larger range than we should have expected' (xvi. 164).

poets best appreciate the kind of poetry that they themselves write: 'Such poetry as a man deliberately writes, such, and such only will he like. . . . Nor is this all; for being conscious of great powers in himself, and those powers of an adverse tendency to those of his author, [Johnson] would be for setting up a foreign jurisdiction over poetry, and making criticism a kind of Procrustes' bed of genius, where he might . . . regulate the passions according to reason.' Johnson's achievement as a critic was circumscribed by the Augustan tradition. Within that tradition he was a great critic. But Augustan standards must not be used to legislate and exclude. The eighteenth-century emphasis on propriety and clarity in diction must not legislate for a poetry in which we can see 'words and images . . . struggling for expression'. Secondly, Johnson was 'without any particular fineness of organic sensibility', while Shakespeare possessed the 'most refined sensibility to nature'. Consequently he was blind to 'the shifting shapes of fancy, the rainbow hues of things', 'the rapid flights', 'the glancing combinations', 'the infinite fluctuations', and 'individual traits'. Yet these constitute the truth of nature to which the critic must always be open or alive. Finally, there is Hazlitt's characteristic allegation of abstraction and generality which in Johnson's case is related directly to his defective sensibility. Feeling does not direct thought: 'Dr. Johnson's general powers of reasoning overlaid his critical susceptibility.' Faced therefore with the choice of a critic who could say all that he felt, and one who felt more than he could say, Hazlitt chose the latter. The 'high-sounding dogmas' (xi. 165) of a critic who dared 'not trust himself with the immediate impressions of things' (vi. 102) was no substitute for the intuitive perception of a critic with 'quick natural sensibility'.

In his criticism of Dryden, Addison, and Johnson, Hazlitt did not relate their deviations from his critical ideal explicitly to his own distrust of abstraction. He emphasized certain aspects of their work which, in the context of the rest of his general critical theory, are obviously connected with this major preoccupation. In criticizing the criticism of his contemporaries, however, he insisted upon a necessary connection between their limitations and their bias towards abstraction. If literature in the early nineteenth century was to safeguard the imaginative and existential nature of man from the encroachments of science or a scientifically oriented philosophy, it was imperative that the Romantic critics should appreciate the dangers of an extreme reaction which, while it recognized the authenticity of the poetic, attempted to subsume it within a more comprehensive theological or philosophical framework. Hazlitt's fear that the Romantic poets and critics might betray their own cause in attempting to defend it brought out into the open his distrust of the abstract tendencies of the age. Abstraction, the greatest vice of the age, is painstakingly pursued and exposed in all its constituent ramifications, whether as the metaphysical, the dogmatic, the theoretical, the preceptive, or the systematic. The detachment of the critic surveying the past is replaced by the urgency of the critic involved with the present. He had little confidence in the critical spirit of an age whose partiality for systems and system-makers he saw best exemplified by the manner of welcome accorded to Godwin's *Political Justice* and the *Edinburgh Review* (xviii. 306). He admired the *Review*'s relative impartiality but he bitterly resented its theoretically inspired injustices:

> In matters of taste and criticism, its tone is sometimes apt to be supercilious and *cavalier* from its habitual faculty of analysing defects and beauties according to given principles. . . . In this latter department it has been guilty of some capital oversights. The chief was its treatment of the *Lyrical Ballads* at their first appearance . . . in its denial of their beauties, because they were included in no school, because they were reducible to no previous standard or theory of poetical excellence.
>
> (xi. 129)[12]

The most serious challenge to his conception of the imaginative element in literature and life came not from Godwin or Jeffrey who in many respects represented the traditions and past attitudes of a previous generation, but from Coleridge and Schlegel who spoke unequivocally for the new century. His criticism of the German critical method brings out very clearly the basic opposition between abstract and non-abstract views of poetry, between an interpretation of poetry as independent and self-authenticating and one which subordinated poetry to philosophy: '[The Germans] have no shades of opinion, but are always straining at a grand systematic conclusion. . . . No question can come before them but they have a large apparatus of logical and metaphysical principles ready to play off upon it' (xvi. 58). Hazlitt greatly admired Schlegel with whom he had much in common. Nevertheless, he could not

---

[12] He rejected the criticism of the *Quarterly* because there was 'nothing liberal, nothing humane' in its judgements (xi. 115).

ignore certain abstract leanings which he considered inimical to a balanced assessment of the nature of poetry and its role in the early nineteenth century. The first of these was Schlegel's tendency to mysticism; the second was his over-dependence upon theory: 'His speculative reasonings on the principles of taste, are often as satisfactory as they are profound. But he sometimes carries the love of theory, and the spirit of partisanship, farther than is at all allowable' (ibid.). Hazlitt attributed Coleridge's decline as a poet and critic and his ultimate failure as a philosopher to the influence of German Transcendental philosophy. Feeling, which for Hazlitt represented the real basis of these activities, was forever being diminished by Coleridge's over-reliance upon the conceptual.[13] This depreciation of the affective element is the constant theme of almost all his criticisms of Coleridge. It served in his view to divorce Coleridge's most subtle speculations from reality: 'He is the man of all others to swim on empty bladders in a sea, without shore or soundings: to drive an empty stage-coach without passengers or lading, and arrive behind his time; to write marginal notes without a text . . . "and discern perfection in the great obscurity of nothing" ' (xviii. 370). Carlyle's criticism of Coleridge in his life of John Sterling is remarkably similar although written from a very different viewpoint.

The critical writings of Charles Lamb and Leigh Hunt did not present the same problems. Both critics abhorred the systematic and theoretical. Neither was committed to any of the more metaphysical Christian doctrines and were temperamentally disinclined to engage in abstract, philosophical speculation. There was much less to fear therefore from Lamb and Hunt. Hazlitt's admiration of the more profound critical genius of Coleridge was always tempered by his distrust of its ultimate tendency and its potentially subversive effect on contemporary critical attitudes. Consequently, his criticism of Lamb and Hunt is more sympathetic. The emphasis shifts from abstraction to feeling. Hunt is distinguished by 'a fineness of tact and sterling sense' (xi. 177), while Lamb is complimented on his 'fine and masterly *tact* in the twilight of genius' (xx. 263). Hunt's catholicity of taste he thinks marred by a failure of expression—an inability to articulate all that he felt—resulting in an air of superficiality militating against a real appreciation of his

---

[13] See J. D. Boulger, *Coleridge as Religious Thinker*, pp. 196–219, for a similar analysis of Coleridge's decline as a poet.

perceptiveness over a wide range of critical interests. Feeling is likewise the source of Lamb's strength as a critic, although he differs from Hunt in that, faultless in the expression of what he felt, he felt too little.[14] His range of critical sympathies was too restricted. In Hazlitt's campaign against the exclusiveness of much of Romantic criticism, Lamb shared with Wordsworth the doubtful privilege of being singled out for special attention—with this difference— that his was the exclusiveness of the critic who was not at the same time a poet of original genius:

> L[amb] makes us mad in this: he wants to cut down everything to a certain standard. He wishes to leave Sancho Panza out of *Don Quixote*, and Partridge out of *Tom Jones*; and to conclude *Robinson Crusoe* when the savages appear. . . . L[amb] explores vast undiscovered, or forgotten, regions of literature; and gropes his way with a fine and masterly *tact* in the twilight of genius; but shuns the beaten path, the broad day. . . . Why then does he vex us by saying, that Sir Walter's [novels] are trash? And that you cannot take any single part and read it aloud, as you can a passage in Milton or Shakespeare, because there is nothing to carry you on but the story.

(xx. 263)

In his criticism of the critics Hazlitt exacted certain demands which he made every attempt to satisfy in his own critical writings. 'To say what I think, and think what I feel' appears to be a modest critical objective until the full implications of such sincerity of feeling are appreciated within the context of his preoccupation with abstraction. He attributed his own unpopularity as a critic to the exclusive and sectarian spirit of the English public. Of its neglect of *The Spirit of the Age*, his greatest work, he wrote: 'If you do not attach yourself to some one set of people and principles, and stick to them through thick and thin, instead of giving your opinion fairly and fully all round, you must expect to have all the world against you, for no other reason than because you express sincerely . . . not only what they say of others, but what is said of themselves' (xvii. 300). His despondency was not altogether justified, for he was not without readers who perceived in his work some of the qualities which he himself most prized in the work of other critics. Keats was perhaps his most enthusiastic admirer: 'I said if there were three things superior in the modern world, they were "the Excursion",

[14] For examples of Lamb's 'exclusiveness', see *Works*, xi. 181; xii. 36; xvii. 65, 318; xx. 270, 275.

"Haydon's Pictures" & "Hazlitt's depth of Taste".'[15] Keats later
changed his mind about *The Excursion* and Haydon's paintings,
but his admiration of Hazlitt's powers as a critic and philosopher
remained unaltered, and in April 1818 he purposed to 'prepare
myself to ask Hazlitt in about a years time the best metaphysical
road I can take'.[16] The quality that most impressed Leigh Hunt
in the *Characters of Shakespear's Plays* was Hazlitt's sincerity or
openness of feeling, what he called that 'very striking susceptibility
with which he changes his own humour and manner according to
the nature of the play he comes upon; like a spectator in a theatre,
who accompanies the turns of the actor's face with his own, now
looking eager, now withdrawn, now staring, now subsided, now
cheerful-mouthed, now sad, now careless, now meditative, now
wound up by social merriment, now relaxed by solitary despondency'.[17] John Scott observed the same quality in the *Lectures on the
Age of Elizabeth* and isolated in characteristic Hazlitt fashion the
three strands of openness, truth to nature in art, and the intuitive
perceptiveness of feeling: 'He catches the mantles of those, whose
celestial flights he regards with devout, but undazzled eye . . . the
hidden charm, the essential principle of power and efficacy, the
original feature, the distinguishing property—to these his sagacity
and taste are drawn, as it were by instinct.'[18] Even Crabb Robinson,
who could never forgive Hazlitt his alleged ill-treatment of
Wordsworth and Coleridge acknowledged him as 'the director of
my taste', affirmed his reputation as a critic to be well-deserved,
and wrote of his review of Schlegel's *Lectures* that he had 'entered
into the sense of the author and evinces a kindred spirit'.[19] This
sincerity of feeling that so impressed his contemporaries differenti-
ates the spirit of Hazlitt's criticism and thought from, for example,
that of De Quincey, one of whose most recent critics has observed
that the attraction for De Quincey of political economy lay in its
'*a priori*, insulated . . . [and] fixed doctrine'.[20]

[15] Keats, *Letters*, I. 204–5.
[16] Ibid., I. 274.
[17] Hunt, *Dramatic Criticism*, p. 169.
[18] *London Magazine*, I (1820), 187–8.
[19] *H. C. Robinson on Books and their Writers*, I. 6, 182.
[20] De Quincey, *New Essays*, p. 22.

CHAPTER NINE

The Spirit of the Age

The Devil take these general terms, not content with
having driven all poetry out [of] the world, at length
they make war upon their own allies, nay their very
parents—dry facts. If it had not been the age of
generalities. . . .

SHELLEY, *Letters*[1]

HAZLITT's theory of abstract ideas provided a philosophical and
psychological rationale for the critical movement towards particularity in the late eighteenth and early nineteenth centuries. His
distrust of abstraction was one that was fully shared by Hurd,
Whiter, and Joseph Warton, as well as by the new Shakespeare
critics and the Scottish aestheticians. Moreover, he repeatedly
endorsed in a variety of ways Hurd's claim that the poet's ability
to break away from the abstract, to penetrate into the complex
particularity of the individual, was specifically related to painting.[2]
It is scarcely surprising therefore that the late eighteenth century's
conception of the spirit of the age had much more in common with
Hazlitt's views on this subject than with Coleridge's or Carlyle's.
There was a growing awareness in the literary criticism of the
period of the dangers to poetry and the values it embodied presented by the increasing importance attached to matters of abstract
speculation. In this equation science and a science-oriented philosophy was only one facet of the larger problem of abstraction. The
same is true of Hazlitt's conception of the spirit of the age. The
nineteenth century employed the concept of the spirit of the age in
two distinct ways: either as a tension between two polar opposites
or as an imbalance of one of these two factors. In the writings of
Coleridge and Carlyle the tension was conceived of as one between
the mechanical and the spiritual, empiricism and idealism. Hazlitt
on the other hand, like some of the writers of the late eighteenth

---

[1] *The Letters of P. B. Shelley*, ed. F. L. Jones (Oxford, 1964), II. 115.
[2] See Chapter IV, n. 25.

century, viewed the problem in terms of an opposition between the imaginative, spiritual or poetic, and the abstract, scientific or philosophical, empirical or idealist. These differing conceptions of what constituted the spirit of the age had far-reaching consequences. They serve to explain why in the writings of Hazlitt and the critics of the late eighteenth century the dominant opposition is between imagination/feeling and reason/understanding, while in Coleridge and Carlyle understanding is distinguished from and opposed to reason. In the case of Coleridge and Hazlitt this difference in emphasis reflects radically divergent theories of abstract ideas.

In 1785 Thomas Reid had warned in general terms of the dangers inherent in accepting the opposition between empiricism and idealism as part of the nature of things.[3] In his own Commonsense philosophy he attempted to steer between the dangers of both forms of abstraction, natural as well as non-natural. With the eighteenth-century critics, however, philosophy of any kind was suspect. Writing in the early 1760s, Adam Smith had warned of the dangerous contemporary bias towards abstraction: 'The thoughts of most men of genius in the country have of late [blank] to abstract and speculative reasonings, which perhaps tend very little to the bettering of our practice [in writing].'[4] Smith's embryonic sense that the cultural well-being of society depended upon maintaining a balance between the two antagonistic principles was one shared in a rather more articulate and developed form by Lord Kames who, in the imbalance of the commercial rather than the scientific or philosophical spirit, foresaw the gravest threat to the national character. Writing at the same time as Smith and several years before the establishment of the Royal Academy in 1768, Kames urged that, if only for utilitarian reasons, much greater attention should be paid to the promotion of the fine arts: 'To promote the Fine Arts in Britain, has become of greater importance than is generally imagined. A flourishing commerce begets opulence . . . inflaming our appetite for pleasure. . . . Riches so employ'd, instead of encouraging vice, will excite both public and private virtue.'[5] Kames's warning of the dangerous consequences for a nation's moral and cultural heritage of the uninhibited growth of an industrial and commercial spirit anticipated similar

[3] See Chapter I, n. 27.
[4] Smith, *Lectures on Rhetoric*, p. 37.
[5] Kames, *Elements of Criticism*, I. vii.

warnings in the nineteenth century by Coleridge, Carlyle, and Arnold, but was unusual in the eighteenth. The gravest threat was seen to stem from the speculative rather than the commercial bias, less from the possibility envisaged by Kames of a new generation of hedonists and an age of immorality than from a fear of a general absorption in speculative theories, philosophical, historical, scientific, social, economic, or aesthetic. Adam Smith was clearly aware of the irreconcilable nature of the conflict between poetic genius and what he termed 'abstract and speculative reasonings', but in alluding to the dangers of this predominance his manner of expression had been circumspect and tentative. The bias to abstration 'perhaps tend[s] very little to the bettering of our practice [in writing]'. For William Duff in his *Essay on Original Genius* (1767) on the other hand there was no question of the deplorable effect on poetic genius resulting from 'the philosophical spirit of the times'.[6] In Richard Hurd's *Letters on Chivalry and Romance* (1762) there is more than a hint of Carlyle's early essays in his lament for the decay of wonder in an age of science.[7]

The most detailed application of this view of the spirit of the age to late eighteenth-century poetry occurs in Warton's *Essay on the Writings and Genius of Pope* in 1756:

> [Perhaps] that philosophical, that geometrical, and systematical spirit so much in vogue, which has spread itself from the sciences even into polite literature, by consulting only REASON, has ... diminished and destroyed SENTIMENT; and made our poets write from and to the HEAD rather than the HEART.[8]

English poetry, he declares, has assumed as a result 'a more sober, and perhaps a more rational air'.[9] More than sixty years were to elapse before the implications of Warton's views were to receive their fullest expression in Hazlitt's criticism of the poets and philosophers of the early nineteenth century. In both writers the spirit of the age is seen in terms not of reason and understanding, mechanism and dynamism, empiricism and some form of transcendental idealism, but of reason and feeling, reason and sentiment, abstraction and poetry, the head versus the heart. These are the

---

[6] Duff, *An Essay on Original Genius*, p. 245.
[7] Hurd, *Letters on Chivalry and Romance* (London, 1762), p. 120.
[8] Warton, *An Essay on the Writings and Genius of Pope*, I. 204.
[9] Ibid., II. 17.

categories underlying Hazlitt's criticism of Byron's dramas in 'On Reason and Imagination', Shelley's poetry in 'On People of Sense', the philosophy of Bentham in 'The New School of Reform', and the philosophy and poetry of Coleridge and the later Wordsworth. In both writers feeling is related to the discrimination of the individual, reason with the general, systematic, and theoretical. The gravest danger to the imaginative principle is not mechanism but abstraction, of which the bias to mechanism is only one aspect. There are of course great differences between the two critics. Their views, although similar, found expression in a variety of different ways. One of the most significant differences is in the matter of tone. The urbane detachment of Warton's analysis is that of the eighteenth-century critic, scholar, and poet, for whom poetry is 'polite literature', a cultural adornment and embellishment unconnected in any significant way with the question of what it is to be a human being. Hazlitt's on the other hand is passionate and obsessive, an insistent, strident, and often disconcerting reminder to those modern critics who would deny the Romantic poets and critics any concern for poetry as a criticism of life.

By the turn of the century the imbalance perceived by the critics of the late eighteenth century was even more pronounced. Yet critical as the situation was in Hazlitt's view, this imbalance is not by itself sufficient, as it is in the case of Coleridge and Carlyle, to account for the constant emphasis in his writings on the necessity for safeguarding the imaginative element in life and literature. An additional factor is operative which, although present in embryonic form in Warton, is altogether absent from the writings of Hazlitt's contemporaries. This factor is his awareness that science and a science-oriented philosophy are not co-extensive with abstraction. Abstraction, or as Wittgenstein terms it 'our craving for generality', also characterizes the philosophies designed to counter the growth of empiricism. While rejecting the empirical answers these philosophers accept the empiricists' questions. Science in consequence exacts its own revenge. The non-natural and supra-rational replace the natural and causal; 'utilitarian, practical facts', as Croce expresses it, are exchanged for 'ideas suspended in a metaphysical heaven'.[10] Since the initial assumption in both cases is the same, however, both share a common basis in abstraction. This point has been best expressed in the twentieth century by Wittgenstein:

[10] Croce, *Aesthetic*, p. 122.

Our craving for generality has another main source: our preoccupation with the method of science. . . . Philosophers constantly see the
method of science before their eyes, and are irresistibly tempted to ask
and answer questions in the way science does. This tendency is the real
source of metaphysics, and leads the philosopher into complete darkness.
. . . Instead of 'craving for generality' I could also have said 'the contemptuous attitude towards the particular case'.[11]

Hazlitt's criticism of the poets and critics of the early nineteenth
century embodies his awareness that the method of science was
built into the non-poetic, non-empirical alternatives proposed by
his contemporaries. Byron and Shelley are thus assimilated to
Bentham in the essays 'On Reason and Imagination', and 'On
People of Sense'. Bentham is linked with Plato, and Plato related to
Coleridge. His criticism of his contemporaries, therefore, was
directed at two enemies—the enemy within and the enemy without. It was the betrayal from within, however, that gave him
greatest cause for alarm and accounts for the obsessive emphasis on
abstraction and generality, philosophical as well as scientific. In so
doing he broke away from the more traditional opposition between
poetry and science to be found in Wordsworth, Coleridge,
Peacock, and Carlyle, in favour of one between poetry and abstraction. He opposed poetry to science, philosophy, and religion,
to idealism as well as empiricism. He rejected any '-ism' that would
subvert the autonomous and self-authenticating nature of poetry.
By enlarging the orthodox opposition in this way he anticipated
a series of critical issues more familiar to us today in the writings of
Arnold, Croce, Lawrence, and Wittgenstein.

The Spirit of the Age was not published until 1825. Its appearance
at that time coincided with a marked change in the philosophical
fortunes of both Bentham and Coleridge. By 1825 Utilitarianism
was no longer the exclusive property of a select group of radical
reformers. It was now beginning to make an impact on a much
wider audience:

When Byron passed away, the feeling he had represented craved
utterance no more. With a sigh we turned to the actual and practical
career of life: we awoke . . . and by a natural reaction addressed ourselves to the active and daily objects which lay before us. . . . Hence
that strong attachment to the Practical, which became so visible a little
time after the death of Byron, and which continues (unabated, or rather

11 Wittgenstein, *The Blue and Brown Books*, p. 18.

increased,) to characterize the temper of the time. Insensibly acted upon by the doctrine of the Utilitarians, we desired to see Utility in every branch of intellectual labour. . . . We were in the situation of a man who, having run a certain career of dreams and extravagance, begins to be prudent and saving, to calculate his conduct, and to look to his estate. Politics thus gradually and commonly absorbed our attention, and we grew to identify ourselves, our feelings, and our cause, with statesmen and economists instead of with poets and refiners. . . . And the interest usually devoted to the imaginative was transferred to the real.[12]

Bulwer-Lytton's analysis here omits one important factor. Poetry had failed to sustain its challenge to empirical philosophy, but the ascendancy established by empirical and Utilitarian theory in the 1820s was not without opposition. Bentham's growing popularity was paralleled by a significant if modest growth in the popularity of Coleridge's philosophical and religious teachings. Coleridge's 'listening public' during the years 1825–34, although small, was influential. Even John Stuart Mill felt compelled in consequence to examine and modify his own allegiance to Bentham: 'I found the fabric of my old and taught opinions giving way in many fresh places, and I never allowed it to fall to pieces, but was incessantly occupied in weaving it anew.'[13] The emergence of a small but definite Coleridgean party Mill assigns to the years 1828–9.[14] In this conflict between two rival systems of abstraction, Bentham vs. Coleridge, empiricism vs. a transcendent theory of metaphysics, Mill felt he had isolated the spirit of the age in early nineteenth-century England. His analysis is similar in many respects to Carlyle's emphasis on the tension between mechanism and dynamism. Its validity, however, is even more limited than Carlyle's. Carlyle in his early writings at least had recognized the existence of poetry, logically as well as historically, as a third factor in the equation. Publicly he minimized its effectiveness as an alternative to his own philosophical and religious rejection of empiricism, but privately he acknowledged that, as expressed in the poetry and prose of Goethe and Schiller, it might contain 'a glimpse of the truth'.[15] Whatever his private misgivings on this score, and however critical of Coleridge's 'metaphysical bric-a-brac', Carlyle put all the weight of his newly acquired authority as an Edinburgh

12 Bulwer, *England and the English*, II. 105–7.
13 Mill, *Autobiography*, p. 110.
14 Ibid., p. 90.
15 See Chapter I, n. 72.

Reviewer behind Coleridge's simplified version of the spirit of the age. By elaborating this dichotomy in terms of its principal spokesmen Mill was also operating in a less general and more personal way within the same traditional and inadequate conception.

The reason for this is not far to seek. Coleridge's self-confessed 'craving after a resting-place for my Thoughts in some *principle*' was one that was fully shared by Mill. The principle in each case was radically different, but the urge to ask questions and find answers, the desire for unity and harmony, are common to both. Like Coleridge, Mill wanted a system: 'When I laid down the last volume of the Traité [by Bentham], I had become a different being. The "principle of utility" . . . fell exactly into its place as the keystone which held together the detached and fragmentary component parts of my knowledge and beliefs. It gave unity to my conceptions of things. I now had opinions; a creed, a doctrine, a philosophy; in one among the best senses of the word, a religion.'[16] It is this common basis in abstraction that gives such insight and sympathy to Mill's analysis of Coleridge's achievement as a philosopher. Even Coleridge's view that the ideal philosophical system would combine the philosophies of Bacon and Plato finds an echo in Mill's attempt to effect a reconciliation or compromise between the empiricist and idealist extremes.[17] It is present in the early essays and was later to vitiate his exposition of his own brand of non-dogmatic Utilitarianism. Empirical and transcendent theories may have a common basis, but as Coleridge realized later the gulf separating them can never be bridged: 'Every man is born an Aristotelian or a Platonist. I do not think it possible that any one born an Aristotelian can become a Platonist; and I am sure no born Platonist can ever change into an Aristotelian. They are the two classes of men, beside which it is next to impossible to conceive a third.'[18] In spite therefore of their status as classic analyses of the various factors at work in a transitional period of English intellectual history, Mill's essays on Bentham and Coleridge are open to serious objection. Their dialectic appertains to the period of his own adolescence and early manhood. Satisfactory as it may be for the years after 1823, it has much less relevance to the years 1796–1822. It not only fails to take into account Coleridge's progress from poetry as

---

[16] Mill, *Autobiography*, p. 47.
[17] Coleridge, *Treatise on Method*, p. 51.
[18] Coleridge, *Works*, VI. 336.

experiential to philosophy as constitutive; it also fails to perceive the triangular nature of the debate in the early nineteenth century. Neither logically nor historically does Mill recognize poetry as a viable alternative to philosophical abstraction. Hence the inadequacy of his therapeutic appreciation of the early poetry of Wordsworth. Poetry is not something to be pillaged for an affective element that can then be used as an additive corrective of an arid and dogmatic Utilitarianism. Nor can it be used as a form of leavening designed to help bridge the gap between two rival systems of philosophy. The Romantic poets and critics were not idle spectators of a trial of strength between two opposing philosophies. Poetry has an existence of its own, not as a system, not as something stated or something known, but as something felt or experienced which, however mysterious and impalpable, is nevertheless authentic. It is the historical manifestation of this possibility in the early nineteenth century that Mill's essays leave out of account. The eventual failure of the English Romantics to prevent this polarization, and the deep-rooted nature of the dichotomy itself in English thought, help to explain why Arnold, in reconstructing a case for poetry later in the century, availed himself of the support of the German Romantics in preference to his immediate predecessors in England, magnifying the achievement of the former at the expense of the latter.

Against this background *The Spirit of the Age* can no longer be regarded as it often has been in the past, even by those who consider it to be his greatest work, as a series of perceptive but disparate and impressionistic sketches of famous contemporaries. Like Chaucer's Prologue, it is and it is not a portrait gallery. The form is important. It frames and isolates each portrait, detaching it from those around it. This should not be overemphasized, however, for in so doing it enables Hazlitt to do justice to the uniqueness of the individual without distorting his analysis in the interest of some more general pattern or theme. It is this discrimination of the particular, rather than the effect of discontinuity inherent in the form, that is important. *The Spirit of the Age* is the apotheosis of his subterranean strategy as an essayist. It is a masterpiece of the kind of indirectness alluded to in the essay 'On Depth and Superficiality' in which he drew the attention of his readers to 'the way in which I work out some of my conclusions underground, before throwing them up on the surface. . . . *Depth* consists then in tracing any number of particular effects to a general principle. . . . It is in fact resolving the concrete into the abstract' (xii. 347, 355). The particularity inherent in the form is reinforced by his Chaucer-like use of conglomerate detail in which descriptions of physical appearance, dress, and personal habits jostle with philosophical analysis, critical commentary, and anecdotal reportage. No portrait is alike. He makes no attempt to systematize his descriptions or insights in the manner of Johnson's *Lives*. The catalogue effect is avoided by a writer who, trained as a painter, was aware that the simultaneity of the spatial art of portraiture was not to be achieved in a temporal art by exhaustive and systematically arranged detail. The haphazard, inconsequential, and slapdash appearance of some of the portraits is deceptive. The detail in Hazlitt's own terms is 'subtle' rather than 'minute'. It is always significant detail which, although 'slight and evanescent at first sight . . . mounts up to a mighty sum in the end . . . an essential part of an important whole' (viii. 39). The general impression arises as he always insisted it should from 'the aggregate of well-founded particulars . . . [not] an abstract theory' (xii. 246). It is through the accumulation of particulars that he pursues his theme of the spirit of the age.

An article written by Hazlitt as drama critic of the *London Magazine* in April 1820 affords an illuminating contrast with his practice in *The Spirit of the Age*. The problem to be solved there was the inability of the poets and novelists of the early nineteenth century to write drama: 'The age we live in is critical, didactic, paradoxical, romantic, but it is not dramatic. . . . Our ancestors could write a tragedy two hundred years ago; they could write a comedy one hundred years ago; why cannot we do the same now?' (xviii. 302–3). In attempting to answer this question Hazlitt provides us with the key to the theme that serves to give unity to the individual portraits of the later work:

We have become a nation of politicians and newsmongers; our inquiries in the streets are no less than after the health of Europe; and in men's faces, we may see strange matters written,—the rise of stocks, the loss of battles, the fall of kingdoms, and the death of kings. The Muse, meanwhile, droops in bye-corners of the mind, and is forced to take up with the refuse of our thoughts. Our attention has been turned, by the current of events, to the general nature of men and things; and we cannot call it heartily back to individual caprices, or head-strong passions, which are the nerves and sinews of Comedy and Tragedy. What is an individual man to a nation? Or what is a nation to an abstract principle? ... A general and speculative interest absorbs the corroding poison, and takes out the sting of our more circumscribed and fiercer passions. We are become public creatures. ... We participate in the general progress of intellect, and the larger vicissitudes of human affairs; but the hugest private sorrow looks dwarfish and puerile. ... If a bias to abstraction is evidently, then, the reigning spirit of the age, dramatic poetry must be allowed to be most irreconcileable with this spirit; it is essentially individual and concrete, both in form and in power. ... It is hardly to be thought that the poet should feel for others in this way, when they have ceased almost to feel for themselves; when the mind is turned habitually out of itself to general, speculative truth, and possibilities of good, and when, in fact, the processes of the understanding, analytical distinctions, and verbal disputes, have superseded all personal and local attachments and antipathies, and have, in a manner, put a stop to the pulsation of the heart ... when we are more in love with a theory than a mistress, and would only crush to atoms those who are of an opposite party to ourselves in taste, philosophy, or politics. ... The poet (let his genius be what it will) can only act by sympathy with the public mind and manners of his age; but these are, at present, not in sympathy, but in opposition to dramatic poetry. ... It would be strange indeed ... if in the same period that produced the Political Justice or the Edinburgh Review, there should be found such an 'unfeathered, two-legged thing' as a real tragedy poet.

(xviii. 304–6)

The basic opposition between dramatic poetry and abstraction once established, Hazlitt then proceeds to examine the dramatic pretensions of some contemporary poets and novelists—Godwin, Wordsworth, Coleridge, Byron, and Scott—in vindication of his view of the spirit of the age. That view did not change in the intervening five years, but his strategy in *The Spirit of the Age* itself is a very different one. His conception in that work emerges powerfully but indirectly through the massing of particulars, most of which, even the most trivial, are related to this central preoccupation. The individual portraits and the work as a whole are conceived and presented dramatically. The reader is left to draw his own conclusions. The dramatic conception of detail that helps to unify the individual sketches also confers unity on the work as a whole. What appears to be a collection of detached portraits is converted into an historical painting of an age. Even the final arrangement of the work directs attention to the underlying theme. The two extremes of abstraction, scientific and metaphysical, are represented in the opening chapters by their principal protagonists: Bentham, Godwin, and Coleridge. Godwin's presence here is explained by Hazlitt's view of him as the unacknowledged and unduly neglected John the Baptist for the Utilitarian doctrines of the early nineteenth century. A similar opposition is to be found in the two essays that follow: Edward Irving and Horne Tooke. As a critic of Benthamism, the friend of Carlyle, and the fashionable voice of a religious orthodoxy, Irving had much more in common with Coleridge than with the arid empiricism of the author of *The Diversions of Purley*. The next group—Scott, Byron, Southey, and Wordsworth —marks the introduction of the third element in the triangular debate. In these portraits Hazlitt was dealing with poets rather than poetry, not with what poetry could achieve, but with what it had achieved. His task was descriptive rather than prescriptive. By 1825 he was no longer concerned with the validity of poetry as an alternative to abstraction. The work is retrospective and in it he determines to what extent contemporary poets have succeeded in sustaining the role he had earlier envisaged for poetry. Only Sir Walter Scott escapes censure. Scott alone is free from abstraction, but for reasons that are not altogether to Scott's credit as a creative writer. The remaining portraits, Mackintosh, Malthus, Gifford, Jeffrey, the group of politicians, are all illustrative in one way or another of the same basic theme.

Hazlitt's criticism of his contemporaries is not of course confined to *The Spirit of the Age*. What is surprising, however, is that the critical perception controlling and organizing the individual portraits in the last and greatest of his critical writings is not only present in a fully developed form but is the subject of his first essay in literary criticism. The circumstances surrounding this first critical endeavour reveal something of the importance he attached even as early as 1813 to the speculative spirit that he felt to be characteristic of the early nineteenth century. In the *Morning Chronicle* of 17 September 1813 the paper's drama critic had attempted to account for the dearth of good modern comedy in terms of the dictatorial powers exercised by the theatrical managers and the lack of financial incentive.[19] Hazlitt's reply, in the form of

---

[19] These two factors, he argues, help to explain the paradox of a barren drama in an age of great poetry: 'That there is no want of poetical genius in this age is abundantly testified by the productions of a Byron, a Scott, a Campbell, and a

a letter to the editor, was so well written that it resulted in his appointment as the *Chronicle's* dramatic critic, and was subsequently published without alteration as 'On Modern Comedy' in *The Round Table*. In his letter he criticized the assumption that good comedy can be legislated back into existence without reference to the cultural climate of contemporary society. He attributed the decline of English comedy to the generalizing spirit which, originating at the beginning of the previous century, had resulted in a regrettable uniformity of nineteenth-century character, conversation, and dress: 'The present prevailing style of conversation is not *personal*, but critical and analytical. It consists almost entirely in the discussion of general topics, in dissertations on philosophy or taste: and Congreve would be able to derive no better hints from the conversations of our toilettes or drawing-rooms, for the exquisite raillery or poignant repartee of his dialogues, than from a deliberation of the Royal Society' (iv. 12). The age, he argues, is necessary to the greatest dramatist. Not even Shakespeare could have written great drama in an age that was 'one dull compound of politics, criticism, chemistry, and metaphysics!' (ibid.). The dramatic impulse and the bias to abstraction characteristic of contemporary society are incompatible. In the first letter this theme is partially obscured by his somewhat dubious emphasis on the tendency of good comedy to dissipate individuality and to compel social uniformity. In this way comedy is self-destructive: 'It is because so many excellent Comedies have been written, that there are none written at present' (iv. 10).

In a second letter, however, in reply to the critic's rejoinder to the first, Hazlitt developed the theme of poetry and abstraction in all its complexity—free on this occasion from the self-conscious paradoxical intent of the newly fledged essayist. The first letter, because of its inclusion in *The Round Table*, is the more widely known; the second is much the more important. Chronology and popularity in this case yield to logical priority. The subject of the second letter is the philosophical framework that forms the basis

---

Moore; and if such men were to dedicate their talents fairly to the stage, there can be little doubt but that we should receive excellent works from them. While we have a number of individuals possessed of such acknowledged poetical talents, it would be singular indeed if some of them should not excel in the drama.' Hazlitt does not take issue with the critic in his argument that good poetry is a guarantee of good drama. Hazlitt replied to the first article on 25 September 1813. The critic's rejoinder appeared on 4 October, and Hazlitt's reply to this on 15 October.

of the first and serves to give it substance. Its relegation to the volume of miscellaneous writings in the collected edition has meant that, like the essay 'The Spirit of Philosophy', its real significance in relation to the rest of his work has never been fully appreciated. The first letter is a carefully contrived essay designed to appeal to a non-philosophical public. Its origins in his pre-occupation with abstraction are concealed and to some extent distorted by his attempt to cultivate a popular style. In the second he is only concerned with establishing the validity of his experiential view of drama and the nature of the intransigent opposition between drama thus interpreted and generality. The tone too is different. The first is light and detached, general and impersonal. The second, perhaps as a result of the patronizing and bantering tone of the critic's reply, is severe and trenchant, polemical and minutely circumstantial. In his reply the critic had countered Hazlitt's doubtful argument that it is because so many excellent comedies have been written that none are written at present, by suggesting that he would be inclined to apply in this instance 'the analogy which we find to hold in almost every other, that relative perfection is only the result of repeated efforts, and that . . . every successive attempt is in general, an improvement on the preceding . . . what has been once done well usually leads to something better.' The greater refinement and abstraction of the nineteenth century merely requires a more refined and philosophical comedy which, for the reasons suggested in his first article, contemporary dramatists are unable to supply. Hazlitt begins by opposing poetry to science, thereby undermining the critic's analogy: 'His hypothesis, that the arts are uniformly progressive, totally fails; it applies to science, and not to art' (xx. 2). He points out that even if dramatists acquainted with the conversation and speculation of refined society could be found, it would be to no avail: 'To suppose that we can go on refining for ever with vivacity and effect, embodying vague abstractions, and particularizing flimsy general-ities,—"shewing the very body of the age, its form and pressure", though it has neither form nor pressure left,—seems to me the height of speculative absurdity' (xx. 11). The relation that the critic perceives between poetry and philosophy is untenable: 'It confounds philosophy with poetry, laboured analysis with intuitive perception, general truth with individual observation' (xx. 9). Imagination, he argues, is the only judge of the individual, as reason is of the abstract. In art as in life the individual is the sole guarantee of the poetic and imaginative. Drama is not remote from life. It is the most substantial, palpable, and concrete of the arts: 'It brings [characters] into action, obtrudes them on the sight, embodies them in habits, in gestures, in dress, in circumstances, and in speech. It renders every thing overt and ostensible, and presents human nature not in its elementary principles or by general reflections, but exhibits its essential quality in all their variety of combination, and furnishes objects for perpetual reflection' (xx. 9–10). He pours scorn on his opponent's suggestions for the improvement of modern comedy:

> He is for refining Comedy into a pure intellectual abstraction, the shadow of a shade. Will he forgive me if I suggest . . . that the drama in general might be constructed on the same abstruse and philosophical principles. As he imagines that the finest Comedies may be formed without individual character, so the deepest Tragedies might be composed without real passion. The slightest and most ridiculous distresses might be improved by the help of art and metaphysical aid, into the most affecting scenes. A young man might naturally be introduced as the hero of a philosophic drama, who had lost the gold medal for a prize poem; or a young lady, whose verses had been severely criticized in the reviews. Nothing could come amiss to this rage for speculative refinement; or the actors might be supposed to come forward, not in any character, but as a sort of Chorus, reciting speeches on the general miseries of human life, or reading alternately a passage out of Seneca's Morals or Voltaire's Candide. . . . But the instant we begin to refine and generalise beyond a certain point, we are reduced to abstraction, and compelled to see things, not as individuals, or as connected with action and circumstances, but as universal truths, applicable in a degree to all things, and in their extent to none, which therefore it would be absurd to predicate of individuals, or to represent to the senses. The habit, too, of detaching these abstract species and fragments of nature, destroys the power of combining them in complex characters, in every degree of force and variety. The concrete and the abstract cannot co-exist in the same mind.
>
> (xx. 9–10)

What is in effect Hazlitt's first critical essay represents the clearest and most unequivocal expression of his life-long conviction that poetry and abstraction are irreconcilable, and that the gravest threat to poetry in the early nineteenth century was not science, but generality. Coleridge's attempt to appropriate the credit for the substance of the first letter and so detract from the obvious originality of the views expressed was singularly ill-advised.[20] Even on the most charitable interpretation his remarks are little more than wishful thinking for there is nothing more characteristic of Hazlitt and less characteristic of Coleridge than the conception of the spirit of the age that is embodied in them. Occurring as they do at the point of transition from philosophy and painting to criticism and essay-writing, these two letters reveal all four to be different facets of a unified response to life as early as 1813 that is radically different from the kind envisaged by Coleridge. His criticism of Coleridge's tragedy in the article on contemporary drama in the *London Magazine* appeals to the same criteria in almost exactly the same language: 'He is of the transcendental German school. He is . . . an ingenious metaphysician, who mistakes scholastic speculations for the intricate windings of the passions, and assigns possible reasons instead of actual motives for the excesses of his characters. He gives us studied special-pleadings for involuntary bursts of feeling, and the needless strain of tinkling sentiments for the point-blank language of nature' (xviii. 309). If we compare this with his criticism of Byron's tragedies in *The Plain Speaker* essay 'On Reason and Imagination', the criteria will be found to be the same whether the date is 1826, 1820, or 1813. The form the abstraction takes in each case is different and Hazlitt's language isolates this difference quite precisely. But there is no doubt that the object of his criticism in both is their 'scouting individuality', and it is this that enables him to relate Byron's tragedies to the scientific abstraction of Bentham's Utilitarianism. The poetry of Shelley in its contempt for the individual is likewise assimilated to the philosophy of Bentham. Hazlitt's perception of the affinities between the poets and the empirical philosophers, the poets' own sincere objections to empiricism notwithstanding, is the most distinctive feature of his criticism of his contemporaries. His awareness of the circuitous and insidious nature of the scientific analogy and the temptations it offered to poets seeking to establish poetry as a form of discourse insusceptible of scientific criteria, serves to explain something of the 'damnable iteration in him' whenever a contemporary is the subject of critical comment.

[20] Coleridge, *Letters*, III. 441: 'In the same paper there is what I should have called a masterly Essay on the causes of the Downfall of the Comic Drama, if I was not perplexed by the distinct recollection of having myself *conversed* the greater part of it at Lamb's.'

One of the most distinctive features of Hazlitt's critical method is his employment of what might be termed control models. A writer comes to serve as an ideal, or is chosen to exemplify a standard in a particular branch of literature: Shakespeare as a dramatist, Bacon as a philosopher, Montaigne as an essayist, Burke as a prose-writer, and Joseph Fawcett as a critic. Each is representative in his own way of Hazlitt's experiential ideal. This critical procedure, however, presents certain difficulties in dealing with an age that is above all an age of abstraction. Wordsworth and Coleridge, Byron and Shelley are clearly ineligible, Wordsworth by virtue of his egotism, Coleridge because of his metaphysical leanings, Byron as a result of his generality and predilection for ethical poetry, and Shelley as a poet of impalpable abstractions. The candidate who fulfils this role in his criticism of his contemporaries is the unlikely figure of Sir Walter Scott. Superficially, Scott the novelist appears to satisfy all his experiential demands. He is always concrete, never abstract; he renders the object present to the reader; he is the most dramatic writer now living; his concern is always for his subject, never for himself, and it is always the subject that the reader sees. He offers a striking contrast in this respect with Lord Byron:

> We like a writer (whether poet or prose-writer) who takes in (or is willing to take in) the range of half the universe in feeling, character, description, much better than we do one who obstinately and invariably shuts himself up in the Bastile of his own ruling passions. . . . [Scott] casts his descriptions in the mould of nature, ever-varying, never tiresome, always interesting and always instructive, instead of casting them constantly in the mould of his own individual impressions. He gives us man as he is, or as he was, in almost every variety of situation, action, and feeling. . . . [Byron] hangs the cloud, the film of his existence over all outward things . . . a curtain intercepts our view, we do not breathe freely the air of nature or of our own thoughts. . . . [Scott] draws aside the curtain, and the veil of egotism is rent, and he shows us the crowd of living men and women, the endless groups, the landscape background, the cloud and the rainbow, and enriches our imaginations. . . . Or to sum up the distinction in one word, Sir Walter Scott is the most *dramatic* writer now living.
>
> (xi. 71–2)

Unlike his contemporaries Scott's 'speculative understanding is empty, flaccid, poor, and dead' (xi. 58). In spite of this, these qualities in Scott are not the qualities of the genuine poet so much as of the dedicated historian. Scott has little or no original genius, no intensity of feeling, and because of these deficiencies represents the historical rather than the poetic experiential ideal. This distinction is most effectively illustrated in *The Plain Speaker* essay, 'Sir Walter Scott, Racine, and Shakespear', in which he argues that 'the creative principle is every where restless and redundant in Shakespear. . . . Sir Walter's mind is full of information, but the *"o'er-informing power"* is not there' (xii. 340).[21] He compares Scott's genius with that of the Duke of Wellington: 'The one gets a hundred thousand men together, and wisely leaves it to them to fight out the battle, for if he meddled with it, he might spoil sport: the other gets an innumerable quantity of facts together, and lets them tell their own story, as best they may' (ibid.). As a genuine poetic spirit therefore Scott is immeasurably the inferior of Wordsworth, Coleridge, and Byron. Nevertheless, the experiential demand which Scott satisfies, even if only at the historical or narrative level, enabled Hazlitt to invoke his work as a novelist against which he might measure the abstraction of his greater contemporaries. This appears to be the principal purpose behind the frequent comparisons between Scott on the one hand, and Byron, Wordsworth, and Godwin on the other.[22] He provides some kind of ideal, however inadequate ultimately, against which he can isolate, measure, and characterize the peculiar form which the bias to abstraction assumed in the early nineteenth century.

Neither Scott's novels nor his poetry, the definition of the latter

---

[21] Hazlitt's frequent comparisons between Scott and Shakespeare (vi. 129; xi. 59–60, 62–3; xviii. 310; xix. 96) are designed to elicit the essential difference between a genius that is imitative and historical, and one that is poetic and creative: 'There is a power in true poetry that lifts the mind from the ground of reality to a higher sphere, that penetrates the inert, scattered, incoherent materials presented to it, and by a force and inspiration of its own, melts and moulds them into sublimity and beauty. But Sir Walter . . . has not this creative impulse, this plastic power, this capacity of reacting on his first impressions. He is a learned, a literal, a *matter-of-fact* expounder of truth or fable. . . . A poet is essentially a *maker* . . . [Scott] has either not the faculty or not the will to impregnate his subject by an effort of pure invention' (xi. 59–60). In *The Plain Speaker* essay he draws attention to his own concern in this favourite comparison of the early nineteenth century: 'Sir Walter Scott has not then imitated Shakespear, but he has given us nature, such as he found and could best describe it; and he resembles him only in this, that he thinks of his characters and never of himself, and pours out his works with . . . unconscious ease' (xii. 345–6). Donald Davie's observation in *The Heyday of Sir Walter Scott* (London, 1961), is misleading: 'It is a long time since anyone coupled the name of Scott, as Hazlitt . . . did, with the name of Shakespeare' (p. 22).

[22] See *Works*, xi. 69–72, 76–7; xii. 319–20; v. 155; xii. 320; vi. 128–30; xvi. 401.

being 'a pleasing superficiality' (xi. 61), is characteristic of the spirit of the age. This is true whether we conceive of that spirit as an imbalance or as a tension. There is no abstraction in his work, but neither is there feeling or imagination. In no sense can it be said of Scott's novels that in them we can see the literature of the age assuming the role of defender of the imaginative element in life. For a writer to be characteristic of the age where this is thought of as a tension, there must be something of the genuinely poetic which is in turn circumscribed by a tendency to abstraction. Only in this way can the writer be said to defend the poetic against the scientific, while at the same time betraying the cause he is in process of defending. Thus, to say of any work that it is characteristic of the spirit of the age is both a compliment and a criticism. Scott escapes the one only by escaping the other, so that a certain spuriousness is implicit in Hazlitt's use of him as a control model. Hazlitt criticized his contemporaries so severely only because he was thoroughly convinced that something intrinsically priceless was in danger of being overlooked or distorted. Nowhere is this more obvious than in his criticism of the poetry of Wordsworth.

Implicit in all his critical observations is a distinction between the genuinely 'poetic' nature of Wordsworth's early poetry and the abstract quality of the later work. Wordsworth's poetry in this respect was 'a pure emanation of the Spirit of the Age' (xi. 86). The term 'poetic' is important here. Unlike Coleridge, Hazlitt never lost sight of the qualities that had initially attracted him to the poetry of Wordsworth at the turn of the century. It never became, as it did for Coleridge, a 'vague, misty, rather than mystic, confusion of God with the world, and the accompanying nature-worship'.[23] Nowhere does he seriously consider the poetry of the 'great decade', as do many modern readers, in terms of mysticism, pantheism, or panentheism. Conscious of his own desire to do justice to what Hunt had called 'that real and interior spirit of things, which modifies and enlivens the mystery of existence',[24] he was disinclined to interpret literally a language that was essentially poetic and thereby confuse the poetic spirit with the pantheistic letter. In his criticism Wordsworth appears as the greatest and most original of his contemporaries. He attributes this pre-eminence to the poet's powers of sentiment and association: 'No one has shown

[23] Coleridge, *Letters, Conversations and Recollections*, I. 107.
[24] See Chapter I, n. 46.

the same imagination in raising trifles into importance.... He exemplifies in an eminent degree the power of *association*; for his poetry has no other source or character.... Each object has become connected with a thousand feelings, a link in the chain of thought, a fibre of his own heart' (xi. 88–9). For Hazlitt, as for Wordsworth himself, it is the feeling that confers importance on the object or event. His greatness as a poet derives almost entirely from his ability to transmute object into symbol through his power of feeling: 'It is this power of habitual sentiment, or of transferring the interest of our conscious existence to whatever gently solicits attention, and is a link in the chain of association . . . that is the striking feature in Mr. Wordsworth's mind and poetry' (viii. 44–5).

Association and sentiment, as Hazlitt uses these terms, are also of course striking features of his own work as an essayist. The two passages from the essays adduced as evidence of his 'pantheism', for example, are couched in an associative language similar to his criticism of the poetic but non-pantheistic poetry of the early Wordsworth.[25] He praises Wordsworth for qualities that in Romantic prose are best exemplified by his own essays. In this respect he is uniquely qualified as a critic of the poetry. The essays, like the poetry, consist in 'seeing nature through the medium of sentiment and passion, as each object is a symbol of the affections and a link in the chain of our endless being'. When Hazlitt in his essay in *The Spirit of the Age* attempts to account for the poet's fondness for the paintings of Rembrandt, he is drawing attention at the same time to the grounds of his own appreciation of both poet and painter: 'His eye also does justice to Rembrandt's fine and masterly effects. In the way in which that artist works something out of nothing, and transforms the stump of a tree, a common figure into an *ideal* object, by the gorgeous light and shade thrown upon it, he perceives an analogy to his own mode of investing the minute details of nature with an atmosphere of sentiment' (xi. 93). Likewise, when he assimilates Wordsworth's poetry to the prose of Rousseau in the essay on the latter in *The Round Table*, he does so in terms of sentiment and association: 'Both create an interest out of nothing, or rather out of their own feelings; both weave numberless recollections into one sentiment; both wind their

---

[25] Ibid. An exception to this is his interpretation of the *Immortality Ode* (iv. 250). His criticism of Wordsworth is best read in the context of the view of sentiment outlined in Chapter II.

own being round whatever object occurs to them (iv. 92). What he is emphasizing throughout is a vision of man's *relationship* to the world, a vision that modern critics of both writers now accept as central to an understanding of their writings as well as of Hazlitt's own essays.[26]

'Sentiment' in the context of his criticism of Wordsworth has a general as well as a specific significance. It is descriptive and evaluative of the early poetry and enables us at the same time to relate that criticism to his conception of the spirit of the age. Wordsworth is not only the greatest of contemporary poets but, as such, is also the chief spokesman for poetry in an age of science. It is unlikely that Hazlitt would have accepted Bulwer-Lytton's view that Wordsworth's poetry had 'repaired to us the want of an immaterial philosophy—it *is* philosophy, and it is of the immaterial school'.[27] What is important for Hazlitt is the poetry and the sentiment, not the philosophy. Nevertheless, like Bulwer-Lytton, he regarded Wordsworth's poetry as a necessary counterbalance to the empirical attempts to reduce the existential and imaginative to the quantifiable and verifiable. This equation is never made explicit in any discussion of sentiment in so far as it relates to Wordsworth, but it is unmistakably present in his defence of sentiment in *The Plain Speaker* essay, 'The New School of Reform'. This essay written in 1826, the year after his account of Wordsworth had appeared in *The Spirit of the Age*, is in the form of an imaginary conversation between representatives of sentiment and scientific reason. In it he defended the poetic achievement of his contemporaries and the 'sentimentalities' of his own essays from the criticism of the Utilitarians. Public utility according to the sentimentalist is not the only criterion of value. The most trivial incidents can and often do possess a significance far in excess of their intrinsic importance:

Reflection recals what sense has once embodied; imagination weaves a thousand associations round it, time endears, regret, hope, fear, innumerable shapes of certain good still hover near it. I hear the sound of village bells—it 'opens all the cells where memory slept'—I see a well-known prospect, my eyes are dim with manifold recollections. What say you? Am I only as a rational being to hear the sound, to see the object

[26] See J. Voisine, 'Un Nouveau Jean-Jacques: William Hazlitt', in his *J.-J. Rousseau en Angleterre à l'Epoque Romantique*, pp. 345–424; C. Salvesen, *The Landscape of Memory* (London, 1965), pp. 175–7, 187–97.

[27] See Chapter I, n. 8.

with my bodily sense? Is all the rest to be dissolved as an empty delusion, by the potent spell of unsparing philosophy? Or rather, have not a thousand real feelings and incidents hung upon these impressions, of which such dim traces and doubtful suggestions are all that is left? And is it not better that truth and nature should speak this imperfect but heartfelt language, than be entirely dumb? And should we not preserve and cherish this precious link that connects together the finer essence of our past and future being by some expressive symbol, rather than suffer all that cheers and sustains life to fall into the dregs of material sensations and blindfold ignorance. There, now, is half a definition of Sentiment.

(xii. 194)

Such a passage sets his criticism of Wordsworth as a poet of sentiment within a more general and entirely characteristic pattern of thought. Sentiment however is only one aspect of that criticism. The opposition between science and poetry does not exhaust the import of his conception of the spirit of the age. The empirical bias is only one aspect of abstraction.

While Wordsworth's early poetry is characteristic of the spirit of the age conceived as a tension between poetry and science, the later poetry and *The Excursion* in particular are characteristic of the same spirit conceived as an overemphasis on abstraction: 'His later philosophic productions have a somewhat different character. They are a departure from, a dereliction of his first principles' (xi. 90). In affecting 'a system without having any intelligible clue to one' (xi. 91), the poet of *The Excursion* had betrayed the genuinely poetic vision of the early poetry. The sentiment of the latter gave way to a 'dusty', 'bread and butter', and 'Sunday-school' philo-sophizing that marked the intrusion of the scientific impulse in a different guise (xvi. 142; xix. 73; iv. 46 n). In designating the poem a 'philosophical pastoral', a 'scholastic romance' (iv. 112), Hazlitt was criticizing the scientific impulse at the root of the philosophical and religious abstraction. The principal difference between this criticism of the poem and Coleridge's is that Hazlitt, like Keats, objected both to the abstraction and the form of the abstraction, to the system as well as the shallow and commonplace nature of Wordsworth's orthodoxy. Coleridge's criticism on the other hand, as his letter to Wordsworth in April 1815 makes abundantly clear, is only directed at the unimaginative nature of the abstraction. Rather than a statement of Wordsworth's religious viewpoint, *The Excursion* he had envisaged was intended to express his own mature and sophisticated metaphysical speculations in the same sphere.

Unfortunately, Hazlitt's criticism of Wordsworth's poetry has been overshadowed, if not totally eclipsed, by Coleridge's. The reasons for this are obvious: the intrinsic merit of Coleridge's analysis in the *Biographia*; the close relationship between the two poets in the period during which their greatest poetry was written; the easy access to a substantial part of his criticism of Wordsworth in a work that has become a classic of English literature; and the importance we attach to his theory of imagination. In Hazlitt's case, however, the criticism of Wordsworth is scattered through twenty volumes of the collected edition of his works. The poet and the critic disliked each other and were at no time on terms of any great intimacy. Moreover, the terms of his criticism—sentiment and the associative nature of the imagination—are unfamiliar and have never achieved the critical currency of Coleridge's theory of imagination. There is a tendency to view them as historical relics of late eighteenth-century aesthetics, without regard to Hazlitt's own highly individual and characteristic use of them. Yet, if we look beyond the dated conceptual labels and compare the criticism of Wordsworth by Hazlitt and Coleridge in its entirety, we shall discover Hazlitt's emphasis on imaginative memory and abstraction to be more consonant in the main with the modern reader's ambivalent response to Wordsworth's poetic achievement. By stressing association and sentiment, he drew attention to the crucial importance of memory and the symbolic significance of objects and events in the poet's past life. Association and sentiment direct our attention in reading Wordsworth to what one writer in another context has interpreted as two different conceptions of time: 'I am not a man who was a boy looking at a tree. I am a man who remembers being a boy looking at a tree. It is the difference between time, the endless row of dead bricks, and time, the retake and coil.'[28] Implicit in Hazlitt's analysis and outmoded critical terminology are certain emphases which are particularly characteristic of the best modern criticism of Wordsworth—imaginative memory, subjective time consciousness, and what one critic in characterizing the poet's relation to Nature has called imaginative or relational monism.[29] Hazlitt's poetic interpretation of the early poetry is a necessary corrective to those pantheistic interpretations that,

[28] William Golding, *Free Fall* (London, 1959), p. 46.
[29] J. Jones, *The Egotistical Sublime* (London, 1954), pp. 54–110.

according to John Jones, confuse imaginative kinship with formal philosophical allegiance.[30] Few would agree with Coleridge that the weakness of Wordsworth's later poetry is that it is the work of a propagandist for a religious and moral *orthodoxy*. Our objection is that he is a propagandist. We object not to the commonplace nature of the beliefs and doctrines of *The Excursion*, but to the poet's attempt to constrain the poetic and imaginative within an abstract system. We reject abstraction in poetry and not, as Coleridge does, this particular brand of abstraction.[31]

The difference between Hazlitt's criticism of *The Excursion* and Coleridge's criticism of the same poem is the result of their differing conceptions of the spirit of the age. This in turn, like their rival philosophies of literature and life, is directly related to their conflicting views on the subject of abstraction. What is true of their criticism of *The Excursion*, however, is equally true of their many other differences over a wide area of specific critical issues. Hazlitt's criticism of Coleridge himself, for example, is the consequence of the same basic conflict. As a philosopher Coleridge inhabits a 'metaphysical Bridewell' (xvi. 141); as a poet and critic he attempts to 'subject the Muse to *transcendental* theories' (xi. 30); and as a dramatist he is 'an ingenious metaphysician' (xviii. 309). The conflict here, as in the case of Wordsworth's later poetry, is between the concrete and the abstract, the poetic and the philosophical. Hazlitt interprets the later work of both poets as the sacrifice of the poetic and imaginative to the religious and philosophical. The precise nature of the sacrifice differs in each case, and this difference Hazlitt captures in his discrimination between the dogmatic and commonplace nature of Wordsworth's orthodox opinions and the subtle and highly abstract metaphysical theorizings of Coleridge.

A recognition of the philosophical basis of Hazlitt's criticism of Coleridge's later development as well as its essential validity is all the more important in that the tendency of modern critics of Coleridge has been to emphasize the tone and to neglect the substance of the charges he levels against Coleridge.[32] Hazlitt's contemptuous and scornful treatment of Coleridge's later work is

[30] Ibid., p. 36.

[31] I have developed this argument at length in two articles, 'Coleridge: Philosopher and Theologian as Literary Critic', *University of Toronto Quarterly*, xxxviii (1968), 17–33; 'Coleridge's Two Voices as a Critic of Wordsworth', *ELH* xxxvi (1969), 361–81.

[32] John Kinnaird's review-article 'The Forgotten Self', *Partisan Review*, xxx

greatly to be regretted. It has done irreparable harm to his own status as a critic and has resulted in perpetuating the animosity of the principals in the critical interpretations of their modern commentators. Nevertheless, his criticism of Coleridge is not the petty and captious spite of an envious rival and malignant enemy intent on destroying Coleridge's credibility with the public. The tone is important, but so too is the substance. More important than an emphasis on either, however, is the recognition that substance and tone are indivisible. The tone of the criticism is the consequence of the irreconcilable nature of the conflicting philosophies of critics who at the turn of the century were united in their experiential view of poetry.

Coleridge in Hazlitt's view was the only person who answered in any degree to his conception of a man of genius. Even as late as 1826 he could still say that he was 'the man of perhaps the greatest ability now living' (xii. 198). His estimate of Coleridge's powers, however, was not based on his works, but was the result of his own acquaintance with the man, his conversations, and his lectures. Of Coleridge's 1808 lectures he wrote: 'Mr. Coleridge . . . some twenty years ago, threw a great stone into the standing pool of criticism, which splashed some persons with the mud, but which gave a motion to the surface and a reverberation to the neighbouring echoes, which has not since subsided' (xi. 28). His mature view of Coleridge finds its best expression in his portrait of him in *The Spirit of the Age*:

There is no man of genius, in whose praise, he descants, but the critic seems to stand above the author . . . nor is there any work of genius that does not come out of his hands like an illuminated Missal, sparkling even in its defects. If Mr. Coleridge had not been the most impressive talker of his age, he would probably have been the finest writer; but he lays down his pen to make sure of an auditor, and mortgages the admiration of posterity for the stare of an idler. . . . All that he has done of moment, he had done twenty years ago: since then, he may be said to have lived on the sound of his own voice. Mr. Coleridge is too rich in intellectual wealth, to need to task himself to any drudgery. . . . He walks abroad in the majesty of an universal understanding, eyeing the 'rich strond', or golden sky above him, and 'goes sounding on his way', in eloquent accents, uncompelled and free !

(xi. 30)

(1963), 302–6, is an excellent but unfortunately isolated instance of how best to discriminate between Hazlitt and Coleridge in terms of their respective philosophies.

Hazlitt then proceeds to a consideration of the individual works in order to ascertain if any of them reflects his own sense of their author's genius. Of *Remorse*, he writes: '[It] is full of beautiful and striking passages, but it does not place the author in the first rank of dramatic writers. But if Mr. Coleridge's works do not place him in that rank, they injure instead of conveying a just idea of the man' (xi. 35). According to Hazlitt only the *Ancient Mariner* gives a just impression of the poet's 'extraordinary powers'. The poetry, the *Ancient Mariner*, and some of the conversational poems excepted, is inferior to the man. The prose is even less accurate as a guide: 'If our author's poetry is inferior to his conversation, his prose is utterly abortive. Hardly a gleam is to be found in it of the brilliancy and richness of those stores of thought and language that he pours out incessantly, when they are lost like drops of water in the ground. The principal work, in which he has attempted to embody his general views of things, is the FRIEND, of which, though it contains some noble passages and fine trains of thought, prolixity and obscurity are the most frequent characteristics' (ibid.).

Hazlitt of course had no access to much of the material that forms an essential part of the modern critic's stock-in-trade—the letters, notebooks, marginalia, reported conversations, and lectures. What did impress him was the great silence of 1800 to 1815 broken only by the publication of the periodical numbers of *The Friend* in 1809 and *Remorse* (1813), written originally in 1797. But of Coleridge's multifarious plans in the early years of the century for works on poetry, morals, logic, metaphysics, and politics—plans with which Hazlitt was doubtless acquainted—nothing was ever completed.[33] It would be tempting to suggest that the tone of Hazlitt's reviews of 1816–17 reflects the frustration and bitter disappointment of one acutely conscious of the disparity between Coleridge's powers and his achievement. This, although it accounts for the elegiac note of the character sketch in *The Spirit of the Age*, is inadequate by itself to explain the acid quality of many of his observations on the works of Coleridge's maturity: *The Statesman's Manual*, the *Biographia*, and the second *Lay Sermon*.[34] Even

---

[33] Coleridge's early projects are usefully listed in J. R. de J. Jackson's *Method and Imagination in Coleridge's Criticism* (London, 1969), pp. 1–20.

[34] *Works*, vii. 114–18, 119–28, 128–9; xvi. 115–38. For his review of *Christabel*, see *Works*, xix. 32–4.

the portrait of 1825 is less an exposure of Coleridge's constitutional
infirmity of purpose than a lament that his transcendent genius
would not be valued by posterity at its true worth. The question
then is why his criticism of Coleridgean abstraction differs markedly
from his criticism of the same element in the work of Wordsworth,
Byron, Shelley, and Godwin. Acutely conscious of the threat
posed by the abstract, subtle in his detection, and relentless in his
criticism of it, these factors by themselves do not satisfactorily
account for this difference. Their conflicting philosophies are
important but are only one element. Disagreement at this level
seldom generates the heat characteristic of Hazlitt's strictures on
Coleridge's development from 1816 onwards. Their philosophical
differences cannot reconcile the diverse elements present in his
criticism: regret and disgust; disappointment and contempt; concern for a just evaluation by posterity of Coleridge's genius and
public criticism of his private life and personal weaknesses. The
solution of this problem lies rather in Hazlitt's view that 'all he has
done of moment, he had done twenty years ago', or as he puts it
rather more provocatively in the *Political Essays*: '*All* that Mr.
Coleridge ever did in poetry, as the *Ancient Mariner, Christabel*, the
Three Graves, his Poems and his Tragedy, he had written, when,
according to his own account, he must have been a very ignorant,
idle, thoughtless person' (vii. 181). Much of what follows in the
development of this solution must of necessity be conjectural.

In these two passages Hazlitt is not merely drawing a distinction
between Coleridge's powers and his achievement, the promise and
the fulfilment. Rather he is directing our attention to two
Coleridges—the poet, critic and philosopher of his youth with
whom he identified himself and his ideals, and of whom he could
say that until he met Coleridge 'I could neither write nor speak'
(xvii. 312), and the philosopher and theologian of the period after
1815 whose metaphysical theorizings were so entirely alien to him.
The tone of Hazlitt's critical strictures reflects his anger and bewilderment, his sense of grievance and of betrayal. It was not that
Coleridge had shown so much promise and had disappointed him,
but that Coleridge, whose energies in the years between 1797 and
1804 had expressed an experiential ideal of poetry and life—best
exemplified in the poetry written at that time by Wordsworth and
by Coleridge himself—had gone over to 'the unclean side'. Thus,
while Hazlitt could contemplate and criticize the abstraction of the

other poets with a certain degree of equanimity, he was unable to regard Coleridge as just another manifestation of the spirit of the age. Coleridge was an exception. The reason for this is that Hazlitt at the turn of the century in all probability conceived of Coleridge, at least in general terms, as the spokesman for the self-authenticating nature of poetry. The evidence for this hypothesis is strong. First, there is the nature of his own criticism and his criticism of Coleridge in particular. The impact on him of his first acquaintance with poets is a recurrent theme. He distinguishes between Coleridge the poet and Coleridge the philosopher, assigning 'all that he has done of moment' to the period of his friendship with Wordsworth. In addition, there is the evidence of Coleridge's own early notebooks and correspondence.

In 1796 Coleridge defended *Religious Musings* from the charge of being too metaphysical by postulating the existence of a poetry of 'lofty & abstract truths'.[35] Two years later, as a result perhaps of his growing familiarity with the poetry of Wordsworth, he conceived his task as a poet very differently: 'I devote myself . . . in poetry, to elevate the imagination & set the affections in right tune by the beauty of the inanimate impregnated, as with a living soul, by the presence of Life.'[36] In 1801 he reviewed his early work in the light of his new conception of poetry and concluded that 'the material forms or intellectual ideas . . . [should not] claim attention for their own sake'.[37] Poetry is no longer seen as a statement of religious or political beliefs, as a system of abstract truths. Instead it is the expression of a personal vision which is not explicitly characterized but which has an essential reference to the feelings, affections, passions, and imaginations of men, and the great appearances of nature. In a letter to Richard Sharp in 1804 Coleridge conjured up his vision of Wordsworth as the great philosophical poet:

I dare affirm that he will hereafter be admitted as the first & greatest philosophical Poet—the only man who has effected a compleat and constant synthesis of Thought & Feeling and combined them with Poetic Forms, with the music of pleasurable passion and with Imagination. . . . I prophesy immortality to his *Recluse*, as the first & finest philosophical Poem, if only it be . . . a Faithful Transcript of his own most august & innocent Life, of his own habitual Feelings & Modes of seeing and hearing.[38]

[35] Coleridge, *Letters*, I. 279.   [36] Ibid., I. 397.
[37] Ibid., II. 666.   [38] Ibid., II. 1034.

The emphasis on Wordsworth's 'own habitual Feelings & Modes of seeing and hearing' implies a poetic and experiential criterion radically different from that envisaged by Coleridge in his letter to Wordsworth in 1815, and in *Table Talk* in which he says that Wordsworth was 'to deliver upon authority a system of philosophy'.[39] If the early letters in which he developed his theories of imagination and of poetry as symbol, and his view of art as organic, are an adequate indication of the subjects of Coleridge's conversations and interests during this period, then Hazlitt's early reverence for Coleridge and his subsequent disenchantment are easily explained. Shawcross has pointed out that the analysis of imagination in the *Biographia* founders on the movement within Coleridge's thought that saw the displacement of imagination by reason. J. D. Boulger has traced the implications of the changes resulting from Coleridge's shift of emphasis from an experiential concept of practical reason to a higher reason intuitive of the ideas of ultimate reality. Chapter III attempted to show that since imagination can be construed on an analogy with practical reason, any change in the latter concept in the direction of a constitutive theory rendered inevitable Coleridge's progressive loss of interest in the imagination. Poetry is subverted by philosophy and religion, imagination by reason, and the affections and feelings of men by an abstract system. Imagination by its very nature was unable to sustain the Platonic weight of his life-long insistence on 'something *one & indivisible*' (1797), 'a resting-place for my Thoughts in some *principle*' (1822).[40] This inherent bias to abstraction evident in Coleridge's early thought rendered inevitable the *volte-face* recorded in the two lay sermons and the central chapters of the *Biographia*. Herein lies perhaps the solution of the problem raised by Hazlitt's criticism: whether we can legitimately argue for two disparate Coleridges, or whether what has been termed a *volte-face* in the thought of the later Coleridge is more accurately and justly described as a development. Both points of view are valid depending on the context. If we emphasize his constant search for order, harmony, and unity, there is no evidence of a lack of continuity, only the abandonment of a premiss untenable given the conditions of his preoccupation with system and stability. If on the other hand, like Hazlitt, we do not give full weight to the reasons underlying

---

[39] Coleridge, *Works*, VI. 403.
[40] Coleridge, *Letters*, I. 349; *Letters, Conversations and Recollections*, II. 136.

Coleridge's early emphasis on imagination, then the tendency will be to view Coleridge, as Coleridge viewed Wordsworth, as a Janus head, not of Spinoza and Dr. Watts on this occasion, but of Shakespeare and Plato.

Given the conflict between their respective philosophies, and the nature of Hazlitt's attitude to Coleridge at the turn of the century, the over-reaction evident in the 1816–17 reviews is much less culpable. It was intolerable to Hazlitt that Coleridge of all people should capitulate to the spirit of the age. Unlike Coleridge in his criticism of Wordsworth, however, Hazlitt made no distinction between public and private criticism. The distasteful feature of the reviews is that in them Hazlitt conducts a private quarrel in a private way in public. The manner in which his sense of grievance is expressed should not blind us to the point at issue between them which is of the greatest importance. By 1825 Hazlitt was able to regard the matter with a greater air of detachment, and what *The Spirit of the Age* portrait lacks in immediacy is compensated by a more balanced series of judgements at once mellow and resigned.

The inescapable conclusion to be drawn from Hazlitt's criticism of Wordsworth and Coleridge is one which, although a commonplace, is in some danger of being overlooked, especially in relation to Coleridge. It is that without the work of the period from 1797–1804 their achievement is considerably less than major. Coleridge's poetry endures by virtue of its quality as poetry; the criticism by virtue of its quality as criticism. But our interest in the philosophy lies not in the quality of the philosophizing so much as in the fact that it is Coleridge's. The *Biographia*, published in 1817, is the clearest exception to Hazlitt's generalization on this point. Yet even the *Biographia*, or at least those parts of it that give it classic status, is anachronistic. The theory of imagination and the criticism of Wordsworth are both retrospective, harking back to the preoccupations and speculations of the early letters and notebooks. They are patently at odds with Coleridge's current thought and with the philosophy of the previous chapters. Hazlitt's criticism is a salutary corrective of the excessive reverence for everything Coleridgean that is such a marked feature of post-war criticism. Modern critics of Coleridge would do well to ponder Lamb's judgement of Hazlitt's strictures on Coleridge: 'Yet there is a kind of respect shines thro' the disrespect that to those who know the rare compound (that is the subject of it) almost balances the reproof, but then those who know him but partially or at a distance are so extremely apt to drop the qualifying part thro' their fingers.'[41]

The abstraction in the work of Wordsworth and Coleridge, however different, is still eminently a religious abstraction. In Byron and Shelley, on the other hand, it is humanistic. Otherwise, the pattern which Hazlitt's criticism of these two poets evinces is somewhat similar. The passion in Byron's poetry, like the feeling in Wordsworth's, is severely circumscribed by the poet's egotism. His thoughts, like Wordsworth's, are commonplace and orthodox. Shelley, his shorter lyrics excepted, occupies the metaphysical extreme which on the religious level is assigned to Coleridge. His poetry attempts 'to embody an abstract theory' (xii. 246). His greatest vice as a poet is his passion for philosophical speculation, with the result that the spirit of poetry is 'sublimed into a high spirit of metaphysical philosophy' (xvi. 265).

Few men, according to Carlyle, are permanently blessed with the felicity of ' "having no system" '.[42] The few who are, according to Hazlitt, are poets. Abstraction is not merely a matter of systems, scientific, religious, philosophical, political, or critical. It is a condition endemic in human nature. Abstraction in the widest sense is the recurrent theme of Romantic poetry and criticism. Perhaps the classic statement among many is Coleridge's in the *Biographia*, when he drew attention to Wordsworth's 'original gift of spreading the tone, the *atmosphere*, and with it the depth and height of the ideal world around forms, incidents, and situations, of which, for the common view, custom had bedimmed all the lustre, had dried up the sparkle and the dew drops. . . . To carry on the feelings of childhood into the powers of manhood; to combine the child's sense of wonder and novelty with the appearances, which every day for perhaps forty years had rendered familiar . . . this is the character and privilege of genius.'[43] Similar views are to be found elsewhere in the writings of Wordsworth, Shelley, Keats, Blake, Carlyle, and Hazlitt. Abstraction, in the form of a life lived according to blind custom and convention, mechanized into a form of automatic non-living, is representative for the Romantics of the

[41] *The Letters of Charles Lamb*, ed. E. V. Lucas (London, 1935), II. 196. See Coleridge, *Letters*, IV. 925, for his own estimate of his best work—an estimate that differs little from Hazlitt's.

[42] Carlyle, *Essays*, III. 2.

[43] Coleridge, *Biographia*, I. 59.

fall of man. It is the 'sleep of death' from which Wordsworth in the Prospectus of *The Excursion* proclaimed he wished to deliver man. It is the condition of the 'poor loveless, ever-anxious crowd' of Coleridge's Dejection Ode. It is related to the fourfold vision of Blake, and to Keats's distinction between the poet as dreamer and the poet as philosopher. A world of pure imagination, a non-abstract world is the lost Paradise of Romantic poetry, a paradise which, according to Coleridge's view of the imagination, must be recreated out of the destruction of the abstract world of sense perception and everyday living. There is no need to resort to pantheism, mysticism, neo-Platonism, or to invoke transcendental orders of being to explain the significance and permanent validity of Romantic poetry at its best. It is a poetry of new relationships in this world—the abstract world seen under the aspect of imagination: 'Its root is in the heart of man: it lifts its head above the stars' (iv. 250).

Hazlitt's self-appointed task as a critic and essayist was to safeguard what has been called the inspired condition of man. His critical effort is a series of intricate and repetitious variations on a theme. In *The Spirit of the Age* the theme is implicit in the variations themselves. It is the culmination of a decade of critical endeavour and a belated acknowledgment of the growing polarization of the abstract impulses characteristic of the age. It is a despairing requiem for the ultimate failure of Romantic poetry, for the imaginative spirit of man in the early nineteenth century. Coleridge was convinced that there were reasons for hope. So too was Carlyle. But for Hazlitt what hope there was lay not in the immediate future but in the nature of poetry itself, and the spirit of man: 'We can no more take away the faculty of the imagination than we can see all objects without light or shade. . . . Poetry is one part of the history of the human mind, though it is neither science nor philosophy' (v. 9).

BIBLIOGRAPHICAL NOTE

All references to Hazlitt are to *The Complete Works of William Hazlitt*, ed. P. P. Howe (London, 1930–4). The arrangement of this edition is as follows:

BIBLIOGRAPHY

A. WILLIAM HAZLITT

BIBLIOGRAPHIES

DOUADY, J. *Liste Chronologique des Oeuvres de William Hazlitt* (Paris, 1906).

KEYNES, G. *Bibliography of William Hazlitt* (London, 1931).

PARK, R. In *The New Cambridge Bibliography of English Literature*, ed. G. Watson (Cambridge, 1969), III. 1230–8.

SCHNEIDER, E. W. In *English Romantic Poets and Essayists: a Review of Research and Criticism*, ed. C. W. and L. H. Houtchens (New York, 1957, 1966 [rev.]), pp. 75–113.

CRITICISM AND BIOGRAPHY

ALBRECHT, W. P. *Hazlitt and the Creative Imagination* (Lawrence, Ka., 1965).

—— *Hazlitt and the Malthusian Controversy*, University of New Mexico Publications in Language and Literature, IV (1950).

ANDREWS, J. 'Bacon and the Dissociation of Sensibility', *N & Q* CXCIX (1954), 484–6, 530–2.

BABCOCK, R. W. 'The Direct Influence of Late Eighteenth Century Shakespeare Criticism on Hazlitt and Coleridge', *MLN* XLV (1930), 377–87.

BAKER, H. *William Hazlitt* (Cambridge, Mass., 1962).

BAKER, H. T. 'Hazlitt as a Shakespearean Critic', *PMLA* XLVII (1932), 191–9.

BULLITT, J. M. 'Hazlitt and the Romantic Conception of the Imagination', *PQ* XXIV (1945), 343–61.

CAIN, R. E. 'David Hume and Adam Smith as Sources of the Concept of Sympathy in Hazlitt', *PELL* I (1965), 133–40.

CALDWELL, J. R. 'Beauty is Truth', *University of California Publications in English*, VIII (1940), 131–53.

CHASE, S. P. 'Hazlitt as a Critic of Art', *PMLA* XXXIX (1924), 179–202.

DÉDÉYAN, C. 'Le Fils d'Alliance: William Hazlitt', in his *Montaigne dans le Romantisme Anglo-Saxon et ses Prolongements Victoriens* (Paris, [1946]), pp. 170–82.

DONOHUE, J. W. 'Hazlitt's Sense of the Dramatic Actor as Tragic Character', *SEL* V (1965), 705–21.

ELLIOTT, E. C. 'Reynolds and Hazlitt', *JAAC* XXI (1962), 73–9.

ELTON, O. In his *A Survey of English Literature, 1780–1830* (London, 1912), II. 357–77.

GARROD, H. W. 'The Place of Hazlitt in English Criticism', in his *Profession of Poetry and Other Lectures* (Oxford, 1929), pp. 93–109.

GATES, P. G. 'Bacon, Keats and Hazlitt', *SAQ* XLVI (1947), 239–51.

GILFILLAN, G. In his *Galleries of Literary Portraits* (Edinburgh, 1857), II. 15–24, 88–95.

HOWE, P. P. *The Life of William Hazlitt* (London, 1922, 1928 [rev.]); ed. F. Swinnerton, 1947.

IRELAND, A. *Hazlitt, Essayist and Critic: Selections from his Writings* (London, 1889), pp. xiii–lxv.

KINNAIRD, J. 'The Forgotten Self', *Partisan Review*, XXX (1963), 302–6.

—— ' "Philo" and Prudence: a New Hazlitt Criticism of Malthus', *BNYPL* LXIX (1965), 153–63.

KLINGOPULOS, G. D. 'Hazlitt as Critic', *EC* VI (1956), 386–403.

LARRABEE, S. A. 'Hazlitt's Criticism and Greek Sculpture', *JHI* II (1941), 77–94.

MacLEAN, C. M. *Born under Saturn: a Biography of William Hazlitt* (London, 1943).

MILNER, P. L. 'William Hazlitt on the Genius of Shakespeare', *Southern Quarterly*, V (1966), 64–71.

MUIR, K. 'Keats and Hazlitt', in *John Keats: a Reassessment*, ed. K. Muir (Liverpool, 1958), pp. 139–58.

NIBLETT, W. R. 'Hazlitt's Contribution to Literary Criticism', *Durham University Journal*, II (1941), 211–22.

NOXON, J. 'Hazlitt as Moral Philosopher', *Ethics*, LXXIII (1963), 279–83.

O'HARA, J. D. 'Hazlitt and the Functions of the Imagination', *PMLA* LXXXI (1966), 552–62.

—— 'Hazlitt and Romantic Criticism of the Fine Arts', *JAAC* XXVII (1968), 73–85.

PATTERSON, C. I. 'Hazlitt as a Critic of Prose Fiction', *PMLA* LXVIII (1953), 1001–16.

PRIESTLEY, J. B. *William Hazlitt* (London, 1960).

SAINTSBURY, G. In his *Essays in English Literature, 1780–1860*, First Series (London, 1890), pp. 135–69.

SALLÉ, J.-C. 'Hazlitt the Associationist', *RES* XV (1964), 38–51.

SALTER, C. H. 'The First English Romantic Art Critics', *Cambridge Review* (8 June 1957), 671–3.

SARGEAUNT, G. M. 'Hazlitt as a Critic of Painting', in his *Classical Spirit* (Bradford, 1936), pp. 206–23.

SCHNEIDER, E. W. *The Aesthetics of William Hazlitt: a Study of the Philosophical Basis of his Criticism* (Philadelphia, 1933, 1952).

SCHNÖCKELBORG, G. *Schlegels Einflus auf Hazlitt als Shakespeare-Kritiker* (Münster, 1931).

SIKES, H. M. 'The Poetic Theory and Practice of Keats: the Record of a Debt to Hazlitt', *PQ* XXXVIII (1959), 401–12.

SMITH, K. In his *Malthusian Controversy* (London, 1951).

STEPHEN, L. In his *Hours in a Library*, Second Series (London, 1876), pp. 290–343.

THORPE, C. D. 'Keats and Hazlitt; a Record of Personal Relationship and Critical Estimate', *PMLA* LXII (1947), 487–502.

TRAWICK, L. M. 'Sources of Hazlitt's "Metaphysical Discovery"', *PQ* XLII (1963), 277–82.

—— 'Hazlitt, Reynolds and the Ideal', *SIR* IV (1965), 240–7.

VOISINE, J. 'Un Nouveau Jean-Jacques: William Hazlitt', in his *J.-J. Rousseau en Angleterre à l'Epoque Romantique: les Ecrits Autobiographiques et la Légende* (Paris, 1956), pp. 345–424.

WHITLEY, A. 'Hazlitt and the Theatre', *University of Texas Studies in English*, XXXIV (1955), 67–100.

WILL, F. 'Two Critics of the Elgin Marbles: Hazlitt and Quatremère de Quincy', *JAAC* XIV (1956), 97–105.

WOOLF, V. In her *Collected Essays* (London, 1966), I. 155–64.

WRIGHT, E. 'Hazlitt and Sainte-Beuve', *Academy* (25 August 1906), 180–1.

ZEITLIN, J. *Hazlitt on English Literature* (New York, 1913), pp. xi–lxxiii.

B. PRIMARY SOURCES

ADDISON, J. *Works*. Ed. R. Hurd (London, 1854–6). 6 vols.

—— *The Spectator*. Ed. D. F. Bond (Oxford, 1965). 5 vols.

ALISON, A. *Essays on the Nature and Principles of Taste* (Edinburgh, 1790).

ARNOLD, M. *Complete Prose Works*. Ed. R. H. Super (Ann Arbor, 1960). 7 vols. published.

The Artist: a Collection of Essays relative to Painting, Poetry, Sculpture, Architecture, the Drama. Ed. P. Hoare (London, 1810). 2 vols.

BARRY, J. *An Inquiry into the Real and Imaginary Obstructions to the Acquisition of the Arts in England* (London, 1775).

BEATTIE, J. *An Essay on the Nature and Immutability of Truth* (Edinburgh, 1770).

—— *Elements of Moral Science* (Edinburgh, 1790–3). 2 vols.

—— *Essays on Poetry and Music* (Edinburgh, 1776).

BELL, C. *Essays on the Anatomy of Expression in Painting* (London, 1806).

BELSHAM, W. *Essays, Philosophical, Historical, and Literary* (London, 1789–91). 2 vols.

BENTHAM, J. *Works*. Ed. J. Bowring (Edinburgh, 1838–43). 11 vols.

BLAIR, H. *Lectures on Rhetoric and Belles Lettres* (Edinburgh, 1783). 2 vols.

BLAKE, W. *Complete Writings*. Ed. G. Keynes (London, 1957, 1966).

BROMLEY, R. A. *A Philosophical and Critical History of the Fine Arts* (London, 1793–5). 2 vols.

BUCHANAN, W. *Memoirs of Painting* (London, 1824). 2 vols.

BULWER, E. L. *England and the English* (London, 1833). 2 vols.

B[URGESS], J. *The Lives of the Most Eminent Modern Painters* (London, 1754).

BURKE, E. *A Philosophical Enquiry into the Origin of our Ideas of the Sublime and Beautiful.* Ed. J. T. Boulton (London, 1958).

BUTLER, J. *Works.* Ed. W. E. Gladstone (Oxford, 1896). 2 vols.

CAMPBELL, G. *The Philosophy of Rhetoric* (London, 1776). 2 vols.

CARLYLE, T. *Works.* Ed. H. D. Traill (London, 1896–9). 30 vols.

COLERIDGE, S. T. *Complete Works.* Ed. W. G. T. Shedd (New York, 1853). 7 vols.

—— *Anima Poetae.* Ed. E. H. Coleridge (London, 1895).

—— *Biographia Literaria.* Ed. J. Shawcross (London, 1907). 2 vols.

—— *Coleridge on Logic and Learning.* Ed. A. D. Snyder (New Haven, 1929).

—— *Coleridge on the Seventeenth Century.* Ed. R. F. Brinkley (Durham, N.C., 1955).

—— *Collected Letters.* Ed. E. L. Griggs (Oxford, 1956). 6 vols. published.

—— *Essays on his own Times.* Ed. S. Coleridge (London, 1850). 3 vols.

—— *Letters, Conversations and Recollections.* Ed. T. Allsop (London, 1836). 2 vols.

—— *The Notebooks.* Ed. K. Coburn (London, 1957). 4 vols. published.

—— *Notes, Theological, Political and Miscellaneous.* Ed. D. Coleridge (London, 1853).

—— *Miscellaneous Criticism.* Ed. T. M. Raysor (London, 1936).

—— *The Philosophical Lectures.* Ed. K. Coburn (London, 1949).

—— *The Political Thought of Coleridge.* Ed. R. J. White (London, 1938).

—— *Shakespearean Criticism.* Ed. T. M. Raysor (London, 1930, 1960). 2 vols.

—— *Treatise on Method.* Ed. A. D. Snyder (New Haven, 1934).

DE QUINCEY, T. *Collected Writings.* Ed. D. Masson (Edinburgh, 1889–90). 14 vols.

—— *Confessions of an English Opium-Eater.* Ed. E. Sackville-West (London, 1950).

—— *New Essays.* Ed. S. M. Tave (Princeton, 1966).

DRYDEN, J. *Essays.* Ed. W. P. Ker (Oxford, 1900). 2 vols.

—— *The Critical Opinions of John Dryden.* Ed. J. M. Aden (Nashville, 1963).

DUBOS, J. B. *Reflexions Critiques sur la Poësie et sur la Peinture* (Paris, 1719). 2 vols.

[DUFF, W.] *An Essay on Original Genius* (London, 1767).

ELLEDGE, S. *Eighteenth-Century Critical Essays* (Ithaca, N.Y., 1961). 2 vols.

GERARD, A. *An Essay on Genius* (London, 1774).

[GILPIN, W.] *An Essay upon Prints* (London, 1768).

GRAY, T. *Correspondence.* Ed. P. Toynbee and L. Whibley (Oxford, 1935). 3 vols.

H[ARRIS], J. *Three Treatises* (London, 1744).

HARTLEY, D. *Observations on Man* (London, 1749). 2 vols.

HAYDON, B. R. *The Diary of Benjamin Robert Haydon.* Ed. W. B. Pope (Cambridge, Mass., 1960–3). 5 vols.

HUNT, L. *Essays: The Indicator, The Seer* (London, 1842).

—— *Leigh Hunt's Dramatic Criticism, 1808–31.* Ed. L. H. and C. W. Houtchens (New York, 1949).

—— *Leigh Hunt's Literary Criticism.* Ed. L. H. and C. W. Houtchens (New York, 1956).

—— *Men, Women, and Books* (London, 1847). 2 vols.

HURD, R. *Letters on Chivalry and Romance* (London, 1762).

—— *Q. Horatii Flacci, Ars Poetica* (London, 1749; 2 vols. 1753; 3 vols. 1776).

JEFFREY, F. [Jeffrey's contributions to the *Edinburgh Review* as listed by D. Nichol Smith in his *Jeffrey's Literary Criticism* (London, 1910)].

JOHNSON, S. *Works* (Oxford, 1825). 9 vols.

—— *The Critical Opinions of Samuel Johnson.* Ed. J. E. Brown (Princeton, 1926, New York, 1961).

—— *Diaries, Prayers, and Annals.* Ed. E. L. McAdam *et al.* (New Haven, 1958).

—— *The Idler and The Adventurer.* Ed. W. J. Bate *et al.* (New Haven, 1963).

—— *Letters.* Ed. R. W. Chapman (Oxford, 1952). 3 vols.

KAMES, H. HOME, LORD. *Elements of Criticism* (Edinburgh, 3 vols. 1762; 2 vols. 1785).

KANT, I. *The Critique of Aesthetic Judgment.* Tr. J. C. Meredith (Oxford, 1928).

—— *The Critique of Practical Reason.* Tr. T. K. Abbott (London, 1879, 1889).

—— *The Moral Law, or Kant's Groundwork of the Metaphysic of Morals.* Tr. H. J. Paton (London, 1948).

KEATS, J. *Letters, 1814–1821.* Ed. H. E. Rollins (Cambridge, Mass., 1958). 2 vols.

KNIGHT, R. PAYNE. *An Analytical Inquiry into the Principles of Taste* (London, 1805).

LAMB, C. *Works.* Ed. E. V. Lucas (London, 1903–5). 7 vols.

LAMOTTE, C. *An Essay upon Poetry and Painting* (London, 1730).

LESLIE, C. R. *Memoirs of the Life of John Constable.* Ed. J. Mayne (London, 1951).

LESSING, G. E. *Selected Prose Works.* Ed. E. Bell (London, 1879).

LOCKHART, J. G. *Lockhart's Literary Criticism.* Ed. M. C. Hildyard (Oxford, 1931).

MACAULAY, T. B. *Complete Works* (London, 1898). 12 vols.

MENGS, A. R. *Works* (London, 1796). 3 vols.

MILL, J. S. *Autobiography.* Ed. J. J. Coss (New York, 1924, 1960).

—— *Mill on Bentham and Coleridge.* Ed. F. R. Leavis (London, 1950).

—— *Utilitarianism, Liberty, Representative Government.* Ed. A. D. Lindsay (London, 1910).

PALEY, W. *Paley's Moral Philosophy.* Ed. R. Whately (London, 1859).

PILES, R. DE. *The Art of Painting* (London, 1706).

—— *The Principles of Painting* (London, 1743).

PRICE, R. *A Review of the Principal Questions in Morals.* Ed. D. D. Raphael (Oxford, 1948).

PRICE, U. *An Essay on the Picturesque* (London, 1794–8). 2 vols.

PRIESTLEY, J. *Joseph Priestley: Selections from his Writings.* Ed. I. A. Brown (University Park, Pa., 1962).

QUATREMÈRE DE QUINCY, A. C. *The Destination of Works of Art and the Use to which they are applied.* Tr. H. Thomson (London, 1821).

—— *An Essay on the Nature, the End, and the Means of Imitation in the Fine Arts.* Tr. J. Kent (London, 1837).

REDGRAVE, R. and S. *A Century of British Painters.* Ed. R. Todd (London, 1947).

REID, T. *Works.* Ed. W. Hamilton (Edinburgh, 1863).

—— *An Inquiry into the Human Mind* (Edinburgh, 1764).

—— *Essays on the Active Powers of Man* (Edinburgh, 1788).

—— *Essays on the Intellectual Powers of Man* (Edinburgh, 1785).

REYNOLDS, J. *Works.* Ed. E. Malone (London, 1797). 2 vols.

—— *Discourses on Art.* Ed. R. Fry (London, 1905); ed. R. R. Wark (San Marino, Calif., 1959).

RICHARDSON, J. *Works* (London, 1792).

—— *An Account of Some of the Statues, Bas-Reliefs, Drawings and Pictures in Italy* (London, 1722).

ROBINSON, H. C. *Henry Crabb Robinson on Books and Their Writers.* Ed. E. J. Morley (London, 1938). 3 vols.

RUSKIN, J. *Works.* Ed. E. T. Cook and A. D. O. Wedderburn (London, 1902–12). 39 vols.

SCHLEGEL, A. W. *A Course of Lectures on Dramatic Art and Literature.* Tr. J. Black (London, 1815). 2 vols.

SCOTT, J. R. *Dissertations, Essays and Parallels* (London, 1804).

SHAFTESBURY, A. A. Cooper, Lord. *Characteristics.* Ed. J. M. Robertson (London, 1900). 2 vols.

SHELLEY, P. B. *Complete Works*. Ed. R. Ingpen and W. E. Peck (London, 1926–30). 10 vols.

SMITH, A. *Lectures on Rhetoric and Belles Lettres*. Ed. J. M. Lothian (London, 1963).

SMITH, D. NICHOL. *Eighteenth Century Essays on Shakespeare* (Oxford, 1903, 1963).

SMITH, G. G. *Elizabethan Critical Essays* (London, 1904). 2 vols.

SPINGARN, J. E. *Critical Essays of the Seventeenth Century* (Oxford, 1908). 3 vols.

STEWART, D. *Elements of the Philosophy of the Human Mind* (London, 3 vols. 1792–1827; ed. G. N. Wright, 1843).

STOCKDALE, P. *Lectures on the Truly Eminent English Poets* (London, 1807). 2 vols.

TURNBULL, G. *A Treatise on Ancient Painting* (London, 1740).

WALPOLE, H. *Anecdotes of Painting in England*. Ed. R. N. Wornum (London, 1849). 3 vols.

WARTON, J. *An Essay on the Writings and Genius of Pope* (London, 1756–82). 2 vols.

WARTON, T. *Observations on the Faery Queen* (London, 1754; 2 vols. 1762).

WEBB, D. *An Inquiry into the Beauties of Painting* (London, 1760).

WINCKELMANN, J. *The History of Ancient Art among the Greeks*. Tr. G. H. Lodge (London, 1850).

—— *Reflections on the Painting and Sculpture of the Greeks*. Tr. H. Fuseli (London, 1765).

WORDSWORTH, W. *Prose Works*. Ed. A. B. Grosart (London, 1876). 3 vols.

—— *The Critical Opinions of William Wordsworth*. Ed. M. L. Peacock (Baltimore, 1950).

WORNUM, R. N. *Lectures on Painting by the Royal Academicians* (London, 1848).

YOUNG, E. *Conjectures on Original Composition* (London, 1759).

C. SECONDARY SOURCES

ABRAMS, M. H. *The Mirror and the Lamp: Romantic Theory and the Critical Tradition* (New York, 1953).

AMARASINGHE, U. *Dryden and Pope in the Early Nineteenth Century: a Study of Changing Literary Taste, 1800–30* (Cambridge, 1962).

ARNHEIM, R. *Art and Visual Perception: a Psychology of the Creative Eye* (London, 1956).

BABBITT, I. *The New Laokoon: an Essay on the Confusion of the Arts* (London, 1910).

BABCOCK, R. W. *The Genesis of Shakespeare Idolatry, 1766–1799: a*

Study in English Criticism of the Late Eighteenth Century (Chapel Hill, 1931).

BARNES, W. H. F. 'Richard Price: a Neglected Eighteenth Century Moralist', *Philosophy*, XVII (1942), 159–73.

BAUER, J. *The London Magazine, 1820–29* (Copenhagen, 1953).

BELL, C. *Art* (London, 1914).

BINYON, L. 'English Poetry in its Relation to Painting and the other Arts', *PBA* VIII (1917–18), 381–402.

BOULGER, J. D. *Coleridge as Religious Thinker* (New Haven, 1961).

BUCKLEY, V. *Poetry and Morality: Studies on the Criticism of Arnold, Eliot and Leavis* (London, 1959).

CLARK, K. *Landscape into Art* (London, 1949).

COLLINGWOOD, R. G. *The Principles of Art* (Oxford, 1938).

CROCE, B. *Aesthetic as Science of Expression and General Linguistic.* Tr. D. Ainslie (London, 1909, 1922 [rev.]).

DOWNIE, R. S. *Government Action and Morality: Some Principles and Concepts of Liberal-Democracy* (London, 1964).

FRY, R. *French, Flemish and British Art* (London, 1951).

—— *Georgian Art, 1760–1820.* Ed. R. R. Tatlock (London, 1929).

—— *Transformations: Critical and Speculative Essays on Art* (London, 1926).

—— *Vision and Design* (London, 1920).

GEORGE, E. *The Life and Death of Benjamin Robert Haydon, 1786–1846* (London, 1948).

GIOVANNINI, G. 'Method in the Study of Literature in its Relation to the other Fine Arts', *JAAC* VIII (1950), 185–95.

GOMBRICH, E. H. *Art and Illusion: a Study in the Psychology of Pictorial Representation* (London, 1960).

—— *Meditations on a Hobby Horse and other Essays on the Theory of Art* (London, 1963).

—— *The Story of Art* (London, 1950).

GRENE, M. *The Knower and the Known* (London, 1966).

HAGSTRUM, J. H. *The Sister Arts: the Tradition of Literary Pictorialism and English Poetry from Dryden to Gray* (Chicago, 1958).

HALÉVY, E. *The Growth of Philosophic Radicalism* (London, 1928, 1952).

HEBB, D. O. *The Organization of Behavior: a Neuropsychological Theory* (New York, 1949).

HIPPLE, W. J. *The Beautiful, the Sublime, and the Picturesque in Eighteenth-Century British Aesthetic Theory* (Carbondale, Ill., 1957).

HUGHES, T. R. 'The London Magazine, 1820–29' (Oxford University Dissertation, 1931). [unpbd].

HUSSEY, C. *The Picturesque: Studies in a Point of View* (London, 1927).

JACK, I. *English Literature, 1815–1832* (Oxford, 1963).

—— *Keats and the Mirror of Art* (Oxford, 1967).

JONES, J. *The Egotistical Sublime: a History of Wordsworth's Imagination* (London, 1954).

JORDAN, J. E. *Thomas de Quincey, Literary Critic: his Method and Achievement* (Berkeley, 1952).

LANDRÉ, L. *Leigh Hunt (1784–1859): Contribution à l'Histoire du Romantisme Anglais* (Paris, 1935–6). 2 vols.

LANGER, S. K. *Reflections on Art: a Source Book of Writings by Artists, Critics, and Philosophers* (Baltimore, 1958).

LEAVIS, F. R. 'Coleridge in Criticism', *Scrutiny*, IX (1940), 57–69.

MABBOTT, J. D. 'Interpretations of Mill's "Utilitarianism"', *Philosophical Quarterly*, VI (1956), 115–20.

MADDEN, W. A. *Matthew Arnold: a Study of the Aesthetic Temperament in Victorian England* (Bloomington, Ind., 1967).

MARCHAND, L. A. *The Athenaeum: a Mirror of Victorian Culture* (Chapel Hill, 1941).

MANWARING, E. W. *Italian Landscape in Eighteenth Century England: a Study chiefly of the Influence of Claude Lorrain and Salvator Rosa on English Taste, 1700–1800* (New York, 1925).

MONRO, D. H. *Godwin's Moral Philosophy* (Oxford, 1953).

MONK, S. H. *The Sublime: a Study of Critical Theories in Eighteenth-Century England* (New York, 1935).

MUIRHEAD, J. H. *Coleridge as Philosopher* (London, 1930).

NESBITT, G. L. *Benthamite Reviewing: the First Twelve Years of the Westminster Review, 1824–36* (New York, 1934).

OGDEN, H. V. S. and M. S. *English Taste in Landscape in the Seventeenth Century* (Ann Arbor, 1955).

POLE, D. *The Later Philosophy of Wittgenstein: a Short Introduction* (London, 1958).

PRICE, H. H. *Perception* (London, 1932, 1950 [rev.], 1954).

—— *Thinking and Experience* (London, 1953).

RAPHAEL, D. D. 'Fallacies in and about Mill's *Utilitarianism*', *Philosophy*, XXX (1955), 344–57.

READ, H. 'Parallels in English Painting and Poetry', in his *In Defence of Shelley and other Essays* (London, 1936), pp. 223–48.

RICHARDS, I. A. *Coleridge on Imagination* (London, 1934).

ROSTON, M. *Prophet and Poet: the Bible and the Growth of Romanticism* (London, 1965).

RYLE, G. *The Concept of Mind* (London, 1949).

SALVESEN, C. *The Landscape of Memory* (London, 1965).

SHACKFORD, M. H. *Wordsworth's Interest in Painters and Pictures* (Wellesley, 1945).

STEVENS, W. 'The Relations between Poetry and Painting', in his *The Necessary Angel: Essays on Reality and the Imagination* (London, 1960).

Tinker, C. B. *Painter and Poet: Studies in the Literary Relations of English Painting* (Cambridge, Mass., 1938).

Topazio, V. W. *D'Holbach's Moral Philosophy* (Geneva, 1956).

Toulmin, S. E. *An Examination of the Place of Reason in Ethics* (Cambridge, 1950).

Urmson, J. O. 'The Interpretation of the Moral Philosophy of J. S. Mill', *Philosophical Quarterly*, III (1953), 33–9.

Wellek, R. *A History of Modern Criticism, 1750–1950* (London, 1955). 6 vols. published.

—— *Immanuel Kant in England, 1793–1838* (Princeton, 1931).

—— *The Rise of English Literary History* (Chapel Hill, 1941).

—— 'The Parallelism between Literature and the Arts', *English Institute Annual*, 1941 (1942), 29–63.

Wittgenstein, L. *Notebooks, 1914–16*. Ed. G. H. von Wright and G. E. M. Anscombe (Oxford, 1961).

—— *Preliminary Studies for the 'Philosophical Investigations' generally known as The Blue and Brown Books* (Oxford, 1958).

—— *Tractatus Logico-Philosophicus* (London, 1922).

Index

Index

religion, 30, 170 n., 226, 228; and Rembrandt, 149, 184, 224; and Rousseau, 67, 183–4, 224–5; and Scott, 222; and sentiment and association, 66–7, 183–4, 224–7; and the spirit of the age, 223–6, 231, 235–6; and vision, 125

Wycherley, William, 177